T0355224

What Do We Mean When We Talk About Meaning?

What Do We Mean When We Talk About Meaning?

STEVEN CASSEDY

OXFORD
UNIVERSITY PRESS

OXFORD
UNIVERSITY PRESS

Oxford University Press is a department of the University of Oxford. It furthers
the University's objective of excellence in research, scholarship, and education
by publishing worldwide. Oxford is a registered trade mark of Oxford University
Press in the UK and certain other countries.

Published in the United States of America by Oxford University Press
198 Madison Avenue, New York, NY 10016, United States of America.

Library of Congress Cataloging-in-Publication Data
Names: Cassedy, Steven, author.
Title: What do we mean when we talk about meaning? / Steven Cassedy.
Description: New York, NY, United States of America : Oxford University Press, [2022] |
Includes bibliographical references and index.
Identifiers: LCCN 2021045022 (print) | LCCN 2021045023 (ebook) |
ISBN 9780190936907 (hardback) | ISBN 9780190936914 |
ISBN 9780190936921 (epub) | ISBN 9780190936938
Subjects: LCSH: Meaning (Philosophy) |
Meaning (Philosophy)—Religious aspects—Christianity.
Classification: LCC B105.M4 C38 2022 (print) |
LCC B105.M4 (ebook) | DDC 121/.68—dc23
LC record available at https://lccn.loc.gov/2021045022
LC ebook record available at https://lccn.loc.gov/2021045023

DOI: 10.1093/oso/9780190936907.001.0001

1 3 5 7 9 8 6 4 2

Printed by Sheridan Books, Inc., United States of America

For Patrice, Mike, Meghan, Liam, Isaac, Eva, Peter, and Sophia, who fill me with love, pride, and awe

Contents

Acknowledgments

Thanks to Patrice, the love of my life, for her invaluable help.

Thanks to Theo Calderara, my editor at Oxford University Press, for his help, from the moment I first inquired about my project to its publication.

Thanks also (in no particular order) to Richard Elliott Friedman, University of Georgia; the late David Goodblatt, *olev ha-sholem*, UC San Diego; Tim Cassedy, Southern Methodist University; James Tartaglia, Keele University; Emily Esfahani Smith, Washington DC; William Breitbart, Memorial Sloan Kettering Cancer Center, NY; William Fitzgerald, King's College London; Julia Mebane, Indiana University; Anthony T. Edwards, UC San Diego; Robert Cancel, UC San Diego; Donna Cancel, San Diego; William Propp, UC San Diego; Richard Spinello, Boston College; Mark Massa, Boston College; Liam Bergin, Boston College; Christian Danz, Vienna University; Todd Kontje, UC San Diego; William Arctander O'Brien, UC San Diego; Anthony Grafton, Princeton University; Eric Watkins, UC San Diego; Clinton Tolley, UC San Diego; Anders Engberg-Pedersen, University of Southern Denmark; Robert H. Abzug, University of Texas, Austin; Alastair Hannay, University of Oslo, Norway; Andrew Finstuen, Boise State University; Rabbi Simon Jacobson, Meaningful Life Center, Brooklyn, NY; Seth Lerer, UC San Diego; Stephen D. Cox, "The Other" (Steve), UC San Diego; Alexandra Popoff, Canada; Inessa Medzhibovskaya, New School, NYC; Beth Holmgren, Duke University; Irina Paperno, UC Berkeley; Alain J.-J. Cohen, UC San Diego; Barbara L. Fredrickson, University of North Carolina, Chapel Hill; Alexander Batthyány, International Academy for Philosophy, Principality of Liechtenstein; Timothy Pytell, California State University, San Bernardino; Robert P. Ebert, Princeton University; Christoph Fehige, Saarland University, Saarbrücken, Germany; Edward Mendelson, Columbia University; Gordon Marino, St. Olaf College; Rabbi Ed Feinstein, Valley Beth Shalom, Encino, CA; Daniel Gardner, MD, San Diego; Matthew Zetumer, MD, San Diego; Henry E. Allison, Boston University; Page duBois, UC San Diego; Alan Jacobs, Baylor University; Martin Leiner, Friedrich-Schiller-Universität Jena, Germany; Eric Brandt, University of Virginia Press.

Introduction

This Ambiguous, Ubiquitous Word

The word is everywhere. We want our lives and activities to be filled with it. We want our job to have some of it—or we complain that our job doesn't have any of it. We talk about trying to find it, or about how other people are trying to find it. We seek out activities for our children that will have it. Religion is all about looking for it. We put the suffix *-ful* after it, to identify those activities, events, and experiences that have it. Then again, we rarely claim actually to have it or, at the end of a quest for it, truly to have found it. We seem mostly to look for it or lament its absence. And so we put the suffix *-less* after it.

Since the second half of the twentieth century, religious leaders of all kinds have used it, often paired with such adjectives as *transcendent, infinite, spiritual, ineffable, ultimate, essential, deepest, authentic, inmost*. An Austrian concentration camp survivor and psychiatrist believed that reaching out for it was fundamental to human nature. A psychologist in the 1950s identified it as a cure for anxiety. A bestselling author and life coach promises that a change in it "can literally change your biochemistry in a matter of minutes" (and, incidentally, make you rich).[1] It can be found everywhere from conversations about big, eternal truths to the title of a Monty Python film.

And yet almost no one ever pauses to define it. That's odd, isn't it? Our English word *meaning* originally had to do almost exclusively with words and signs. At its broadest and simplest, it can refer to what we derive from or find in anything that is the object of *interpretation*: words, stories, myths, dreams, signs, symbols, oracles, even events that appear mysterious and in need of explanation (what was the *meaning* of the worldwide die-off of frogs?). But that's not—or not quite—what *meaning* means in the contexts I've just mentioned. Almost no one ever explicitly tells us what *meaning* means in any of these contexts. Instead, we find synonyms. Topping the list are *purpose* and *value*. In most cases, we know only by implication that these terms are synonyms. In *The Purpose Driven Life*, evangelical pastor Rick Warren uses the word *meaning* interchangeably with the word *purpose*. Several pages into

What Do We Mean When We Talk About Meaning? Steven Cassedy, Oxford University Press. © Oxford University Press 2022. DOI: 10.1093/oso/9780190936907.003.0001

the book, he writes this: "For thousands of years, brilliant philosophers have discussed and speculated about the meaning of life. Philosophy is an important subject and has its uses, but when it comes to determining the purpose of life, even the wisest philosophers are just guessing."[2] The two sentences make no sense unless "meaning of life" and "purpose of life" are synonymous, and yet Rev. Warren never sees any reason to say explicitly that they are. When the Pew Forum on Religion and Public Life conducted surveys in 2007 and 2012 to determine the level of religious affiliation among Americans, the question apparently designed to capture the common ground between the religious and the non-religious was this: "How often, if at all, do you think about the meaning and purpose of life?" "Meaning and purpose" sometimes appears to be a single noun. In an article in a professional psychology journal, a group of researchers drawing a distinction between a happy life and a meaningful life wrote this: "Meaningfulness is presumably both a cognitive and an emotional assessment of whether one's life has purpose and value."[3] But, of course, beyond this statement, *meaning, meaningfulness, purpose,* and *value* are never defined—strange, given that the aim is to offer a scientific description of "a meaningful life" and thereby to explain why it's measurably preferable to just "a happy life."

Sometimes a writer will actually attempt a definition, but with very few exceptions the definitions are not really definitions at all, since usually at best they're vague and at worst they're simply circular. In *A Secular Age* (2007), Catholic philosopher Charles Taylor uses the word *meaning* dozens of times (though strangely, despite its obvious centrality, it does not warrant an entry in the index). Here's what he offers by way of a definition: early in the book, Taylor is writing about "our responses, the significance, importance, meaning, we find in things." "I want to use for these the generic term 'meaning,'" he goes on, "even though there is in principle a danger of confusion with linguistic meaning. Here I'm using it in the sense in which we talk about 'the meaning of life,' or of a relationship as having great 'meaning' for us."[4] To put it gently, telling us first that *meaning* means "meaning" and "significance" and next that it means the same thing that it means in the phrase "the meaning of life" doesn't really narrow things down very much.

Where it often gets perplexing is in the surprisingly large number of books and scholarly articles devoted to "the meaning of life," which is its own cottage industry. Apparently if you set out to write a book on "the meaning of life," you and your readers already know what the title phrase means—not, of course, in the sense that you know the answer to the question "What is the meaning of life?" but in the sense that you have a pretty good idea what the question itself—and the word *meaning* in the question—means. So some authors never bother to define *meaning* at all. John Cottingham, for example, begins *On the Meaning of Life* (2003) with "The Question That Won't Go Away" ("What are we really asking when we ask about the meaning of life?") and answers it like this: "Partly, it seems, we are asking about our relationship with the rest of the universe—who we are and how we came to be here." By a few pages later, he's already adopted an understanding of the word *meaning* but forgotten to tell us what it is.[5] Others do offer a definition, often with strange results. Terry Eagleton, in his often funny and entertaining *The Meaning of Life* (2007), approaches the task in the negative, by looking at the word *meaningless*. Here's his explanation of what people feel when they find life "meaningless": "that their lives lack *significance*." And what does *significance* (by contrast with *meaning*) mean? Well, "to lack significance means to lack point, substance, purpose, quality, value, and direction."[6] So *meaning* can be replaced with *significance*, and *significance* can be replaced with the six nouns that complete Eagleton's sentence. Does this help? For Dennis Ford, in *The Search for Meaning: A Short History* (2007), *meaning* (used interchangeably with *purpose*) is "a vehicle for introducing students to the fundamental epistemological, ontological, and axiological dimensions of religion, philosophy, and ethics."[7] But what does the word mean? Ford never says. And for Thaddeus Metz, in *Meaning in Life: An Analytic Study* (2013), *meaningful* means "significant," "important," and "matters" (as in "it matters"), and *meaning* means "something that is finally, and not merely instrumentally, valuable."[8]

Think about the bind this puts us in when we encounter this word not in casual conversation but in works of scholarship, where we'd like to presume that authors have reflected carefully on their topics and have paid attention to the words they use—especially a word that is *the topic of the book*. *Meaning* may go undefined altogether, in which case we have to guess what it means. Or it may be defined through the use of such words as *purpose* and *value*, to choose only two out of (as we'll soon see) many. This raises another problem. Speaking of only these two words, we have to pause and ask how the word *meaning*, but only in certain contexts, came to mean the same thing as the word *purpose* and the word *value*. Why not just use the words *purpose* and *value*, if that's what we're talking about? I can't say that the *meaning* of a hammer is to drive nails, nor can I say that the *meaning* of a particular Rolex watch is twelve thousand dollars. So why can I say that "the meaning of life" is to love my neighbor, or say that my life has "no meaning" when what I'm really saying is that my life has no *value* and I'm about to shoot myself?

To be sure, there are countless words whose entries in a good dictionary will include a wide range of meanings, some of them only remotely related to others. The question is whether you can see *why* a given word has come to mean both definition 2 and the very different definition 3a. How does a word that fundamentally has to do with signs, words, stories, and other things that, well, mean or signify something come to mean "purpose" and "value"? How does it come to mean all the other things it appears to mean, apart from "signify"? If you look at the list of examples I began with and many that I'll come to later, you'll see that *meaning* can also mean "essence," "very important truth," "reason to go on living," "thing that good people do," "explanatory framework," or "God," to name just a few. So, with this of all words, we can't help realizing (1) that it's come to mean many different things (lots of words do that), (2) that it's hard to figure out how it came to mean many of those things, and (3) that, apart from contexts where it has to do with basic signifying, most of the time we are left guessing what in the world it *does* mean. It often seems to mean, you know, something really lofty, something weighty and important.

How do other European languages express these notions? We'll see that the English word *meaning* in the senses I've been referring to absorbed some of the meanings of the equivalent words in other languages—German above all and, to a lesser extent, French and Russian. But the words in those are only *roughly* equivalent to English *meaning*, so that when, say, a work by Albert Camus appears in English and the translator renders the word *sens* with the word *meaning*, two things happen. First, the reader of the translation likely understands the English word *meaning* slightly differently from how the French reader of the original understands *sens*. Second, because of the context of the original and because of the necessity of using *meaning* as the equivalent, the English word begins to take on a set of nuances that it otherwise lacks in our language. The French and German words have to do with both direction (so *le sens de la vie* and *der Sinn des Lebens* can suggest a direction that life can take) and sense experience, and the Russian word has to do with thought (so *smysl zhizni* can suggest a way that we think about life).

But English *meaning* is peculiar among the European equivalents (Danish too, as we'll see later) in that it is derived directly from a verb. It starts out technically as a gerund, or verbal noun. The verb *to mean*, like its cognates in other Germanic languages, means primarily "to intend" and "to signify," whether of persons ("I mean no harm") or of objects, words, and signs ("What meaneth the noise of the great shout?"). The gerund *meaning*, therefore, denotes the act of intending or signifying, or, most commonly, the product of either—the thing that someone intended or the thing that an object, word, or sign "points to" (metaphorically speaking).[9] This has profound consequences for our English word. Presumably the sentence "The meaning of X is Y" can be replaced with the sentence "X means Y." "The meaning of *car* is 'automobile'" is equivalent to "*Car* means 'automobile.'"

So, what about *meaning* in the senses we're looking at? If someone were to compose the sentence "The meaning of life is X," could that sentence be replaced by the sentence "Life means X"? Is the sentence "The meaning of life is to love your neighbor" the same as "Life means to love your neighbor"? Here we run into a problem. The question "What is the meaning of life?" is surely not *exactly* the same as "What does life mean?" In many of the examples at the beginning of this chapter and in so many of the instances we see in popular and academic writing, sentences featuring *meaning* simply can't be recast as sentences with the verb *to mean*. *Meaning* is so often something we seek, find, give to something, or experience. "Faith will come to him who passionately yearns for ultimate meaning, who is alert to the sublime dignity of being," wrote Rabbi Abraham Joshua Heschel.[10] "Through salvation our past has been forgiven, our present is given meaning, and our future is secured," writes Rick Warren.[11] Tony Robbins writes that Viktor Frankl and other survivors of Nazi concentration camps "found meaning even in their extreme suffering. It was a higher meaning, a deeper meaning that kept them going." He continues: "Find the empowering meaning in anything, and wealth in its deepest sense will be yours today" (though the meaning that brings you wealth is probably not the same one that camp inmates found in suffering).[12] How can you rewrite any of these sentences and use the verb *to mean* instead of the noun *meaning*? You can't.

And yet, in a work that contains numerous instances of the word *meaning*, Rabbi Heschel also wrote this, the last of an extraordinary series of sentences beginning with the same two words: "God means: What is behind our soul is beyond our spirit; what is at the source of our selves is at the goal of our ways."[13] Could he have written "The meaning of God is . . ."? That's hard to say, because we can't be sure whether Heschel is saying that the word *God* signifies the words that follow or whether he's saying that God, the divine being, intends what is expressed in those words. In fact, it would be impossible to translate this sentence into German, Russian, or French without distortion, because you wouldn't know whether to use a verb that means "signifies" (something a word does) or a verb that means "intends" (something a person—or God—does). You'd have to choose.

Our English *meaning* means both, and this should remind us that the English word functions in a way that sets it apart from the only roughly equivalent words in German, French, and Russian. The verb *to mean* lurks behind it, often giving explicit or implicit agency to whatever has it. Once I "give my life meaning," my life takes on the power both to signify and to intend. Once I "find meaning in my life," it's my life that yields up something to me, even though I was the one in the act of seeking.

Still, as we've already seen, "signifying" and "intending" don't exhaust the meanings of *meaning*, since there are all those other meanings I've spoken of—"purpose" and "value" above all. How did our *meaning* acquire these other meanings? To a considerable extent, it was through the translation of the only roughly equivalent words in German and French. This is particularly true in negative statements. The German sentence that would get translated into English as "My life has no meaning" could be understood variously as "My life has no direction" (therefore, by extension, no purpose), "My life makes no sense" (that is, I don't understand it), or "My life signifies nothing" (whatever *that* means). The equivalent Russian sentence would likely be understood as the second or third of these options (with perhaps the first only by implication, depending on the context). In *The Myth of Sisyphus*, Camus forcefully asserted the equivalence of *meaning* (*le sens*) and *value* by equating the question of whether life isn't worth living ("ne vaut pas la peine d'être vécue") with the question of the meaning of life ("le sens de la vie").[14] And yet to a French-speaker, the phrase expressing the possibility that life has no meaning ("qu'elle n'a point de sens") cannot fail to come across, at least in part, as "Life makes no sense," that is, I don't understand it, my mind can't grasp it. But translate the phrase into English, and you come away with the idea that life is missing some sort of inexpressible and essential quality—which brings us back to the distinctive nature of the English *meaning*. If I, a French-speaker, say, "La vie n'a point de sens," then, to the extent that I'm understood as saying life makes no sense, I'm focusing attention on myself and my mind: *I* don't understand life. But when I, an English-speaker, say, "Life has no meaning," then, because of the verbal origin of *meaning*, I'm focusing attention on *life*, as *it* fails to yield up to me the essential something-or-other that the word *meaning* is felt to denote. It's not my failing; it's a failing of life.

In the chapters to come, I'll show how, over the last two-plus centuries, the English word *meaning* has accumulated the large set of meanings and connotations it now boasts when used in settings of the sort I've described—call them, for want of a better term, *metaphysical* (understood broadly and *very* loosely). Many of these arose through translation from German, French, and Russian.

The large set of meanings and connotations has given this word a most peculiar status. As we'll see, the word *meaning* frequently shifts among these meanings and connotations in a single work by a single writer. Or a single speech by a single speaker, sometimes even within a single paragraph. And almost no one stops to define it, so we the readers and listeners carry the burden of deciding what in the world it means here, and then here, and then over here. Given that in the metaphysical contexts I'm referring to it almost invariably suggests something weighty, important, and, above all, mysterious, these shifting and uncertain meanings can be a huge problem: what in heaven's name does the speaker mean by *meaning*? Does it somehow consistently retain the resonance of its primary and original meaning, the one that has to do with signifying? After all, *meaning* strongly suggests that we're engaged in some sort of interpretive act, that we're treating objects in our experience as though they were signs that point beyond themselves to something else. Or does it possess meanings and connotations that simply escape the orbit of that original meaning altogether? In the end, without definitively resolving this question, we might say that the word *meaning* is persistently ambiguous. Who wants to give a definition, when the word floats around so happily in a sea of indeterminacy, just as long as we understand that something very deep is being hinted at? And when we feel the agency that the English word, by contrast with its European equivalents, suggests, we have the added benefit of living in the world of Baudelaire's stunning sonnet "Correspondances" (from *Les fleurs du mal*, 1857), where man "passes through forests of symbols / That observe him with familiar glances." Yes, "familiar," but without revealing any concrete, explicit truths. Familiar but mysterious.

So the story, which starts farther back than the last couple of centuries, goes something like this: In the world of the Jewish scriptures and in ancient Greece there is virtually nothing like this use of *meaning* and its equivalents in other modern European languages. In part, this is lexical. Biblical Hebrew and Aramaic simply lack a word that is equivalent to *meaning*, featuring instead a word that has to do with *interpreting,* as in the case of mysterious dreams. Ancient Greek has the lexical means to present discussions of both *signifying* and *interpreting*, and it's easy to find such discussions—say, in connection with oracular pronouncements and in connection with the study of literary texts. But the noun that is equivalent to our *meaning* is exceedingly rare in ancient Greek, and there is little in the way of metaphorically finding something like "meaning" in, say, the everyday world, the heavens, or "life." Instances of what we might, in modern terms, describe as "looking for a meaning or meanings" apart from conventional signifying objects (words, signs with commonly accepted referents) tend to be restricted in the ancient world to unique occurrences—a troubling dream, mysterious writing on a wall, strange pronouncements by an oracular voice.

The oldest precursor to our modern metaphorical/metaphysical use of *meaning* is a tendency in early Christianity to conflate the Divine Scriptures with the world or the heavens, so that one could speak metaphorically of "reading" the world or the heavens and thus seeking *meanings* (plural) that lie beyond direct experience, just as the Scriptures yield up meanings beyond the literal. But the meanings that are discovered have not broadened so as to include anything like "the meaning of life" (which in Latin would be *sensus vitae*). That phrase first emerges in German-speaking lands in the late eighteenth and early nineteenth centuries, during the Romantic era, when the notion becomes absolutized, so that *meaning* appears in the singular, as the metaphysically grand, mysterious, often indefinable, and generally unattainable object of a human quest. The German word that is used in this and similar phrases is *Sinn*. Its various sub-meanings do not match up exactly with those of English *meaning*, but *meaning* is how *Sinn* is almost invariably rendered in English. By the middle of the nineteenth century, English and American writers were using *meaning* in a way that mimicked the German equivalent, to express a mysterious essence in the world that invites, but generally does not yield to, an attempted act of interpretation. Nor did the word itself, perpetually polyvalent and ambiguous, yield to an attempted act of interpretation.

At the end of the nineteenth century and beginning of the twentieth, as English translations of nineteenth-century Russian classics flooded the market, English-speaking readers encountered, above all in Tolstoy, a veritable barrage of musings on "the meaning of life." For Count Tolstoy (as he was always referred to in this era), the Russian word (*smysl*) that gets translated into English as *meaning* vacillated between the idea of "goal" or "list of actions you should take," on one hand, and some sort of ineffable spiritual or religious truth, on the other. Tolstoy's slightly older contemporary Dostoevsky, though he wrote far less frequently about "the meaning of life," looks ahead to what will become a dominant usage in English starting in the mid-twentieth century (though it's unlikely he was directly responsible for it). The issue arose for Dostoevsky in connection with the loss of faith that he decried in his homeland, something that had led to an epidemic of suicides in the 1870s. He appears to have needed a phrase that would denote, from a secular perspective, what was missing in the lives of those who had renounced—or never embraced—religion. Such people lack a belief in the immortality of their souls, he claimed, and that belief alone can give us access to "the highest meaning of life," which in turn supplies us with the urge to continue living. Missing "the highest meaning of life" can lead you to kill yourself. Dostoevsky, whose works first appeared in English at a time when translations of Tolstoy had been out for years, did not initially attract the same level of attention abroad as the Count. When he finally did catch on, it was for qualities entirely different from those that drew readers to Tolstoy.

Starting in the mid-twentieth century, German theologian Paul Tillich and Austrian psychiatrist Viktor Frankl helped to establish for *meaning* the array of senses that would allow the word to function in both secular and religious contexts, as well as in psychotherapy and self-help. In both instances, this was thanks to the peculiar nature of *Sinn* as the two writers used it in their German writings. *Sinn* was almost always translated into English as *meaning*. Tillich and Frankl both began writing prolifically in English, and when they did, they consistently used *meaning* as the English equivalent of the German word. Thus, in Tillich, English-language readers began to encounter *meaning* as a theological term with a wide reach of senses, including "God." And in Frankl they encountered the word as a name for (among others) something that, on being found, rescues the despairing from despair. Tillich helped steer Americans through the post–World War II "Age of Anxiety," a time when, despite outward appearances and polling data showing sky-high levels of conventional faith in God, Americans were struggling mightily with the very real possibility that there might not be any such being, that He might be dead. And Frankl took psychotherapy in a decidedly new direction, as new schools, especially those focused on *meaning* as an agent of rescue from hopelessness among the terminally ill, sprang up, and (perhaps unwittingly) helped to found and guide the modern self-help movement. Attempts by these figures themselves or by readers to define *meaning* invariably fail—not because the writer in a given instance is missing the clarity that the explanatory task demands but because the word functions properly only when it is ambiguous.

By the end of the twentieth century, *meaning* had found a home in the climate of puzzlement and speculation occasioned by the increasing sense that the world had grown and was continuing to grow more secular, or at least less religious in the conventional sense of the term. Among the "developed" nations, the phenomenon is particularly striking in the United States, which resisted secularization far longer than, say, France or the Scandinavian countries. Tillich and others had already laid the groundwork for what happened here. Once conventional religious terms (the theistic God, for example) began to lose their secure place, the need arose for something that could generically comprise both the older conceptions and whatever else had come along to take their place—and comprise them in a way that would be valid for the conventionally religious, the less conventionally religious, and the non-religious. That something, of course, was most commonly *meaning* or "meaning and purpose" (sometimes "meaning and value"). Conventional believers could agree that they found meaning and purpose in such conventional religious ideas as a theistic God. Less conventional believers—Paul Tillich, for example—could construct such phrases as "ultimate meaning" as alternatives to a theistic God, while also using *meaning* prolifically to suggest a host of related concepts. Pope John Paul II's encyclical on the sanctity of life, *Evangelium Vitae* (1995), contains thirty-one instances of *meaning*, including six instances of "meaning of life." And entirely secular people could speak about their own quests for meaning and purpose. *Meaning* was used in these contexts, by the religious and the non-religious alike, not only as a substitute expression for *God* but also to point to a variety of essential qualities that appear to defy definition in concrete, empirical terms.

At the end of this story is this word *meaning*, which has accumulated a capacious store of meanings. Lots of words have several meanings. But what sets this one apart, in the contexts I will refer to, is that speakers and writers make little or no effort to specify with precision which meaning they are using. That's because they are often using several at once but without explicitly saying so—perhaps without even knowing so. It's the very fluidity that gives *meaning* its peculiar resonance and mystique and that allows it to live with equal comfort in the writings of secular scientists and the official decrees of Catholic popes. That's the ambiguity that lends this word its peculiar and characteristic power—what makes it the quintessentially modern word.

1

The Ancient World Got Along Without It Until the Rise of Christianity

Ancient Hebrew (and Aramaic)

Let's begin with the Jewish scriptures. If I wish to make the claim that nothing equivalent to the English *meaning*, in the senses I listed in the Introduction, occurs in these writings, I'll need to know what I'm looking for. First, is there a non-modern Hebrew word that's equivalent to English *meaning* in our word's primitive, original sense—that is, having to do with signifying? Second, is there anything equivalent to the other senses of *meaning*, the ones I'm attempting to claim are of much more recent vintage? The first question is fairly easy to answer. To answer the second requires that we look for contexts in the Hebrew Bible that resemble those in the modern world in which our word *meaning* appears in the newer senses. If we find any such contexts, then we can ask if there's a Hebrew word that functions in the same way as our English word functions in such expressions as "the meaning of life."

Where in the Hebrew Bible does the notion of *meaning* in its primitive sense arise? The King James Version (KJV) of the Old Testament includes only one instance of the word *meaning*—in the Book of Daniel. The verb *to mean* occurs in various forms in a handful of places, but in no instance does it translate a Hebrew (or Aramaic) verb with the same sense as our verb *to mean*. In some cases, there is no corresponding word at all in the Hebrew (or Aramaic) text, and the English word is italicized in the KJV to show that the translators added it for clarity. For example, we read, "What *meanest* thou by all this drove which I met?" (Genesis 33:8). But, translated literally, the underlying Hebrew text is "Who to you [is] this company that I met?" The King James translators had Esau ask Jacob what his *intention* was, even though the original Hebrew has nothing of the sort. In Deuteronomy, after Moses has assembled the Israelites and given them the Ten Commandments, he says to them, in the King James Version, "*And* when thy son asketh thee in time to come, saying, What *mean* the testimonies, and the statutes, and

What Do We Mean When We Talk About Meaning? Steven Cassedy, Oxford University Press. © Oxford University Press 2022. DOI: 10.1093/oso/9780190936907.003.0002

the judgments, which the Lord our God hath commanded you? Then thou shalt say unto thy son, We were Pharaoh's bondmen in Egypt" (6:20–21). But, as the italics indicate, there's nothing in the original Hebrew that corresponds to "mean." Translated literally, the Hebrew in that place reads, "What [are] the testimonies and the statutes and the judgments that God our lord commanded you?" To be sure, the answer to the question is not a list of the testimonies, statutes, and judgments but an explanation of how they came about. Again, Hebrew has no verb that tells us, "Here's an explanation." In fact, even the verb *to be*, in the present tense, is only implied in Hebrew. Similarly, in "What *meaneth* the noise of the great shout?" (1 Samuel 4:6), where once again the English verb is easily used in the sense of "is the explanation of," there is no verb at all in the Hebrew text. Literally translated, this question reads, "What [is] the voice of this great shout?" Clearly the speakers (the Philistines) are asking for an explanation, but Hebrew does not offer a verb that allows them to communicate that explicitly.

What about contexts in which *meaning* or *to mean* would be the natural way of expressing the thought and in which the idea appears to be *signification*? There are a handful in the Hebrew Bible. Genesis 40, for example, tells the story of Pharaoh's butler and baker, who offended their master. Pharaoh claps the two men into the prison where Joseph is being held (after the wife of Potiphar has falsely accused Joseph of attempting to "lie with" her). One night the baker and the butler each dream a dream, and each is troubled by his dream. In the modern world, our impulse would be to ask what the *meaning* of a dream is or what the dream *means*, making *dream* the source of whatever is to be yielded up. The mid-twentieth-century Revised Standard Version renders the story like this: "And one night they both dreamed—the butler and the baker of the king of Egypt, who were confined in the prison— each his own dream, and each dream with its own *meaning*. When Joseph came to them in the morning and saw them, they were troubled. So he asked Pharaoh's officers who were with him in custody in his master's house, 'Why are your faces downcast today?' They said to him, 'We have had dreams, and there is no one to interpret them.' And Joseph said to them, 'Do not interpretations belong to God? Tell them to me, I pray you'" (Genesis 40:5–8, my emphasis).

The only substantive difference between this translation and the King James is in the first sentence, which in the KJV runs like this: "And they dreamed a dream both of them, each man his dream in one night, each man according to the *interpretation* of his dream, the butler and the baker of the king of Egypt, which were bound in the prison" (my emphasis). Where the modern version has *meaning*, the king's translators put *interpretation*. They were right. The Hebrew root for what shows up in the Revised Standard Version as *meaning, interpret*, and *interpretation* is the same: *p-t-r*. In verbal form (*patar*) it means "interpret," and in nominal form (*pitron*) it means "interpretation." The action it denotes belongs to the person perceiving the mysterious object (in this case, a dream), *not* to the mysterious object. In the Hebrew Bible, dreams don't *mean*. They don't do anything but get dreamed. Someone with powers conferred by God *interprets* them, because, as we learn in the following chapter, where Pharaoh himself is now the dreamer, God *makes known* (*higgid*), via dreams and then via the *interpreter* (*poter*) *of* those dreams, once again Joseph, what he is about to do (Genesis 41:25).

The other major place where what we would think of as *meaning* comes up is the Book of Daniel. Here, in another story of exile, once again (as in the case of Pharaoh's dream) there is a dream dreamed by a non-Jewish ruler, once again the dream requires interpretation, and once again a Jew gives that interpretation. Because the Book of Daniel is written not in Hebrew but in the closely related Semitic language Aramaic, the verbal root, *p-sh-r*, is slightly different from, though etymologically cognate with, the Hebrew *p-t-r*. In chapter 5, we have what might suggest the most literal notion of *meaning*, the famous story of the writing on the wall. Today we'd ask what the *meaning* of the writing is or what the writing *means*. But King Belshazzar says to Daniel, "I have heard that you are able to make interpretation [literally "to interpret interpretation," since verb and noun are from the same root] and loosen knots [that is, solve problems]; now if you can read the writing and make known to me its interpretation, in purple will you be clothed" (Daniel 5:16, my translation). Daniel answers with an account of the overreaching transgressions that the king and his father, Nebuchadnezzar, have committed, and then proceeds to his explanation of the writing. The Jewish Publication Society translation renders the opening of Daniel's explanation in the way we would naturally express the thought today: "This is the writing that is inscribed: MENE MENE TEKEL UPHARSIN. And this is its meaning" (5:25–26). But, translated literally, what Daniel says is "This is the *interpretation* [*peshar*] of the speech" (5:26, my emphasis). He then pronounces each of the words that the mysterious hand has written on the wall and *interprets* each one for the king: "MENE [*mene*], God has numbered [*menah*] your kingdom and brought it to an end," and so on (Daniel 5:26, my translation). So, we might say that this part of Daniel's answer to the king, what he declares to be the interpretation, constitutes the *meaning* of the writing on the wall, under-stood as something that this writing "contains." But neither biblical Hebrew nor Aramaic has a word for that.

What about *meaning* as in "the meaning of life"? Needless to say, there's no passage in the Hebrew Bible that could be literally translated as "the meaning of life" since, as we've just seen, there's no word that corresponds to our word *meaning*, not to mention that the Hebrew word for "life" does not custom-arily refer to human lived experience and its duration (though, oddly, one of the few exceptions occurs in Ecclesiastes 2:17, where the speaker declares, "I hated life"). But does the *idea* (as best we can specify what this idea is) occur in the Hebrew Bible? The *locus classicus* for ancient Jewish "existen-tial despair," to speak anachronistically, is Ecclesiastes, one of the "Wisdom Books" of the Hebrew Bible. Tradition attributes this book to King Solomon, which would place it as early as the tenth century BCE. More recent critical scholars, however, place it anywhere from as early as the fifth to as late as the third century BCE.[1] That the subject of the book is "the meaning of life" or, perhaps more accurately, "the meaninglessness of life," as we understand these expressions in the modern world, appears to be almost a truism. That's not surprising, given how the book starts off: "Vapor of vapors, said Kohelet [the speaker], vapor of vapors, all is vapor. What profit is there to a man in all the labor at which he labors under the heavens?" (Ecclesiastes 1:2–3, my translation). That sounds like a ripe context for pondering "the meaning of life," doesn't it?

In *The Message: The Bible in Contemporary Language*, a modern, highly colloquial translation created between 1993 and 2002, Presbyterian pastor Eugene H. Peterson uses the word *meaning* liberally in Ecclesiastes. A few lines after the despondent opening, we read this: "Everything's boring, utterly boring—no one can find any meaning in it" (1:8). Literal translation: "All words [or "all things," *devarim*] are wearisome, a man cannot speak [them], the eye is not satisfied with seeing, and the ear is not fulfilled with hearing." Nothing even close to our word *meaning*, and yet, translated into our modern language, it almost rings true. Peterson has included his own chapter subheadings throughout *The Message*, and in chapter 7 of Ecclesiastes, one section bears the subheading "How to Interpret the Meaning of Life." "I con-centrated with all my might," we read there, "studying and exploring and seeking wisdom—the meaning of life" (7:24). And since this section spills over into the following chapter, we're not surprised to read this opening verse: "There's nothing better than being wise, / Knowing how to interpret the meaning of life. / Wisdom puts light in the eyes, / And gives gentleness to words and manners" (Ecclesiastes 8:1). Again, the original text contains nothing remotely resembling "the meaning of life" in either of these two passages. Literally translated, they read, "What is, [is] far off and deep, deep; who can find it?" (7:24) and "Who is like the wise man, and who knows the interpretation [*pesher*; the Aramaic word is used here] of a thing [or "word," *davar*]? The wisdom of a man lights up his face, and the boldness of his face is changed" (8:1). True, the word *pesher*, "interpretation," actually appears in 8:1, and it applies to *davar*, which could mean, from least to most specific, "thing," "matter," "word," or, in this context (as the Jewish Publication Society translators construe it), the "adage" that follows (about the wisdom of a man). If it's the least specific, then we might render it in modern colloquial English as "Who knows how to interpret stuff?" If that's what Kohelet was asking, then we might rightly say he was asking a question rather similar to "What is the meaning of life?" But just *rather* similar. The rhetorical question points to the failure of the interpreter to interpret, not to the failure of "stuff" to yield up its secrets. And if it's just "stuff" or "things," then the substance of this passage doesn't quite rise to the level of wondering about life itself.[2] And if there's a grand sense of mystery associated with life itself, as possibly hinted at in the passage from Ecclesiastes, that mystery is certainly not associated with the notion of seeking something that today we might call *meaning*.

Greece

If we travel northwest across the Mediterranean from the locus of these ancient writings, we discover a language featuring terms much more closely matched to English than can be found in ancient Hebrew. Greek has a verb whose semantic reach substantially overlaps with that of English *to mean*, though it largely lacks the element of *intention*. An equivalent to the noun *meaning* exists, but it is extremely rare. What Greek civilization does offer, however, is a number of remarkably sophisticated theories of meaning, if by *meaning* we understand "signification," what signs, words, and language do.

Underlying all conversation about signifying in ancient Greek is a group of nouns that mean "token," "sign," "omen," "name" (or, in a discussion of grammar, "noun")—something, that is, that stands for or points to something else. *Symbolon*, the source of our word *symbol*, comes from a verb that means, literally, "throw together," thus "join" or "unite." At its most basic level, *symbolon* refers to an object, such as a knucklebone (*astragalos*), that two parties to an agreement broke in two, so that in the future each party could prove his identity by being able to join ("throw together") his part with that of the other party. By extension, *symbolon* comes to mean "token," "tally" (originally, in English, a notched stick cut lengthwise, like the *symbolon*, so that the two pieces could be matched up as proof of an agreement) or, more generally, anything that refers to anything else. *Onoma*, the most basic word for "name" or "noun," gives the verb *onomazō*, "to name" or, by extension, "to mean" (signify).

Most important, however, is the cluster of words stemming from *sēma*, meaning "sign," "mark," "token," "omen," "signal"—anything that "stands for," "points to," or "represents" someone or something. From this root word we get the verb *sēmainō*, "to indicate, point by a sign," "to give signs," "to signify," "to mean." It's largely through the use of this verb and a number of other terms derived from *sēma* that we get Greek theories of meaning. Though there are numerous such theories, we can get a good idea of what a conversation about the signifying powers of language sounded like from the late fifth through the fourth century BCE by looking at Plato's *Cratylus* and a number of works by Aristotle. *Cratylus* rose to notoriety in the early years of modern linguistics for presenting the notion that names bear more than an arbitrary connection with the things they refer to. Whatever we might think of this notion, which Socrates illustrates with example after example in the dialogue, *signifying* is a fairly simple matter. A given noun or name *means* a certain thing. Thus when Socrates and Hermogenes are deciding whether the correct name for Hector's son should be Astyanax, as the Trojan men called him, or Scamandrius, as the women called him, Socrates chooses the former name because, like the name Hector, it is Greek. As he explains, "*Anax* and *hektōr* mean [*sēmainei*] roughly the same thing, both of them being names of kingly things [*basilika*]."[3] Thus the answer to the question "What do the words *anax* and *hektōr* mean?" would be "*basilika*." But in the *Cratylus*, there is no noun to indicate the function that the word *basilika* serves in this specific passage. That is, there is no generic term for the something that *any* particular word yields up when we hear or read it—what in English we would call that word's *meaning*.

In Aristotle, the picture is far more elaborate. The treatise *Peri hermēneias* (the English title is *On Interpretation*) would appear at first glance to be about the act of retrieving *meaning*. There's some debate about the Greek word used in the title of this work, *hermēneia*, which can certainly refer to the act of interpreting or explaining something but which can also refer to the act of expressing something. *Peri hermēneias*, it turns out, has relatively little to tell us about interpreting things, but it has plenty to say about *signifying*. Aristotle didn't buy the idea that words bear some sort of organic connection with the things they signify. In fact, he assigned "the things they signify" an astonishingly abstract and modern-sounding status. At the very beginning of the treatise, having covered the relationship between words and thoughts (words are *symbola*, "tokens," of *pathēmata*, "affections," in oneself), Aristotle makes the bold claim that nouns/names *mean* things independently of the truth or falsehood of those things. Thus the noun *tragelaphos*, "goat-stag," *means* something, whether or not there is truly such a thing in the world as a "goat-stag" (and everyone knows there isn't). On the basis partly of this provocative example, Aristotle goes on to claim that separate parts of names don't mean anything by themselves—thus this definition of *onoma*, "name": "A name, then, is a sound that is meaningful [*sēmantikē*] by convention [*kata synthēkēn*], without a tense [because it's not a verb], of which no part taken separately is meaningful [*sēmantikon*]."[4] The adjective that I've translated as "meaningful," *sēmantikos*, tells us that what it modifies (here, *sound* and *part*) carries out the action of the verb *sēmainō*, "to mean." Given the odd status of what gets *meant*, I think we can safely say that *sēmainō* denotes the act of *meaning* or *signifying* in the most basic sense, that is, simply "pointing at," "indicating," without regard for the status of what we're pointing at or indicating. Similarly, at the level of sentences or other extended utterances, we're looking at sounds that *mean*, but where the individual parts taken separately, that is, *words*, can also *mean* (because that, we just learned, is what words do).

In another treatise, the *Rhetoric*, Aristotle says that names/nouns are "imitations" (*mimēmata*), though he does not say of what. "And the voice, the most imitative of all parts of us," he goes on to say, "was there at the beginning."[5] Aristotle would appear to be lapsing into Cratylism, with the suggestion that names carry a natural resemblance to what they imitate—at least those that sound like what they imitate. Whatever he had in mind, he soon returns to the *signifying* power of language. The topic is good prose style and the need for clarity. "Speech [*logos*] being a sort of sign [*sēmeion*]," he says, "if it does not make clear, it will not do its own work."[6] If speech is only a sign and not an imitation, then there is a distinction between the sound of words and what they signify. Aristotle confirms this view when he cites Licymnius, a rhetorician who appears in Plato's *Phaedrus*, as claiming that "the beauty of a name . . . is in the sounds or in that-which-is-signified [*to sēmainomenon*]."[7]

Here is one of the handful of instances in the Greek language (that is, of course, in the extant texts) where a word appears that denotes something like our word *meaning*. Technically it's a passive participle of the verb *sēmainō*, used as a substantive (that is, as a noun). Thus: "something signified," "thing meant," "meaning." It suggests that when we encounter a word we perform an act of recovery for something that, so to speak, lies behind it; that is, we perform an act of *interpretation*. That act is all the more pronounced if words signify largely by convention rather than by sonic resemblance or by some other sort of organic connection. We need to get beyond the word itself to the something that it points to.

This sense of both signifying and interpreting would seem to comport easily with the notion of a "meaning of life" that is understood as a mysterious something lying behind the everyday appearances of our lives, something that we recover through an extraordinary act of interpretation or understanding. We could then say that the effort to find that something resembles the effort to find the *sēmainomenon* of a word, and then we could speak, if only figuratively, of a *sēmainomenon* of life—life now being analogous to a name. But, to begin with, the word *sēmainomenon* is extremely rare in classical Greek (again, in the extant texts). Greeks such as Plato and Aristotle might very well have developed fairly elaborate ideas about signifying, including ideas about the relationship between something that signifies and something that gets signified, but the "something that gets signified" did not achieve the sort of status that would have resulted in its acquiring its own frequently used noun. As we know from English, "What does X mean?" is not always identical to "What is the meaning of X?," even when we're speaking literally about, say, the meaning of a word. In Greek, it's difficult to imagine even a literal context in which someone would ask, "What is the *sēmainomenon* of X?" It's even more difficult to imagine a figurative context—for example, where X is *life*. An educated ancient Greek (I'm guessing, of course) would think you were asking about the word—either *zoē* or *bios*—and would also think that you'd come up with an extremely bizarre way of phrasing the question.

Now, what about oracles, dreams, and other stuff that signifies or "means" in a less direct way than words are supposed to do? If we're asking whether there's anything analogous in ancient Greece to "looking for the meaning of life," where we imagine an act of interpretation that uncovers a mysterious and hidden something-or-other behind a mysterious but perceptible something-that-serves-as-a-sign, does the answer lie in accounts of divination and interpretation? Here we find a rather odd picture. The something-or-other that we start with initially comes through a medium of some sort, who transmits the something-or-other not directly but by means of signs and riddles. These in turn require the services of yet another intermediary whose function is to *interpret* the signs and riddles—that is, to say explicitly what the medium and the signs and riddles said only confusingly. The medium is usually called a *mantis*, and the activity of transmission that the *mantis* carries out is conveyed by a verb or noun from the same root. That primitive root, -*man*-, has to do with rapture and ecstasy, as in *mania*. Translating these words into English is tricky, since there's nothing truly equivalent in our language. *Oracle* leads to problems, because it denotes both the medium and the thing conveyed. *Prophet* doesn't serve because it's taken from the Greek word *prophētēs*, which in some cases denotes the interpreter of what the *mantis* conveys. *Seer* is wrong, since it suggests that the person so designated *sees*, whereas some mediums *hear*. *Diviner* and *divination* are better: they etymologically carry an association with gods, and what a *mantis* delivers generally comes from a god. For want of a better choice, I'll use *divination* for the activity (after all, the god Apollo is usually lurking behind the scenes) and stick with the Greek word *mantis* for the person who carries out the activity.

You might recall that the *Iliad* opens with a dispute between Agamemnon and Achilles. Apollo has visited a plague upon the Achaians (Greeks). The daughter of his priest Chryses has been taken captive by Agamemnon, who, smitten with his prize and wishing to keep her, refuses to accept the priest's offer of ransom. Everyone seems to know this, yet Achilles, in an attempt to prove the obvious to his rival, proposes the natural course of action when we need to know what Apollo is up to: "But come, let's ask some *mantis* or priest or even a dream interpreter—for after all a dream too comes from Zeus—who might tell why Phoebus Apollo is so angry."[8] Luckily, such a man is there in the crowd—Kalchas, described as "the best of the augurs" (bird-interpreters). What can Kalchas offer? He is one "who knew things present, things future, things past, and led the ships of the Achaians into Troy, by means of that divination power [*mantosynē*] that Phoebus Apollo bestows."[9] So if we're asking, "To what—say, something equivalent to our *meaning*—does Kalchas's divination power give him access?," we have one answer in the phrase that begins with "things present." It's worth pointing out a peculiarity of Greek: the word I translated as "knew" is actually a tense of the verb "to see." In Greek, "I have seen" (perfect tense) implies—and thus means the same thing as—"I know." For Kalchas, *seeing* appears to be the key. He fears retribution from Agamemnon if he tells the truth, so Achilles promises him protection: "Taking courage, do tell the divine vision [*theopropion*] that you have seen [i.e., know]."[10] Kalchas sees and reveals a *theopropion*; again, we have a direct object of a verb of seeing or revealing. In this case, the thing seen and revealed already contains the idea of seeing, since *theopropion* is constructed from the word for "god" and from a verb (*prepō*) having to do with seeing: "stuff that gods see." So, is there something equivalent to our *meaning*, as today we might ask Kalchas, "What is the meaning of this plague?" Yes, but only if by *meaning* we understand "explanation." Kalchas knows past, present, and future and sees "stuff that gods see." "Stuff that gods see" is not exactly the same thing as *meaning*: it's certainly what gets retrieved and conveyed when an augur, by means of his special powers, obeys the order "Reveal to us the reason for which Apollo is upset with us." But there's no generic word for the thing retrieved, as in our question "What's the meaning of this plague?"

The most celebrated *mantis*, of course, is the Pythia, commonly referred to as the Delphic Oracle. Lots of confusion has grown up around this figure, who has conventionally been represented in modern times as speaking exclusively in wild and inarticulate ravings. Classicist Joseph Fontenrose debunked this image years ago, demonstrating that in virtually all extant accounts the mantic woman speaks rationally and intelligibly.[11] Either way, her function is to transmit, which she does sometimes by simply speaking for Apollo in the first person, as if rendering his words directly, and sometimes by speaking in the third person. Even if she was represented as speaking Apollo's words directly, the belief was not uncommon that the words spoken at Delphi were a distortion of whatever was being transmitted. So in the late sixth or early fifth century BCE, in one of the many mysterious fragments that have survived from what was apparently a single work, the pre-Socratic philosopher Heraclitus wrote this: "The lord [*anax*] whose divination [*manteion*] is the one in Delphi neither speaks nor conceals but gives signs [*sēmainei*]."[12] Lovely statement, both because, as just a fragment, it is mysterious by nature and because its very topic is mysterious communication. "The lord" no doubt refers to Apollo, but no one knows what the context was here. Did Heraclitus mention the Pythia in the next line? That verb at the end of the sentence: it's the one that can also be translated as "means," though it would be a bit odd to say, "The lord . . . neither speaks nor conceals but means." So Apollo "gives signs," and since it's at Delphi, he gives them via the Pythia, placing someone who consults her at one or two removes from—what? The thing that Apollo said? The thing that he distorted by neither speaking nor concealing it before letting the Pythia have her way with it? Whatever it is, it doesn't have a name. We can't call it *sēmainomenon*, "that-which-is-signified," "the meaning," as in Aristotle, because signifying is not what's going on here. "Making signs" is.

But the Pythia was not the only one who claimed to speak for—or from— Apollo. There's Cassandra, in Aeschylus's *Agamemnon*. She's introduced as simply a captive that the titular hero has brought home as a prize from the war with Troy. At first when she enters, she stands silent, as Agamemnon's wife, Clytemnestra, tries to figure out what to do with her. The chorus naturally assumes the young woman doesn't speak the language and is thus in need of an interpreter (*hermēneus*, one who carries out *hermēneia*, as in Aristotle's work on that topic). It turns out that Cassandra needs a different sort of *hermēneus*; she begins to speak in Greek, but, unlike the Pythia, she speaks in wild, ecstatic exclamations.

A rich lexicon of terms is brought in to identify what Cassandra does and what she is. The minute she opens her mouth, as a stream of inarticulate sounds and "O Apollo!" issue forth, the chorus says, "She seems to be about to proclaim," using a verb (*khraō*) that refers specifically to oracular proclamations. The chorus speaks of her "mantic fame" but also refers to her indirectly as a *prophētēs* ("We don't need any prophets around here"). The chorus calls the things she says *manteumata* (mantic utterances) and tells us she speaks in riddles (*ainigmata*, from which our word *enigma* comes).[13]

Of course, like the Athenian spectators watching this tragedy, we know full well what's going to happen, just as we know full well that "what's going to happen" (*to mellon*) is what Cassandra is telling us. Once that comes to pass, as Cassandra tells the chorus, "you, taking pity on me, will declare me a *mantis* of truth [*alēthomantis*]."[14] So, Cassandra has access to the truth (*alētheia*) and conveys it to us. The chorus repeatedly refers to Cassandra's utterances as *thesphata*, literally "sayings from a god."[15] While spewing out one grim prognostication after another, Cassandra says, "These testimonies [*martyria*—our word *martyr* comes from a word that means "witness"] I trust," and the chorus tells her, "You appear to be foretelling [*thespizein*, literally "to godspeak"] trustworthy things [*pista*]."[16] Yet, even though she has "testimonies" as well as access to the truth and to trustworthy things, grasping what she's saying is no easy feat. At one point she complains that the chorus is not understanding her, even though she knows Greek pretty well. The chorus responds, "And [just like] the Pythian sayings, [what you say is] equally hard to understand."[17] There's a reason for this that is peculiar to Cassandra, among Apollo's various mantic mediums. Cassandra, we find out, had promised to bear Apollo a child but then broke her word. In retaliation, the god condemned her to carry out her mantic arts without being understood. So, presumably Apollo sends something her way, she voices that something, and baffled listeners seek to interpret it. Once again, that something has no generic name, unless perhaps *truth* or *what's going to happen* can be considered a generic name. The verb for signifying, *sēmainō*, is used in this tragedy only in the sense of "to give a signal" or "to portend," never in the sense of "to mean." There is thus nothing corresponding to our *meaning*, in the sense of something that's recovered through an act of interpretation.

Fontenrose notwithstanding, some ancients clearly believed that the message conveyed by a *mantis*, even if not expressed in ecstatic ravings, required the services of a *prophētēs*, "interpreter" (also "foreteller"). In Plato's *Timaeus*, probably written sometime before the middle of the fourth century BCE, the titular participant in the dialogue explains the complicated process of transmission in a section devoted to bodily organs and their functions. The liver, it turns out, is the seat of divination (*manteia*). Given the literally lowly situation of this organ (beneath the diaphragm), it is not surprising that the divination it carries out merits little respect. But the passage that Timaeus devotes to the liver clarifies the relation between divination and interpretation and thus implicitly gives us the links in the chain that extend from an otherworldly original source to us:

> It is customary to set the race of interpreters [*prophētai*] as judges over godly [*entheos*] divinations [*manteiais*], whom [that is, the interpreters] some people call diviners [*manteis*] themselves, not knowing that these [interpreters] are not diviners but expounders [*hypokritai*] of speech and visions that come through riddles; and they should be called not diviners but, more justly, interpreters [*prophētai*] of those who divine. The nature of the liver—namely, for the purpose of divination—is such that it has come to be located where we say it is. And yet, of course, during the time that each person is alive, the liver receives signs [*sēmeia*] that are more visible, but once deprived of life it [the liver] becomes blind and receives divinations [*manteia*] that are obscure rather than signifying [*sēmainein*] something clear.[18]

Divinations are thus a messy business. As Timaeus has explained just before this passage, we deal with divinations not when we are in our right minds but when we are sleeping or otherwise impaired. That's why, when it comes to divinations, we need the services of a *prophētēs*, who can interpret. Thus the *mantis*—or anyone engaged in divining—gives signs, and the *prophētēs* tells you what the signs mean. But, as before, we have to ask: what is the original thing that comes to us by such a complicated route? Something turns into divinations, which are received by a *mantis*, who turns them into signs, which are received and presumably understood by an interpreter. But what is that original something? Again, there is no name for it, and, given the ambiguity of the verb *sēmainō*, which in this context can mean either "signify" or simply "give signs," we couldn't offer *sēmainomenon* as the name of the thing that a person consulting a *mantis* or a *prophētēs* finally receives.

Ancient Greece, of course, featured a two-realm worldview, that of Plato, whose dialogues famously present an account of ideas (*ideai*) that transcend the world of ordinary perception. These ideas have names—"the good," "the beautiful," "being," and so forth—and they are regarded as having always existed. But nowhere are they likened to a *meaning* that we retrieve as we do from words in a written text. And, to the extent that acts of interpretation are employed in efforts to uncover mysteries of various sorts that come our way, "life" itself is not among those mysteries, nor is there any talk of something that we might translate as *meaning* and that, in the singular, is construed as a kind of absolute, mysterious something.

Latin, by contrast, has a range of words that correspond, in varying ways and to varying degrees, to some of the various senses of our word *meaning* in ordinary usage. It also became the language of choice for conveying another two-realm worldview, that of early Christianity. That's where we'll first find *meaning* used as the object of a metaphysical interpretive quest into a mysterious, invisible realm separate from the realm of direct experience. And it's where signification, reading, and interpretation will begin to acquire elasticity, as they get stretched from their primitive, more literal senses to include larger, increasingly nebulous objects.

2

Christianity, Scripture, and "Reading" the World, from Augustine to Bishop Berkeley

Reading the World with Saint Augustine (and Others)

If our English word *meaning* in ordinary usage means "signifying," that is, what signs, words, and stories do, or "thing signified," that is, what signs, words, and stories "point to," then in order for us to use the word and its associated concept in connection with something that is not normally thought of as signifying—say, life, nature, the world—we must take the structure of signifying and translate it to that something. Just as we regard a sign or word, even one that bears some sort of perceptible resemblance to what it signifies (and "what it signifies" encompasses a whole range of possibilities), as an intermediary between us and what it signifies, we must now regard life, nature, or the world as an intermediary between us and something mysterious that, figuratively speaking, lies behind it, something that it "points to." And just as we read a sign or a printed word, we can imagine that we're "reading" the world or nature, which now metaphorically takes on the character of a written text.

German philosopher Hans Blumenberg (1920–1996) investigated the notion of "reading" the world in *Die Lesbarkeit der Welt* (The readability of the world, 1981). The notion of reading the world, and thus the notion of finding in the world something that might be translated into English as *meaning*, arises as early as Augustine (354–430), and it happens in connection with Augustine's rejection of Gnosticism. As Blumenberg presents it, the argument goes like this: Gnosticism accepts the existence of a realm of Platonic ideas, together with the belief that the ideas and the Demiurge that created them were always already there. Christian theology, by contrast, rests on the acceptance of *creatio ex nihilo*, characterized as an act that, in its absolute

What Do We Mean When We Talk About Meaning? Steven Cassedy, Oxford University Press. © Oxford University Press 2022. DOI: 10.1093/oso/9780190936907.003.0003

quality, reflects the ultimate arbitrariness of the Creator's will. When we humans become investigators of nature, we are thus condemned to the role of interpreters, confronting signs and searching for a meaning that lies behind them. "At the same time, however," Blumenberg writes, "man as investigator of nature is limited to what the Creator, conceived as [a] jealous [God], might wish to divulge of his secret . . . and yet at the same time there arise the formulae whose historical interpretation can reveal and legitimize the field of his [man's] curiosity, laying the groundwork for his own Demiurgics."[1] The world now comes to be seen as a book, which stands in a peculiar relationship to the actual book of Scripture, and there arises a division of humankind into those who know how to "read" and those who do not.

The question comes up in Augustine's extended commentary on the Psalms, *Enarrationes in Psalmos* (Exposition of the Psalms), in connection with the language of Psalm 46 (45 in the Septuagint numbering that Augustine used), whose first three lines read, "God is our refuge and strength, a very present help in trouble. Therefore will not we fear, though the earth be removed, and though the mountains be carried into the midst of the sea; Though the waters thereof roar and be troubled, though the mountains shake with the swelling thereof. Selah" (Psalm 46:1–3, KJV). Augustine naturally reads the Jewish scriptures from the vantage point of Christian history, and his task consequently is to interpret them as prophetic of, or simply as illuminating, that history. The implicit question is, "Are mountains ever literally carried into the midst of the sea?" The answer is, "No, it's a metaphor." For even when Jesus said, "If ye have faith as a grain of mustard seed, ye shall say unto this mountain, Remove hence to yonder place; and it shall remove; and nothing shall be impossible unto you" (Matthew 17:20), what he really meant was not that mountains will actually move but that, as Augustine phrases it, "through your most faithful preaching, it will be done, so that this mountain, that is, I myself, will be preached among the Gentiles, glorified among the Gentiles, recognized among the Gentiles." The mountain is Jesus, and the sea is the Gentiles, among whom Jesus has appeared, in order that he may "be preached."

How does reading the book of the world fit into this picture, and how does a metaphor function in that "book"? It turns out that the book of the world reflects what was predicted in the book of Scriptures, so even the illiterate can "read." Here is how Augustine explains it: "What then follows from the fact that the mountains were moved into the heart of the sea? Attend and see the truth. For these things, when they were said, were obscure, since they had not yet happened. But today, who does not know them, now that they have been accomplished? The divine page [actual Scripture] should be a book to you, that you may hear these things; the circle of the world should be a book to you, that you may see these things. In *that* book [actual Scripture], no one reads except those who know the alphabet; [but] in the world as a whole even the uneducated may read."[2] The evidence of your senses *in the world* will show you not mountains but the truth of Jesus among the Gentiles. Needless to say, it takes a reader—a literate one, in the literal sense of the word, and a very smart one, at that—to have discovered the *meaning* of the text in the actual Scriptures, something that requires a fairly sophisticated act of interpretation. Presumably the illiterate reader of the world has no need of the intermediate step (the image of the mountains in the sea) in order to see the reality of a world that has resulted from Jesus' presence among the Gentiles.

All this makes a certain kind of sense, but there's a step in the historical process that Blumenberg leaves out. The authority that Augustine invokes in his commentary on the Psalms is *Scriptura Dei*, the Scripture of God, or the "book" that a smart reader reads and interprets in order to discover meanings that are prophetic of (Christian) history. Does the expression *Scriptura Dei* refer vaguely to "God's writings," in the sense of God's utterances as recorded by or dictated to human beings? Or is it an expression equivalent to what we denote today when we say "the Bible," that is, in the Christian sense, a fixed collection of writings, organized into two testaments with their constituent books, and all printed together (or capable of being printed together) as a single, portable object?

Of course, it's not precisely either. But let's assume that Augustine is referring to his era's equivalent of what Christians today call "the Bible." What is it, and what does it look like? Even though "the Bible" today, as to what it contains and in what order, might vary slightly from one Christian sect or denomination to another (and even though contents and order might be the subject of heated debate among sects and denominations), the notion of a fixed collection, printed in a single, portable book, is accepted without controversy today, at least outside scholarly circles, and has been for centuries. But let's not forget that the process, known as *canon formation*, by which the contents of the Christian Bible and the order of those contents were established, continued for centuries, even after the specifically Christian writings constituting what would come to be called the New Testament were composed (from around 60 CE till the end of the first century or the early decades of the second). Steps in the process included the widely accepted designation of certain texts as "scripture" (*graphē* in Greek), suggesting authoritative and divine status; the establishment, within Judaism, of a fixed canon of texts constituting the Jewish scriptures (as distinguished from the Old Testament, which is a Christian conception), something that, itself, continued for several centuries after the early Christian era; the acceptance of texts from the Jewish scriptures as enjoying the status of scripture among Christians (as early as the first century CE); the emergence of the idea of two "covenants" or "testaments," one represented in the texts of Judaism and one represented in the newer texts of Christianity, and the introduction of the word *diathēkē* ("testament," "covenant") to denote each of the two collections of texts (sometime in the second half of the second century CE); the stabilization and fixing of the contents of the two testaments; the publication of these writings either as two separate testaments or as both testaments in one object; the dissemination of these publications across a sizable area in such a way that, either through private possession or through public reading, a sizable number of people had access to them.

By the end of the fourth century CE, when Augustine began work on *Enarrationes*, two crucial developments had taken place. First, the canon for the two testaments had been settled, not down to the last detail and not by ecclesiastical authority (that would have to wait more than a millennium for the Council of Trent, which issued its decree on the canon of scriptures in 1546), but in such a way that it seems safe to conclude there was general agreement in the Christian church on the broad outlines of the contents, if not on the ordering of those contents. Though modern-day scholars of canon formation present an often bewildering array of views about the various stages of canon formation and the dates of those stages (the Jewish scriptures among Jews, the Pauline writings, the Gospels, the Old and New Testaments, the complete Bible), a series of steps in the second half of the fourth century CE indicates at the very least substantial agreement among churchmen who wielded considerable authority in their own eras. Chief among them are these two: Eusebius (c. 260–c. 340), bishop of Caesarea (Palestine) from about 314 CE till the end of his life, is credited with fixing the New Testament canon. His *Church History*, finished around 325 CE, included a list of twenty-seven books making up the New Testament. Though Eusebius did not explicitly use the word *canon*, this is the list that became standard down to the present day.[3] Then, in 367, Athanasius, bishop of Alexandria from 328 to 373, in his annual letter announcing the date of Easter (an episcopal duty), chose to include a passage on the Divine Scriptures. He gave the complete list of books for both testaments, but, unlike Eusebius earlier in the century, Athanasius was confident in explicitly asserting the absolutely canonical status of these books. The Old Testament list, apart from the order of the books, is virtually identical to the list in modern-day Christian Bibles. The New Testament list is entirely identical to the list in modern-day Christian Bibles, again except for the order of the books.[4]

Augustine himself gave an account of the scriptural canon in 396 CE, in his treatise *On Christian Doctrine* (*De doctrina christiana*, sometimes translated as *On Christian Teaching*). Like Athanasius before him, he uses the term *canon* and its corresponding adjective *canonicus*. Having advised his reader that, "in the matter of the canonical scriptures, he should follow as much as possible the authority of the catholic churches among which properly are those that have deserved to have apostolic seats and to receive epistles," Augustine announces his list like this: "The whole canon of scripture . . . consists of these books" and then presents his list. His Old Testament includes five books that Athanasius did not count as canonical but, apart from the order of the books, is otherwise identical. His list of New Testament books, apart from the order, is the same as Athanasius's.[5] With minor changes to the list of Old Testament books, Augustine's list remained the same to the end of his life.[6] It is thus safe to say that, despite minor disagreement on various issues, by the end of the fourth century a consensus had emerged both on the broad outlines of the Old Testament and on the exact contents of the New Testament, such that a writer could be confident that *scriptura divina* (divine Scripture) or *scriptura Dei* (Scripture of God), with due allowance for minor variations, would suggest the same thing to Christians over a very broad area—just as today, when we hear someone begin a sentence with "The Bible says," we don't pause to wonder whether the Bible in question is the one used in the Catholic Church or the one used in Episcopal congregations.

A key to the other development I mentioned may be found in the sentence "In *that* book, no one reads except those who know the alphabet." The Latin phrase that I've translated as "in that book" is *in istis codicibus*, literally "in those codices." In the previous sentence ("The divine page should be a book to you . . . the circle of the world should be a book to you"), Augustine had used the generic word *liber* (any sort of book). "In those codices" tells us that the physical object Augustine envisions when he speaks of reading Scripture is a codex, that is, a stack of pages attached together, very much like a modern book, by contrast with a scroll, the preferred format for the Jewish scriptures among the Jews themselves. What does this tell us, beyond a simple fact about the physical form of Augustine's sacred texts?

New Testament scholar and book historian Harry Y. Gamble has written a history of early Christian texts, the physical form in which they were produced, and the manner of their dissemination. Four elements of the story have a bearing on our discussion. First, the codex is the physical form of the book that came to be adopted in Christian communities between the second and the fourth centuries CE. The codex, more than the scroll, allowed for the inclusion of several texts in one volume, and it allowed the reader to read those texts out of sequence much more easily.[7] Second, because of its practical advantages, including its compactness and its portability, the codex came to be widely used in Christian religious life, whether or not for liturgical purposes. Gamble points out that codices, as they became increasingly common, circulated among congregations more than among individuals. They thus became "practical instruments of a variety of religious purposes."[8] As, for example, the Pauline letters took on first scriptural authority and then canonical status, the codex allowed for their wide distribution as well as for their easy public and private reading. Third, the wider distribution of codices than of scrolls, the relatively high level of literacy (paltry, of course, by today's standards) that developed among early Christians, and the practice of reading religious texts aloud in public resulted in the exposure of a greater number of people to Scripture. Fourth, by the time of Augustine, Christianity had come to show a powerful orientation toward the written word, as, in Gamble's words, texts had become "the essential instruments of Christian life."[9] The idea is that even illiterate people who were exposed to Scripture by hearing someone read it aloud understood that what they were hearing was, well, Scripture—that is, *the written Word*.

Augustine's choice of the word *codex* for actual Scripture, by contrast with the "Scripture" of the world, indicates that he is envisioning the physical object, with handwritten words on leaves of parchment or papyrus, that you hold in your hands or place on a desk and *read*. But, as his discussion in the nearly contemporaneous *De doctrina christiana* shows, the contents of the physical codex or codices that he has in mind conform to a standard that by now, at the very end of the fourth century CE and beginning of the fifth, has in its broad outlines been widely accepted. Now, by contrast with the world of two centuries earlier, *Scriptura Dei* or *Scriptura divina* denotes a body of written texts that, apart from quibbles about a handful of them and minor variations in their order, are basically the same for all Christians. And that implies that the literate person qualified to read those texts is engaged in acts of interpretation and meaning-seeking in the most basic and literal sense. That's what you do when you read a written text: you seek and find meaning. In fact, that's the entire mission of the *Enarrationes in Psalmos*: seeking and finding the correct meaning in a text where such meaning is presumably difficult to find. The entire work, sentence by sentence, is a demonstration of Augustine's skill at this activity.

But Augustine did not simply demonstrate his skill at interpretation; he wrote about it explicitly, in Book II of *De doctrina christiana*, the book in which he presents his list of canonical Scriptures. More precisely, Book II gives a theory of signs and meaning. Augustine begins his account, as we might expect, with a definition. "For a sign," he writes, "is a thing that, beyond the appearance that it brings to the senses, causes something else to enter our thoughts."[10] Twice in the first two paragraphs Augustine uses the phrase *praeter se significare*, "to signify/point to, something beyond itself"— phrasing remarkably similar to modern definitions of *sign*. Signs fall into two categories: natural signs (*signa naturalia*) and what would be translated literally as "given signs" (*signa data*). Here's how Augustine explains the distinction: "Natural [signs] are those that, without will or desire to signify beyond themselves, cause something else [other than themselves] to be known, as [for example] smoke signifies fire."[11] The second type is generally translated as "conventional signs," but Augustine has a good reason for his word choice, which is to emphasize the intentional nature of these signs: someone (or some creature) *gives* them. "Given signs, in truth," he writes, "are those that all living things give each other for the purpose of showing, as much as possible, the motions of their mind or things that they have sensed or understood." For the purpose of the "given sign" is "to draw out and transfer to the mind of another that which he who is giving the sign bears from his own mind."[12]

But here is the key feature of "given signs" that makes them relevant to Christian doctrine: "Even the signs given by God [*signa divinitus data*] that are contained in the holy Scriptures are shown [*indicata*] to us by the men who wrote them down."[13] The signs we find in the Divine Scriptures are *given* signs, which means that they carry the intention of the author who gave them. In the passages that follow this statement, Augustine writes of what at first glance sounds like *meaning*. The issue is complicated by his use of two closely related words: *sensum* and *sensus*, both of which are derived from the verb *sentire*, "to perceive by the senses." *Sensum* (neuter past participle of *sentire*, used as a substantive) means "thought," "idea," and, by extension, "meaning" or "intention." *Sensus* (fourth declension noun), as Augustine uses it here, means "sense" (as in the five senses), though it is also used to denote the sense or meaning of a word. At the most basic level, what happens when we use signs is we communicate our ideas/thoughts/meanings (*sensa*) by means of signs, and those signs relate to our various senses (*sensūs*). Among signs, words enjoy primacy of place: "For words," writes Augustine, "acquired primacy for signifying those things that have been conceived in the mind if someone wishes to put those things forth. . . . An innumerable multitude of signs by which men pass along their thoughts is constituted in words."[14]

Much of the rest of Book II is taken up with the question of translation. Here, once again, Augustine addresses the notion of using words in order to convey what can be rendered as *meaning*, though Augustine now uses the word *sententia*, which carries the idea of the speaker's or author's intended thought. It is thus close to the English *meaning*, to the extent that our word suggests not only the thought but also the intention of the speaker (what the speaker *means*—assuming, of course, that what gets signified is what the speaker intends). The aim of the translator, Augustine explains, must be to translate not just words but thoughts/meanings (*sententiae*), and this requires a sound knowledge of the languages that are being translated (in this case into Latin). When we evaluate a translation, we are attempting to establish whether errors may be detected, which suggests that a correct meaning, in the original language, underlies the translation.[15] What is ultimately at stake is *truth* and its relation to the language that expresses (or fails to express) it. Augustine devotes several paragraphs of Book II to the capacity of language to bring out truth. He makes five related assertions: (1) truth is presented in *sententiae*, (2) those *sententiae* appear in Holy Scripture, (3) *sententiae* can be true or false, (4) truth depends also on the sequence of thought (*connexio*) in the presentation, and (5) sequence of thought was instituted by God. As Augustine puts it: "The truth of thoughts/meanings is to be sought in the holy books of the Church. The truth itself of sequences of thought [*connexionum*] is not instituted by men but [merely] observed and noted [by men], in order that they [men] may either learn or teach it [the truth]. For truth is perpetual and is instituted by God in the reason of things [*in rerum ratione*]."[16]

Let's look again at what Augustine wrote about the two "books." The distinction he draws is between actual reading, that is, reading characters printed in a codex or scroll, and the figurative "reading" of the world. This is not the only place in the *Enarrationes* that he conflates sacred texts with something outside those texts. His commentary on Psalm 8 includes an extended passage that establishes an equivalence between the Scriptures and the heavens. His analysis turns on this passage in the Psalm: "For I shall see your heavens, the works of your fingers, and the moon and the stars that you brought forth" (8:4). Here is what Augustine wrote:

> We read that the Law was written by the finger of God and given through Moses, His holy servant; by which finger of God many have come to understand the Holy Spirit. So, if by "fingers of God" we rightly understand these very same ministers [referenced earlier] who are filled with the Holy Spirit—on account of the same Spirit that operates in them, since it is by them that Divine Scripture has been composed for us all—then we are being consistent in understanding that, in this passage, the books of both Testaments are being called "the heavens." It was said of Moses himself by the magicians of Pharaoh, when they were bested by him, "This is the finger of God" [Exodus 8:19]. And it is written, "Heaven is folded up like a book" [Isaiah 34:4], and even if this is said of this ethereal heaven [that is, the actual heaven or sky], still, in conformity with the same likeness, the heavens of books [that is, the heavens that *are* the sacred books] are named by allegory. "For I shall see your heavens," he [the Psalmist] says, "the works of your fingers," that is, I shall discern and understand the Scriptures, which, by your ministers through the operation of the Holy Spirit, you have written down.
>
> Accordingly, the heavens named earlier may be understood as the same books, where he [the Psalmist] says, "For your glory is raised above the heavens," so that the entire sense [*sensus*] is, "For your glory is raised above the heavens": Your glory surpasses the utterances of all the Scriptures; out of the mouth of infants and sucklings you have brought renown, so that those who wish to attain knowledge of your glory, which is elevated above Scriptures, because it goes beyond and surpasses the proclamations of all words and languages, might begin with faith in the Scriptures. Therefore, God brought the Scriptures down to the [mental] capacity of infants and sucklings, as it is sung in another Psalm: "He brought down heaven and came down" [Psalm 18:9].... Hence is destroyed the rash and blind promiser of the truth, who is the enemy and the defender [of the truth] when the heavens are seen as the works of the fingers of God, that is, when the Scriptures, brought down to the slowness of infants, are understood and

[when,] through the humbleness of historical belief, which is born in time, [the Scriptures] lift up these infants, well nourished and strengthened, toward the things that they [the Scriptures] have confirmed, to the sublimity of the understanding of things eternal. Clearly these heavens, that is, these books, are the works of God's fingers, for truly they were composed by the Holy Spirit operating in the saints.[17]

Naturally the attentive reader will note that Augustine appears to be saying something here that is at odds with what he says about Psalm 46. There he suggested that in order to read the actual Scriptures you needed to be literate, while even a simple man (*idiota* in Latin) can read the "Scriptures" of the world. Here, by contrast, he claims that God made the actual Scriptures accessible to the slow minds of infants and sucklings, who are then lifted up "to the sublimity of the understanding of things eternal." But what matters for our purposes here is not that in one passage the dim-witted metaphorically "read" only the book of nature whereas in another they literally read the Scriptures themselves, but that in both passages all of us, from the dim-witted on up, are taking something that isn't a book and reading it as if it *were* a book. The simple man "reads" the world. Infants and sucklings, via their literal reading of Scripture, are "reading" the heavens and the "things eternal" therein. The act of interpreting, that is, seeking meaning (*sensus, sententia, intellectus*), is thus directed not at texts written down in codices (or scrolls) but at what we now treat as a text (though it isn't one literally): heaven and earth. If literal texts contain signs, in the form of words, then heaven and earth contain signs of a different sort, but signs nonetheless. Like the signs that are words, these signs point *praeter se*, beyond themselves. What they point to are "things eternal," God's truth uncorrupted by "the rash and blind promiser." They are, from the perspective of mere mortals, intrinsically open to dispute and therefore ambiguous, for who among us can claim with absolute authority to have discovered God's truth, to have looked directly at things eternal? No, such things are shrouded in mystery and subject to interpretive acts that can never be guaranteed to reveal an absolute truth. Signs appear to carry multiple meanings.

Here is the step that will lead the way, centuries later, to talk of "the meaning of life" and equivalent phrases in European languages other than English (where *meaning* appears in the singular but is always deeply ambiguous and polyvalent). The nexus of words that we find in Latin offers a set of nuances slightly different from the ones we find in the English *meaning*.

As we've seen, *sensus* and *sententia* are connected with senses and feeling, not only on the part of the giver of meaning (*sententia* suggests the intended thought—even personal opinion—formed in the mind of the speaker or author) but also on the part of the receiver of meaning. *Intellectus* is connected with the *mind* of the receiver of meaning (the *understanding* that the receiver forms from what is conveyed). *Significatio* and the verb *significare* are generally associated more often with the *sign*, the thing that points *praeter se*, beyond itself, and less often with the author or speaker who signifies something. But the activity that Augustine describes takes the interpreting we carry out when we read an actual written text and transposes it to the world or heavens. And in order for this transposition to work, we must presuppose a separation between, on the one side, what we directly perceive in this world (or the heavens) and, on the other, a realm that we hold to be beyond (*praeter*), where certain truths and qualities, hidden to plain view, reside. The world we perceive is thus filled with signs, which point to those truths and qualities, represented as *meanings*.

Centuries later, Blumenberg writes, the medieval theologian Hugh of St. Victor (c. 1096–c. 1141) simply represented the world as a book written by God, in which the creatures of the world are likened to signs and words. Humanity is divided into the foolish, who don't know how to read, and the wise, who do. "And thus," wrote Hugh, "there is no one for whom the works of God are not wondrous, and, just as the foolish man admires [only] the spectacle in them, whereas the wise man, through that which he sees outside, examines the profound thinking of God's wisdom, so does one man in one and the same Scripture merely commend the color and formation of the shapes, whereas another man truly praises the meaning and significance [*sensum et significationem*]."[18] Hugh, in drawing a clear distinction between the man who doesn't know how to read (both literally and figuratively) and the man who does, also draws a clear distinction between the objects that both men see—God's creatures, in the case of nature; letters of the alphabet, in the case of Scripture—and what lies behind those objects. He also supplies two names for what lies behind: *sensus* and *significatio*.

Thirteenth-century Italian theologian St. Bonaventure (1221–1274) drew a distinction similar to the one that Hugh had drawn in the previous century—between literacy and illiteracy, figuratively understood—but on slightly different grounds. Here it was not simply the capacity of some people to "read" (whether in the literal or figurative sense) but rather the very nature of the figurative book of the world. Before the Fall, Bonaventure argued, God had given his creatures their true names, so that man could "read" the book of the world. But after the Fall, man no longer had his earlier knowledge of creatures, a knowledge that originally brought man back to God. The result was that now the book of the world was dead and a new book was in order. That book was the Scriptures. Bonaventure makes this claim in *Collationes in hexaëmeron* (Collations on the six days [of Creation]), a work devoted to the Creation story, including an elaborate theory of interpretation and meaning. Meaning in Scripture, Bonaventure explains, is multiple:

> Thus Scripture has numerous meanings [*intellectūs*], for thus must be the voice of God, that it may be sublime. The rest of the sciences are content with one sense [*unō sensū*], but in this one the sense is multiform, and both language and things signify. In other [sciences], only the language [signifies], because each doctrine is determined by the signs that fit it; hence written words and language, of which the written words are fundamental, are signs of meanings [*intellectuum*]; and because the meanings are proportioned and delimited, so also is the language itself, so that a name, once established, cannot be used equivocally [*aequivocē*]. God is the cause of souls and of language formed from the soul and of the things that language is about.

Thus God's language has multiple meanings (literal, allegorical, anagogical, moral), which Bonaventure now proceeds to enumerate.

The core of Bonaventure's argument regards what happens when we can no longer "read" the world itself and therefore need to move over to reading God's new book. What happens is that we suddenly have to confront words that are used *aequivocē*, literally "with equal voice," which is to say, words that mean several things at once. And the reason for this state of affairs is the passage from *homo stans*, "man standing up," to *homo cadens*, "man falling," that is, man before the Fall and man after the Fall.

> It is certain that man, while still standing, had knowledge of created things and, through the representation of those things, was carried up into God, to praise, venerate, and love Him. And creatures are there for this purpose, and they are thus led back to God. But man having fallen, since he lost that knowledge, there was no one who could lead the creatures back to God. Hence it was as if this book, namely the world, had perished and been erased. It was therefore necessary that there be another book, by

which the first one [the world] might be illuminated, so that it could take on the metaphors of things. This book, then, is the book of Scripture, which sets up the similarities, the properties, and the metaphors of things written in the book of the world. Thus the book of Scripture is reparative of the whole world toward God, that He may be praised, venerated, and loved. Hence, if you ask what a serpent means [*valet*, literally "is worth"] to you or of what use it is to you, [the answer is that] it means [*valet*] more to you than the whole world, because it teaches you prudence, just as the ant teaches wisdom. Solomon [Proverbs 6:6]: *Go to the ant, thou Sluggard, study her ways, and be wise.* And Matthew [10:16]: *Be ye therefore wise as serpents.*[19]

Meanings, in other words, no longer reside in the world, at least not in a form perceptible to human beings. Instead they reside in Scripture, so that now, post-Fall, the meaning of a creature (what the creature "is worth") is revealed to us *in words*. But the words, as we've just read, bear multiple meanings, with the result that not only is a creature in the world twice removed from us (so that meaning travels from creature through Scriptural word to us) but the words that yield up that creature's meaning require several layers of interpretation. After the Fall, ambiguity and polyvalence are built in.

This is certainly different from what we saw in Augustine and in Hugh of St. Victor, but it does not alter the fundamental structure that we see in both. In fact, in the conceptions of all three writers, certain truths and qualities are thought to dwell in a realm removed from that of direct experience, with the result that seeking those truths and qualities may be likened to seeking meanings in a written text. Objects in our direct experience come to be seen as signs, and those signs point beyond to truths and qualities that, by analogy, are seen as *meanings* (as denoted by the collection of Latin nouns we've examined).

The World Loses Its Meaning in the
Protestant Reformation

And then something big happened. As historian of science Peter Harrison has explained, the Protestant Reformation brought about a dramatic change in the approach to Holy Scripture. *Sōlā scriptūrā* (by Scripture alone), the motto of the Reformation, pushed readers to seek fixed, literal meanings, in place of allegorical readings, in the holy texts. Such a method of reading,

Harrison claims, replaced the system we find in St. Hugh, where both Book and world are sources of revelation in which written passages (the Book) and natural objects (the world) serve as microcosms that stand in for the macrocosms that are God's truths. Put more simply: under the older conception, both words (in Scripture) and things (in the world of nature) had meanings. Under the new, Protestant conception, only words had meaning; objects didn't. Harrison explains:

> The sacred rite which had lain at the heart of medieval culture was replaced by a text, symbolic objects gave way to words, ritual practices were eclipsed by propositional beliefs and dogmas. . . . Meaning and intelligibility were ascribed to words and texts, but denied to living things and inanimate objects. The natural world, once the indispensable medium between words and eternal truths, lost its meanings, and became opaque to those hermeneutical procedures which had once elucidated it. It was left to an emerging natural science to reinvest the created order with intelligibility. Thus was one of the hallmarks of modernity, the triumph of the written text and the identification of its meaning with authorial intention, to give rise to another—that systematic, materialistic understanding of the world embodied in the privileged discourses of natural science.[20]

By the end of the seventeenth century, Harrison says, when natural science has established its dominance—Newton's *Principia mathematica* having been published in 1687—the process is essentially complete:

> At the very beginning of the medieval period, the book of nature was written in symbols which were laden with various meanings, but which were not related to each other in any systematic way. Nature was a vast lexicon in which objects were given meanings, but grammatical and syntactic linkages between the elements of the language were completely absent. By the end of the seventeenth century the wheel has come full circle. Natural objects have been stripped of their intrinsic meanings, and even their qualities and essences have gone. In the physics of Descartes and Newton, simple natural objects are denuded of all but basic quantitative properties. In this new language of nature, syntax has triumphed over semantics.[21]

That is to say, order has triumphed over meanings. As Harrison puts it in the concluding chapter of his study, two "hallmarks of modernity," "the identification of the meaning of a text with its author's intention, and the privileged status of scientific discourse," have a common origin, because the new approach to texts "created the conditions which made possible the emergence of modern science."[22] Thus, to credit Harrison's argument, the practice of regarding individual objects in the world as bearing meanings, at least in Protestant lands, has fallen into disuse. The posture we adopt relative to the world under the new outlook is thus empirical rather than hermeneutical.

And Regains It in Bishop Berkeley

The moment that Harrison describes, following the end of the seventeenth century, is precisely the moment when George Berkeley (1685–1753) steps into the picture. On first glance, one might understandably think that Berkeley's views were a throwback to the era that Harrison claims to have been superseded by the modern, scientific worldview, for the devout Anglican bishop resorted to the by then antiquated notion of nature as a book—or at least as something created by an Author and designed to be read. But Berkeley has offered a twist that sets his thinking apart from the medieval view that Harrison describes. The topic that represented Berkeley's starting point was *vision*—not mystical vision, not prophetic vision, but the ordinary faculty that we employ in our ordinary concourse with the world. While the purpose of this faculty is as mundane as can be—namely, to preserve and protect us—it is handicapped by a condition that lies at the very foundation of Berkeley's entire philosophical enterprise: it gives us no direct access to any of the objects whose existence we nonetheless suppose—precisely so that we might negotiate our way around and among them. Here is what he wrote in *An Essay Towards a New Theory of Vision* (1709):

> Upon the whole, I think we may fairly conclude, that the proper Objects of Vision constitute an universal Language of the Author of Nature, whereby we are instructed how to regulate our Actions, in order to attain those things, that are necessary to the Preservation and Well-being of our Bodies, as also to avoid whatever may be hurtful and destructive of them. It is by their Information that we are principally guided in all the Transactions and Concerns of Life. And the manner wherein they signify, and mark unto us the Objects which are at a Distance, is the same with that of Languages and Signs of Humane Appointment; which do not suggest the things signified,

by any Likeness or Identity of Nature, but only by an habitual Connexion, that Experience has made us to observe between them.[23]

At the very end of this work, Berkeley draws a much more explicit analogy between vision and understanding language. He has been seeking to demonstrate that geometric abstractions, such as planes and solids, cannot be "Objects of Sight"—that there can be no "pure Spirit" capable of knowing or seeing such abstractions. Why? "Because we cannot, without great Pains," Berkeley writes, "cleverly separate and disentangle in our Thoughts the proper Objects of Sight from those of Touch which are connected with them." A pure abstraction, erroneously considered as an object of perception, is always anchored in real experience and cannot be artificially divorced from such experience. The impossibility of perceiving a pure abstraction, he says, "will not seem strange to us, if we consider how hard it is, for any one to hear the Words of his Native Language pronounced in his Ears without understanding them. Though he endeavour to disunite the Meaning from the Sound, it will nevertheless intrude into his Thoughts, and he shall find it extreme difficult, if not impossible, to put himself exactly in the Posture of a Foreigner, that never learned the Language, so as to be affected barely with the Sounds themselves, and not perceive the Signification annexed to them."[24] Per the analogy, words are to objects of sight as meaning (or signification) is to objects of touch.

So, we might say, as a recent scholar does, that Berkeley's is a *semiotic* theory of vision, because it is founded on the notion that seeing is a matter of recovering meanings from signs whose connections with those meanings are purely conventional and arbitrary—as are the connections between the words in human language and the meanings associated with *them*.[25] What signs? Berkeley was famous for asserting that the direct knowledge we have is knowledge of *ideas*, that is, that physical objects in the world are already constituted, for the mind, as ideas. What our "visive faculty" directly grasps is thus mere ideas, which are "intromitted" to our senses and which, functioning as signs, point to other ideas, these other ideas standing for what, in all innocence, we believe to be actual things in the world. In a subsequent work titled *Three Dialogues Between Hylas and Philonous* (1713), Berkeley referred to this outlook as *immaterialism*, because he denied the existence of matter outside the mind. Later generations would refer to the outlook as *idealism* (a term that Berkeley himself never used), more specifically *ontological* or *metaphysical idealism*, that is, a philosophy locating the foundation of reality exclusively in the mind—and either suggesting or explicitly insisting that nothing exists outside the mind. I'll have more to say about idealism in Chapter 3.

Berkeley expanded his theory of vision into a full-blown epistemology in *A Treatise Concerning the Principles of Human Knowledge*, published one year after the essay on vision. Here the philosophy of immaterialism received its fullest expression, including the famous claim that when it comes to "the absolute existence of unthinking things without any relation to their being perceived," "their *esse* is *percipi*," that is, their existence, or being (*esse*), is founded entirely in their being perceived. Put differently, we have no warrant for asserting the existence of anything that is independent of our minds. We are thus are at the mercy of faculties of mind whose operation Berkeley repeatedly likened to grasping meanings from words.

And here Berkeley brings back from an earlier era the image of the book. He has just made the apparently paradoxical claim that while we can never be sure of the existence of the objects of our perception, we can nonetheless *study* nature in order to discover its general laws and can be quite sure that the observations we make are the result "of God's goodness and kindness to men in the administration of the world."[26] He then writes this:

> As in reading other books a wise man will choose to fix his thoughts on the sense and apply it to use, rather than lay them out in grammatical remarks on the language; so, in perusing the volume of nature, it seems beneath the dignity of the mind to affect an exactness in reducing each particular phenomenon to general rules, or showing how it follows from them. We should propose to ourselves nobler views, namely, to recreate and exalt the mind with a prospect of the beauty, order, extent, and variety of natural things: hence, by proper inferences, to enlarge our notions of the grandeur, wisdom, and beneficence of the Creator; and lastly, to make the several parts of the creation, so far as in us lies, subservient to the ends they were designed for, God's glory, and the sustentation and comfort of ourselves and fellow-creatures.[27]

At the risk of oversimplifying Berkeley's thinking, we might say that (1) objects in the world exist only as a function of our perception, (2) our "visive faculty" nonetheless serves the pragmatic purpose of allowing us to negotiate our way in the world with as little harm to ourselves as possible, (3) the world does yield to our attempt to establish general laws that govern its workings, and (4) one thing we may be sure of is that the world is a direct expression of the "Author of nature," whose "book" we read for its "sense," inferring from it the existence of its Author.

Now this might sound for all the world like a slightly modernized version of the "book of nature" theology we found in Christianity from its early centuries through the Middle Ages. After all, Berkeley represents us, in our everyday concourse with the world, as assigning meanings or sense to the signs that we perceive there. But, to begin with, he has forcefully denied the very existence of such objects in the world as gave rise to the hermeneutical practices of an earlier generation of Christian theologians. Objects do not exist outside perception; *esse* is *percipi*. And yet Berkeley claimed, perhaps surprisingly, that we can nonetheless observe and measure the external objects we perceive. He was, on the whole, accepting of modern science as represented in Newtonian physics (with reservations about certain issues). In fact, Berkeley's philosophy is considered a form of empiricism, with the understanding, first, that the term *empiricism* emphasizes measurement-based observation plus a controlled experimental method, and, second, that we qualify *empiricism* with the proviso that it does not imply the existence of material substance independent of the mind.[28] One commentator has argued that, for Berkeley, Scripture takes precedence over the book of nature, that the world is a "divine milieu," and that the book of nature is primarily revelatory of God's providence.[29] But even if we credit this interpretation, there is no warrant for representing us human subjects as being on a perpetual hermeneutic quest for mysterious "meanings" that lie hidden behind what we take to be objects of our perception. If Harrison is right, that sort of quest had faded away around the time of Berkeley's birth. In an idealist (or "immaterialist") worldview, the "meanings" are nothing more than the objects whose existence we suppose—not particular divine or otherworldly essences and truths belonging to individual objects. The supposed world of those supposed objects might very well reveal the providence of a beneficent Creator, but individual objects do not, like the words in Scripture, yield up specific meanings whose discovery depends on the deployment of special hermeneutical skills.

Before too long, however, the pendulum would swing. The Age of Enlightenment to which the modern scientific worldview had given rise would soon provoke an impassioned reaction, and the quest for meaning would be back, but in a radically altered form. Meaning would now be absolutized, in the singular, and would carry more mystery, polyvalence, and ambiguity than ever.

3

Idealism and Romanticism

From the Language of Nature to *the* Meaning of Life (or the World)

Hamann Defies the Enlightenment and Revives the Book of Nature

Where we begin to see a glimmer of what will shortly blossom into *meaning* in the singular as a mysterious essence lurking behind appearances in the world is in an extremely odd . . . what to call him? Johann Georg Hamann (1730–1788) can hardly be described as a philosopher, if by *philosopher* we intend to denote the author of a coherent and systematic body of thought on topics to which, well, philosophers conventionally turned their attention at the time that Hamann lived. Hamann, who held no academic position, who wrote no full-length books, who in fact never produced *anything* that resembles what a philosopher might write, positioned himself as a kind of sniping troublemaker in the period that traditional histories of ideas characterize as the transition from Enlightenment to Romanticism and idealism. It would be equally misleading to call Hamann a theologian, if we expect the term *theologian* to suggest the author of a systematic body of thought on religious matters. And yet, paradoxically, it would be entirely accurate to claim that, when it comes to the quest for meanings that lie behind appearances, Hamann's view forms part of a theology—only an extremely unconventional and unsystematic one.

If you attempt to read any of Hamann's writings, you'll quickly see why the scholarship on him reflects such a diversity of opinions about how to interpret and classify him. Filled with a maddening array of esoteric allusions (to texts in the numerous ancient and modern languages he had learned), brimming with irony whose target, especially to readers today, is often elusive, displaying almost nothing resembling a coherently developed argument of the sort we demand of college students, they have challenged intellectual historians who seek the safety and security that recognizable categories offer.

What Do We Mean When We Talk About Meaning? Steven Cassedy, Oxford University Press. © Oxford University Press 2022. DOI: 10.1093/oso/9780190936907.003.0004

It's not even clear what to call them. Essays? Pieces? And yet these writings nonetheless yield up a set of themes, attitudes, pictures of the world, call them what you like, that are revealing for the notion of reading—and seeking meaning in—the world.

It seems safe to claim, for example, that Hamann had no use for abstractions, rigid systems, or any epistemological view that insisted on a clear distinction between "ordinary" knowledge and faith or belief (*Glaube* in German means both). He was deeply religious, in his own peculiar way, seeing evidence of God's revelation throughout nature to such a pervasive extent that, to him, all knowledge rested on faith/belief. In an era that spawned a number of quaint (by today's standards) theories about the origin of language—Rousseau's imaginative fantasy in *Discourse on the Origin and Basis of Inequality Among Men* (1755) and Johann Gottfried Herder's much more sober *Treatise on the Origin of Language* (1772), about which more shortly, are the most prominent—Hamann embedded language in the very fabric of the world itself, which he viewed as God's text.

If there is one consistent principle in Hamann's theology, it is divine condescension, God's lowering himself in order to appear in the world. The classic New Testament passage that expresses this principle is a short stretch of verses in Paul's Epistle to the Philippians. The English New Revised Standard Version captures the essential concept: "Let the same mind be in you that was in Christ Jesus, who, though he was in the form of God, did not regard equality with God as something to be exploited, but emptied himself, taking the form of a slave, being born in human likeness. And being found in human form, he humbled himself and became obedient to the point of death—even death on a cross. Therefore God also highly exalted him and gave him the name that is above every name, so that at the name of Jesus every knee should bend, in heaven and on earth and under the earth, and every tongue should confess that Jesus Christ is Lord, to the glory of God the Father" (Philippians 2:5–11). The subject of the first two sentences is not God but Jesus, and the idea is that, though he "was in the form of God," Jesus by design lowered himself so as not to be God's equal. The Greek verb rendered here, accurately, as "emptied himself" (*kenoō*) gives us the noun *kenosis*, an "emptying," and the corresponding adjective *kenotic*, both of which have been pressed into service to convey the idea that Christ emptied himself of divinity in order to walk in humble form among us—even as a slave, even to the point of death on the cross—together with the paradoxical corollary that, having been humbled, he was thereby exalted by God. A kenotic theology is thus one that emphasizes emptying, humbling, or condescension as characterizing what might otherwise simply be referred to as the Incarnation.[1]

The Philippians passage is one of Hamann's favorites, appearing numerous times in his writings, quoted or paraphrased from the standard German translation by Luther. One in particular stands out, because it joins together the kenotic idea with the notion of the book. It's from a characteristically odd essay titled *Aesthetica in nuce* (Aesthetics in a nutshell, 1762). The topic of the essay appears to be interpretation, so it is not surprising that Hamann should speak of books. But, as in Augustine and the medieval theologians, *book* refers not only to a physical codex but also to nature and the world. Here's what Hamann wrote:

> The opinions of wise men are ways of reading nature, and the pronouncements of religious scholars are ways of reading Scripture. The author is the best interpreter of his own words. He may speak through creatures, through events, or through blood and fire and smoke, which is what the language of holiness consists in.
>
> The the world] contains examples of general concepts that God revealed to [his] creatures through creation. The books of the covenant [presumably Torah] contain examples of secret articles that God wished to reveal to men through men. The unity of the creator is reflected down to the dialect of his works, in all of which there is a tone of immeasurable height and depth! Proof of the most glorious majesty and the emptiest renunciation![2]

The giveaway reference to the kenotic passage in Philippians is the word I've translated as *renunciation*. The German word, *Entäußerung*, corresponds to the verb that Luther used to render the Greek word for "to empty." It literally means something like "cast out," but in normal usage it means "give up," "renounce." So, in Luther's Bible, Jesus "cast himself out" or "renounced himself." But Hamann knew the Greek original ("emptied himself"), so he qualified the renunciation as "emptiest" (*leersten*). The rest of the passage is about interpretation and revelation, but couched in terms that emphasize the paradoxical, kenotic coincidence of high and low. To the extent that it's possible to glean a theory of interpretation from this passage, we could say that God revealed two sorts of truths or meanings to us, his creatures: on one hand, general concepts (whatever Hamann intends by this expression) via created nature itself and, on the other, "secret articles" (perhaps the laws included in Torah) via men, understood either as those who wrote down the words in Scripture or as the one (Moses) who brought the "articles" to his fellow men. Whatever the precise sense of this passage, it's clear that Hamann is reviving the twin "book of nature"/"book of Scripture" model according to which in the first instance (nature) we "read" (figuratively speaking) and in the second we read (literally speaking) meanings. Given that in the first instance we are speaking of God's creation and in the second we are speaking of God's language, both of which exist owing to an act of condescension (mere creatures, mere profane words of "dialect"), we can understand God's revelation as something that comes to us, like Jesus himself, by such an act of condescension. And of course the act of interpretation by which we discover the *meaning* of both the figurative "book" and the literal Book yields not only depth but "immeasurable height."

A few years earlier, Hamann had written another strange little piece, titled *Brocken* (Fragments, 1759), in which he referred to the book of nature and more directly focused on the position of the human subject in confrontation with that "book." The title of the essay is a reference to the Gospel story of the Feeding of the Five Thousand. After Jesus has miraculously nourished the multitude with only five loaves and two fish, he orders his disciples to gather up the leftover fragments (*Brocken*) so that nothing will be wasted. The fragments miraculously fill twelve baskets. Hamann spins this story into a lesson on the bounties that nature has given us: just as the disciples ended up with more than they ever expected (a bit like the *dayenu* chant at a Passover seder: just a little would have been enough, yet God gave us so much more), so nature has provided us with so much from just five senses. The senses (*die Sinne*) are limiting, and yet we find meaning or sense (*Sinn*) in the world. How? "Our life consists in a union of the visible part with a higher being that we deduce only from its effects."[3] Knowledge is not purely empirical. How else to understand the origin of evil?

But Hamann puts a peculiar spin on the rather contrived analogy he has drawn between Jesus' five loaves and our five senses. He takes us back to the Greek world of divination, which now serves as a fit context for a non-empirical, anti-Enlightenment theory of knowledge. Here's what he writes at the very beginning of *Brocken*:

> We see precisely this miracle of godly blessing in the crowd of sciences and arts. What a storehouse the history of scholarship makes! And what is it all based on? Five barley loaves, five senses that we possess in common with unreasoning beasts. Not only the entire warehouse of reason but the very

treasure vault of faith rests on this stock. Our [faculty of] reason is similar to that blind Theban soothsayer Tiresias, to whom his daughter, Manto,
described the flight of birds. He prophesied from her reports. Faith, says
the Apostle, comes through the hearing [sense], through the hearing of the
Word of God (Romans, 10:17).[4]

In Chapter 1, I wrote about the practice of divination in ancient Greece and
the role of the *mantis*, receiver of visions and signs, and the *prophētēs*, interpreter of visions and signs. In the Tiresias story, the daughter's name tells
us that she is the *mantis* (receiving the visions and signs and passing them
on to her father, who can't see them). Hamann, using the Greek-based word
instead of the verb corresponding to "soothsayer" (*Wahrsager*), tells us that
Tiresias "prophesied" (*prophezeyte*). With his solid knowledge of Greek,
Hamann appears to be choosing his words carefully, so that prophesying is
understood as "interpreting" rather than as foretelling. Our much-vaunted
reason—and here is Hamann's dig at the Enlightenment—is actually *prophetic*, in the sense of *interpretive*, and in our ordinary concourse with the
world we carry out the same sort of activity as blind Tiresias, interpreting on
the basis of visions and signs transmitted by the *mantis* of our senses.

In *Aesthetica in nuce*, Hamann did not speak explicitly of *meaning* or *sense*
in connection with "the book." In *Brocken*, he did. "Whence," he asks, "comes
the view in which the arts of divination stand and the large number of them
that are founded on nothing more than a misunderstanding of our instinct
or natural reason? We are all capable of being prophets. All the phenomena
of nature are dreams, visions, riddles that have their meaning [*Bedeutung*],
their secret sense [*Sinn*]. The Book of Nature and that of History are nothing
more than ciphers, hidden signs, which require the key that interprets Holy
Writ and that is the object of its inspiration."[5] Knowledge is prophetic, which
is to say interpretive. It is not founded on the Enlightenment's notion of a
faculty of reason that is universal among human subjects. And the name for
what the prophetic faculty finds is *Bedeutung* or *Sinn*.

The Fuzziness of the Key German Word

Here is a good place to say something about the German word *Sinn*, since it
lies at the origin of speculation, not only in German but in other European
languages as well, about "the meaning of life."[6] The modern-day German

phrase that is translated into English as "the meaning of life" is *der Sinn des Lebens*. But English *meaning* and German *Sinn* are far from identical, and the use of one for the other in translation can lead to serious misunderstandings. In the Introduction, I mentioned that *meaning* is a verbal noun, or gerund, and that, as a consequence, it can suggest agency or, at the very least, action: someone or something is carrying out the action denoted by the verb *to mean*. The closest equivalent in German is *Bedeutung*, also a verbal noun, suggesting the idea that someone or something is carrying out the action denoted by the verb *bedeuten*, "to signify." Like English *meaning*, *Bedeutung* offers the possibility of phrasing a thought about meaning with a grammatical subject and the verb *bedeuten*: "Was bedeutet dieses Wort?" (What does this word mean?). *Meaning* and *Bedeutung*, however, are not identical, because, like its German etymological cousin *meinen*, *to mean* can signify "to intend" (as in, "I didn't mean to offend you"). For the usages that we're examining in this book, in particular in connection with "life," *Sinn* has been the standard German word—rarely *Bedeutung*. And because, as I hope to show, English *meaning* in these usages, while not initially equivalent to *Sinn*, has accumulated a number of nuances that stem from the German word, it's worthwhile pointing out the peculiarities of that word, in particular those features that set it apart from English *meaning*.[7]

A greatly simplified account of the German word *Sinn* would go something like this: Though its history is a bit murky and though etymologies vary from dictionary to dictionary, it appears to have begun its life signifying "change of place," "movement," and, by extension, "direction." In its causative form, it is related to our verb *to send* (that is, to cause something or someone to move to a destination). At a certain moment early in its history, it takes on a number of mental notions, such as "attend to," "be concerned about," perhaps because such notions suggest that the mind (figuratively speaking) *moves* toward an object. The most authoritative and capacious dictionary of the German language, the colossal *Deutsches Wörterbuch*, begun in the mid-nineteenth century by the brothers Grimm (of fairy tale fame), includes a list of two dozen definitions for *Sinn*, including "the inner being of a person"; the mental/spiritual character of a person; "will, desire, inclination"; consciousness; "understanding, smartness, deliberation." In the plural, it denotes the five senses. The editors introduce the list with the striking statement that, in a given instance of this word, it is often difficult to settle on any single one of the definitions they provide. In fact, they state, even a strict organization of the definitions is impracticable, "since, given the fluidity of the boundaries and, in most cases, the indeterminacy and generality of the meaning [*Bedeutung*], the exact nuance often cannot be ascertained with certainty, and, in addition, not infrequently several meanings [*Bedeutungen*] blend together in the concept of the word."

While the extremely lengthy entry for *Sinn* includes no reference to the phrase *der Sinn des Lebens*, there is one definition (number 22) that appears to be most helpful for an understanding of that phrase. At first glance, it marks the transition that shorter and simpler etymological accounts note in the definition of *Sinn*, from "direction" or "movement" to qualities of mind and "meaning," as of a word.[8] But definition 22 in the Grimm dictionary also reflects the indeterminacy that, in the view of the editors, characterizes the entire group of definitions: "In modern times, *Sinn* is customarily and commonly [used] for the meaning [*Bedeutung*], the opinion [*Meinung*], the spiritual content, the intention [*Tendenz*] of an expression, a work, or (more rarely) an action, as distinguished from its wording [*Wortlaut*] or its outward appearance." The illustrative examples include passages asserting incomprehension, that is, in which a listener hears the words but fails to grasp the *Sinn*; passages asserting comprehension of the *Sinn* but not of the words; and passages asserting multiple meanings (*Bedeutungen*) and therefore the possibility of multiple interpretations for a single word. To the extent that *Sinn* conveys fuzziness and fails to denote something precise, it functions very much like the English *sense*, as when we say that a certain word or expression "gives a sense of"—followed by a list of possible choices.[9]

So, even in a simple phrase, such as *der Sinn eines Wortes*, the German can suggest something rather different from the English phrase "the meaning of a word." To begin with, in English, if what you're seeking is a dictionary definition of a particular word X—say, it's the first time you've heard X and you don't know *what it means*—you can easily ask, "What's the meaning of X?" An answer that begins with "The meaning of X is . . ." can end with a dictionary definition. In German, if you're seeking a dictionary definition of X, you're unlikely to start with "Was ist der Sinn von X?" And an answer that begins with "Der Sinn von X ist . . . " is likely to end with a list of connotations rather than with a dictionary definition. If the sentence ends with a dictionary definition, it's more likely to begin with "Die Bedeutung von X ist . . ." (or, much more commonly, it will be phrased "X bedeutet . . .").

This peculiar meaning status of the German word *Sinn* implicitly points to an equally peculiar epistemological and hermeneutical situation. If *Sinn* not only tends to be vague but also marks a separation, opposition, barrier between itself and the object conveying it, then it fosters uncertainty and imposes an interpretive burden on the perceiver. In ordinary usage, *Sinn* is more likely to be connotative; English *meaning* is more likely to be denotative, as are the German noun *Bedeutung* and verb *bedeuten*. If we take a look back at those passages from the Jewish scriptures that I briefly mentioned in Chapter 1, where the interpretation of a dream is at issue and where there is a single, correct interpretation, modern English translations often use the word *meaning* (something that the dream possesses) instead of, or in addition to, the more strictly accurate *interpretation* (something that someone does to the dream). Like many translators, Martin Luther opted for both *meaning* and *interpretation*. For *meaning*, the word he used was not *Sinn* but *Bedeutung* or the verb *bedeuten*, since in the cases of both Joseph and Daniel, there is no fuzziness about what the dreams in question conveyed: given what was at stake, neither Joseph nor Daniel could have plausibly offered up a collection of possible interpretations, asking, respectively, Pharaoh and Belshazzar to make a selection without any guidance. No, assuming that, in our translation from the Hebrew (Joseph) and Aramaic (Daniel), we're using the language of signification and not the language of interpretation, there needs to be a one-for-one correspondence here between sign and signified. The source here is God, so that's *Bedeutung*, not *Sinn*.[10]

And this appears to be how Hamann understood the two words. Dreams, visions, and riddles have a *Bedeutung* or a *Sinn*, but only *Sinn* is qualified with "secret." When it comes time for Hamann to pose the age-old question of how evil can have arisen in a world that was created by a good God, given that the question is paradoxical at its core, *Sinn* is the word he uses: "This philosophical curiosity, which is so surprised and troubled about the origin of evil, must be regarded almost as a dark consciousness of the divine likeness in our reason, as a ὕστερον πρότερον [hysteron proteron, the inversion of logical order in speech], whose true sense [*Sinn*] must be taken in the reverse way, in whose transposition there lies a Cabbala, a secret understanding."[11] Heaven only knows exactly what Hamann is trying to say here, but since the murkiness of his prose matches the mystery and murkiness of his topic (*Cabbala*, with this spelling, in Hamann's era and earlier was often used to refer not specifically to the Jewish mystical tradition but simply to something mysterious or esoteric), not only is *Sinn* the right word, but it would probably be misleading to translate it into English as *meaning*. It really is a *sense* of the thing that Hamann has in mind, and that *makes sense* in an essay that focuses on *the senses* and the limitations that they impose on us creatures of reason.

That Key German Word in Immanuel Kant's Transcendental Idealism

There's no denying that Hamann was an idiosyncratic writer with a modest following, so it would be difficult to claim that his linguistic and stylistic habits had a significant and measurable impact on future generations. A far more seminal thinker was his contemporary Immanuel Kant (1724–1804), whose works show the full array of meanings for *Sinn* and, as hardly needs to be said, had the impact on future generations that Hamann's didn't. In fact, one might claim without too much exaggeration that his use of the word *Sinn* and words constructed from it lies at the heart of what he referred to as his philosophy of *transcendental idealism*.

Kant was (for his era) a rather elderly gentleman when he wrote and published the works for which he is justly renowned: the *Critique of Pure Reason* (1781, rev. ed. 1787), the *Critique of Practical Reason* (1788), and the *Critique of Judgment* (1790). One facile way of describing the path of his thought in his "pre-critical" period, that is, before the composition of the *Critique of Pure Reason*, is to say that over a period of decades he wrestled his way free of a widely accepted mid-eighteenth-century conception of metaphysics. In this conception, metaphysics was understood as a science that takes what Kant would later list as its three principal ideas—God, freedom of will, and immortality—plus the teleological notion of purposes (or "ends") in nature and seeks to integrate them into a coherent worldview as directly knowable qualities.

In 1766, he published a work that baffled and continues to baffle his readers. It was titled *Träume eines Geistersehers, erläutert durch Träume der Metaphysik*, which might be translated "Dreams of a spirit-seer, illustrated through dreams of metaphysics" (thought the main title could also be rendered as "Dreams of a ghost-seer"). The jocular title and the often jocular tone of the writing throughout belie what most scholars take to be the highly serious nature of the question Kant addresses in this book. Put in its simplest terms, that question is "Can beings and forces from the immaterial world make direct contact with our cognitive faculties?" Or, to refer back to the title, can there be such a thing as a ghost-seer/spirit-seer, that is, someone who *literally* sees ghosts, or are dreams the only things a ghost-seer/spirit-seer "sees"? Kant's point of entry into the question is a discussion of meaning and sense (*Bedeutung* and *Sinn*). In the disingenuous tone that he intentionally adopted for this book, Kant explains: "I don't know if there are such things as *spirits/ghosts* [*Geister*], and, what's more, I don't even know what the word *spirit/ghost* [*Geist*] means [*bedeute*]. Since, however, I have often used it myself or heard others use it, something must surely be understood by it, whether this something is a mere fantasy or something real. In order to disclose its concealed meaning [*Bedeutung*], I shall hold up my poorly understood concept against the many various instances of its use, and, by observing those instances where it fits and those where it does not, hope to unfold its hidden sense [*Sinn*]."[12] Here and in several other instances, while *Sinn* appears to be roughly synonymous with *Bedeutung*, the key notion is *secret* or *concealed*. *Sinn* appears to substitute for *Bedeutung* when effort is required to uncover it, when interpretation is called for.

What apparently prompted Kant to address the question of ghost/spirit-seeing in the first place, and to address it in the strange way that he did, was a multivolume opus by the Swedish mystic Emanuel Swedenborg (1688–1772). *Arcana cœlestia* (Heavenly mysteries, 1749–1756) is purportedly a work of Christian theology based on a set of unconventional beliefs peculiar to its author. Swedenborg saw the world as separated into two planes of existence, one spiritual and the other worldly. The two planes are related to each other through a series of correspondences. At the most basic level, for example, God as creator corresponds to the created world, and the spiritual plane of the human mind corresponds to the natural plane of the human mind. In a bygone era, God had written a book, the "Ancient Word," which revealed the correspondences between the two planes of existence. Over time, humanity lost the ability to understand the correspondences, and most of the Ancient Word was lost, except for the part consisting of the first eleven chapters of Genesis. For this reason, in modern times it falls to one who is gifted in the art of seeing correspondences to interpret Scripture. That, of course, is where Swedenborg comes in. Once again, as in Augustine, Hugh, St. Bonaventure, and, more recently, Bishop Berkeley, we have a book—in this case, a literal one (the Bible) and a mythical one (the Ancient Word) very much resembling a book of nature—that challenges the interpreter to discover its hidden meanings. *Arcana cœlestia*, written in Latin, is filled with references to the distinction between "outer sense" (*sensus externus*), the sense of words that pertains to the empirically experienced world, and "inner sense" (*sensus internus*), the sense that is hidden behind the outer sense. Swedenborg's task was to find the inner sense in texts, but this task reveals truths not only about words in the Bible but about the material world as well, behind whose phenomena lie hidden senses or meanings.

What's more, Swedenborg was widely acclaimed for what we would call today psychic powers. For example, on one occasion, as he was sitting at dinner with friends in Gothenburg, he accurately reported the outbreak of a fire hundreds of miles away in Stockholm *as it was occurring* in real time, even though it would have taken several days for news of the fire to reach him by messenger. On another occasion, he accurately told a woman, unknown to him, where in her own house to find a receipt that rescued her from a mistaken attempt to collect a debt from her. In Swedenborg's era, one could certainly credit or not credit stories about his prophetic powers, just as one could accept or not accept his peculiar theology. But for Kant, both the *Arcana cœlestia* and the stories about its author carried a very specific import, since both the book and the stories explicitly or implicitly asserted not just the possibility but the reality of direct communication between an immaterial world and the material world. Swedenborg's theology and life experiences demonstrated the realization of the metaphysics that Kant had been struggling with for years, but they also brought home the stark recognition that if such a metaphysics were to come true, what we'd be talking about is spirit-seeing or ghost-seeing.

Kant was savage in his judgment of Swedenborg's book. It is, he wrote, eight volumes' worth of *Unsinn*—nonsense. It is devoted to "the discovery of the secret sense [*Sinn*] in the first two books of Moses," but Swedenborg's extravagant interpretations of Scripture interest Kant less than the outlandish things the mystic has purported actually to see and to hear with his own eyes and ears. For most troubling about Swedenborg's book is that all of it appears to stem from a kind of derangement. Kant calls it *Täuschung der Sinne*, literally "deception of the senses," which results in *Wahnsinn*, "delusion of the senses." Deception and delusion lie at the foundation of the "airship of metaphysics," he says (before the Montgolfier brothers successfully launched their first balloons in the early 1780s, *Luftschiff*, "airship," meant something like "pipe dream"). *Sinn* is thus central to the serious philosophical problem that Kant treats semi-humorously in *Träume eines Geistersehers*. So far, it means "meaning," "sense" (the sense of a thing), and "sense" both as one of the five senses and as "right mind"—thus *Unsinn* and *Wahnsinn*.

But nowhere do the peculiarities of the German *Sinn* come into relief more fully in *Träume eines Geistersehers* than in the passage where Kant describes what he views as truly the essence of Swedenborg's system of beliefs.

A principal concept in Swedenborg's wild fancy is this: corporeal beings do not have their own subsistence but exist solely through the spirit world [*Geisterwelt*], although each body exists not through just one spirit but through all taken together. Hence knowledge of material things has a double meaning [*Bedeutung*]: an outer sense [*einen äußerlichen Sinn*] in relation to matter among themselves [that is, among the material things] and an inner sense [*einen innern*], to the extent that, as effects [that is, since they are the effects of causes], they point to the powers of the spirit world that are their causes. Thus the body of man shows a relation of its parts among themselves according to material laws; but to the extent that it is supported by the spirit that lives in it, its limbs and their functions possess the value of indicating those powers of the soul to whose effects they owe their shape, activity, and permanence. This inner sense [*dieser innere Sinn*] is unknown to man, and it is this that Swedenborg, whose inner core is opened up, wished to make known to man. With all other objects in the visible world, it is the same. They have, as I have said, one meaning [*Bedeutung*] as things, which is minor, and another as signs, which is greater. This is also the origin of the new interpretations of [Holy] Scripture that he has sought to do. For the inner sense [*der innere Sinn*], that is, the symbolic relationship of all the things recounted therein to the spirit world, is, as he fancies it, the core of their value, and what is left over is only the shell. What is important, however, in this symbolic connection of corporeal things, [understood] as images, to the inner spiritual condition consists in this: all spirits present themselves to each other under the guise of extended [that is, having extension in space] shapes, and, at the same time, the influences of all these spiritual beings among themselves create the appearance of still other extended beings and, as it were, of a material world whose images are nothing more than symbols of their inner condition and yet at the same time cause such a clear and solid deception of the senses [*Täuschung des Sinnes*] that this deception is identical to the actual sensation of such objects. (A future interpreter will conclude from this that Swedenborg is an *idealist*, because he denies the matter of this world its own subsistence and considers it to be perhaps merely a linked appearance arising from the connection to the spirit world.)[13]

To make a somewhat more complicated story simple, the recognition that bringing the conventional conception of metaphysics to fruition would mean proposing a system of delusional "ghost-seeing" is allegedly what led Kant to take the bold step that laid the groundwork for the *Critique of Pure Reason*.[14] A few pages after the passage I just quoted, he wrote this key statement: "Metaphysics is a science of *the boundaries of human reason*. And since a small country always has many boundaries and thus finds it advantageous to know its possessions well and to defend them rather than blindly to seek out conquests, so the use of the aforementioned science is the least known and at the same time the most important, as it is reached rather late and only after long experience."[15] Over the next decade and a half, Kant worked out the "critical program" and wrote the *Critique of Pure Reason*. Now the project would be to discover the *limits* of human reason rather than to prove that reason could reach over into the areas that conventional metaphysics had presumptuously mapped out for itself. To use the crude language of Kant's anti-Swedenborg screed, those areas were the "spirit world." But the spirit world is a vague and imprecise phrase for what lies beyond the "boundaries" that Kant mentioned in *Träume eines Geistersehers*. With the *Critique* would come a more precise delineation. The faculty that grants us access to the empirically observable world would receive the more modest name *Verstand* (understanding), rather than *Vernunft* (reason), and would operate according to a set of a priori (existing independently of and prior to experience) rules of logic, called the "pure concepts of understanding."

This is certainly not the place to offer a lengthy summary and analysis of the *Critique of Pure Reason*, but for our present purposes it's worth stating that the word *Sinn*, alone and in compounds, is integral to the articulation of the project in that work. In fact, in the preface to the revised "B" edition that Kant published in 1787, we can find not only a concise preview of the main lines of argument in the *Critique* but also a concise presentation of the function of *Sinn*. We have no direct access to things in themselves in the world outside our senses. Instead, we are at the mercy of our *Sinnlichkeit* (usually translated "sensibility") or our *sinnliche Anschauung* (translated "sensible intuition"), by which Kant denotes our sensory faculty, which can yield only appearances (*Erscheinungen*) of things existing in the *Sinnenwelt* (sensible world).[16] Thus in the Preface to the B edition Kant uses, for the only time in the entire *Critique*, the word *übersinnlich* ("supersensible," "beyond the reach of our sensory perception") as a term for what is *not* directly accessible to us.[17] It is also here that he lists the three ideas (as he terms them in a later footnote) that are the proper object of the newly defined metaphysics: God, freedom, and immortality, followed by the famous statement "I have therefore had to get rid of knowledge, in order to make room for faith"—a quotable though simplistic way of asserting that only a faculty other than ordinary empirical knowledge (with its origin in *Sinnlichkeit*) can grasp these metaphysical ideas.[18] These ideas live at a yet greater remove from ordinary knowledge, as they are not based even in sensible intuition.

In the *Critique of Pure Reason*, Kant has imported a pair of phrases that he had ridiculed in *Träume eines Geistersehers*: "inner sense" and "outer sense," conferring on them meanings different from those they enjoyed in the work of Swedenborg. In these expressions, *Sinn* is associated with our cognitive faculties and is not a property of an external object, sign, or symbol. Outer sense has to do with our existence in the external world of experience. Inner sense is more complicated. It had appeared in a very early essay, where Kant used the phrase to denote the power to make judgments—the power, that is, that distinguishes rational beings from non-rational beings. Inner sense, Kant wrote, is the capacity "to make one's own representations the object of one's thinking."[19] In the *Critique of Pure Reason*, however, inner sense initially appears to be roughly synonymous with *Sinnlichkeit*, since it has to do with the reception of intuitions from the outside world, while also having as its object the soul.

So far, *Sinn* in the *Critique of Pure Reason* has been associated exclusively with mental faculties. In a small number of instances, however, Kant uses the word, as he had done in *Träume eines Geistersehers*, in the definition it had acquired relatively late in its history, the one that can be translated into English as "meaning" or "sense," as of a word or expression, except that he uses it, together with *Bedeutung*, in connection with objects in the world. For example: "If an act of knowing is to have objective reality, that is, refer to an object and have meaning and sense [*Bedeutung und Sinn*] in that object, then the object must in some way be given."[20] Or this statement about the pure concepts of understanding, where *Sinn* shares space with *sinnlich*: "Our sensible [*sinnliche*] and empirical intuition alone can accord them [the concepts] sense and meaning [*Sinn und Bedeutung*]."[21]

The word *Sinn*, its multiple denotations and connotations, and the words that are formed from it thus form a nexus that to a considerable extent matches up with the epistemology that Kant presents in the *Critique of Pure Reason*. Like the Latin *sensum/sensus/sentientia*, *Sinn* conveys both the receiving, sentient mind and the properties of objects that the mind cognizes and interprets. Kant defined transcendental idealism like this, in the first edition of the *Critique*: "By *transcendental idealism*, I understand the doctrine according to which we regard all appearance as mere representations, and not as things in themselves, and accordingly regard time and space as mere sensible [*sinnliche*] forms of our intuition, not as determinations given in advance of themselves or as conditions of objects considered as things in themselves."[22] Kant did not make grand, mysterious statements about the meaning (*Sinn*) of the world or life. Such statements, by contemporaries, began to appear at the very end of Kant's life and would continue unabated thereafter, leading to the modern construction "the meaning of life" (and its equivalents in other languages). In all likelihood, the sage of Königsberg would have treated such statements with the same contempt that he showed for the *Unsinn* of Swedenborg.

"The World Must Be Romanticized"

"Nur ein Künstler kann den Sinn des Lebens errathen."[23] Thus wrote, at the age of twenty-five, in just this fragmentary form with no accompanying explanation, the astonishing Friedrich Freiherr von Hardenberg (1772–1801), popularly known after his early death as Novalis. If this isn't the very first instance of the phrase *Sinn des Lebens*, it is certainly among the earliest. But how to translate it? If someone wrote the sentence today in German, we would simply render it "Only an artist can guess the meaning of life." But that's because of the history that I will shortly tell, in which the English *meaning* comes to be seen as equivalent to the German *Sinn* in this phrase. What did Novalis mean by it? Like many of his contemporaries, Novalis was fond of writing fragments of this sort, and since by their nature fragments largely lack a context (unless you consider other fragments printed in the same series to be a context), it's always tricky to assign a firm meaning to any one of them. That was often the point. The more isolated, the more mysterious, and the more surprising a fragment is, then the more it requires interpretation and emphasizes the gap between the written words and some truth lying behind them.[24] So, what did Novalis have in mind in using this word, and how do we render it in English?

It appears with almost obsessive frequency, and Novalis uses it in a diversity of often overlapping senses, confirming the validity of the Grimm dictionary's observation about "the fluidity of the boundaries and, in most cases, the indeterminacy and generality of the meaning" of the word *Sinn*. Consider, for example, this extended reflection, written in 1798, on what Novalis refers to as "the moral sense" (in which I have translated every instance of *Sinn* as *sense*):

> We must seek to be magicians in order to be capable of being properly moral. The more moral, then the more in harmony with God, the more godly, and the more bound to God. Only through the moral sense does God become distinct to us. The moral sense is the sense for existence, without external inclination, the sense for bonds, the sense for the highest, the sense for harmony, the sense for freely chosen, invented, and yet collective life and being, the sense for the thing in itself, the genuine divination sense (to divine: to perceive something without cause or contact). The word *sense*, which suggests mediate knowledge, contact, mingling [presumably with the outside world], is of course not entirely fitting here but is an infinite expression, just as there exist infinite quantities. The actual matter [that is, what *Sinn* actually means] can, in case of need, be expressed only approximately. It is non-sense [*Nichtsinn*], or it is sense [*Sinn*], against which that actual thing is non-sense [*Nichtsinn*].[25]

Sinn here is something inside us that faces outward, like the five senses. It is impossible to define precisely, Novalis claims, even in just this use, where it is connected with morality.

When it came to speaking of the senses, Novalis was writing at a peculiar moment in the history of science. The mid-eighteenth century had seen the rise of what could be described as the precursor movement to modern neuroscience (a word that was not coined till the early 1960s). The topic of interest was tissue irritability and nerve response. Laboratory experiments designed to provide evidence that would lead to an understanding of these phenomena involved the related notions of *irritability* (the tendency of muscles to respond to physical excitation) and *sensibility* (the capacity of nerves and the brain to receive sensation). Latin was beginning to give way to European vernacular languages for the communication of scientific ideas. In treatises written in Latin, the name for the force or object that causes muscle excitation or nervous sensation was *stimulus*, whose literal meaning is "goad" or "prod." The word was enlisted initially to denote the experimental instruments (needles and prods of various sorts) that were used to excite muscle and nerve responses in test animals. Subsequently, it came to denote abstractly any source of excitation or sensation. As Germans began to write scientific treatises in the vernacular, they decided, in a fit of Romantically inspired linguistic nationalism, to spurn Latin and Greek terms in favor of native German words. The classic scientific work on irritability and sensibility was composed in Latin by the Swiss-German physiologist Albrecht von Haller. It was titled *De partibus corporis humani sensilibus et irritabilibus* (On the sensible and irritable parts of the human body, 1752). It was shot through with references to *stimuli*. When the work was translated into von Haller's native language in 1753, the word *stimulus* was rendered in German as *Reiz*, a word that, before being pressed into scientific service in this translation, meant primarily "excitation" (in the erotic sense) or "charm." German readers with access to scientific material were thus exposed to physiological discussions rich in references to *die Sinne*, *Reize* (stimuli), and *Reizbarkeit* (stimulability).

Even Immanuel Kant appears to have familiarized himself with the new scientific discoveries. As a mysterious footnote to *Träume eines Geistersehers* appears to show, Kant had discovered the concept of the stimulability of nerves as early as the mid-1760s.[26] Much later, at the age of seventy-four, he published a work titled *Anthropology from a Pragmatic Perspective* concerning the "theory of knowledge of man." Though the idea of the book was to show that such a theory should be "pragmatic," that is, based on action and freedom, rather than physiological, Kant devoted a huge amount of space to precisely the physiology of knowledge, including an account of the five senses and the response of some of them to a stimulus (*Reiz*).[27]

It is in this context that we should attempt to understand several of Novalis's fragmentary writings from the last couple of years of the eighteenth century, writings in which *der Sinn* and *die Sinne* are central. Here's a Novalis fragment from roughly the period when Kant wrote his *Anthropology*:

> We have 2 systems of senses, that, as different as they might appear, are nonetheless most intimately intertwined with one another. One system is called the body, the other the soul. The former exists in dependence on external stimuli [*Reitzen*, in Novalis's spelling] whose embodiment we call nature or the external world. The latter stands originally in dependence on an embodiment of internal stimuli that we call the spirit, or the spirit world.[28]

In this passage, the German *Sinn* without any doubt denotes the senses, though Novalis has introduced the peculiar suggestion that there are two systems of such senses. Another fragment from the same era presents a real challenge not only to the translator but to the German reader as well. For now, I'll continue to translate *Sinn* as *sense*.

> *On non-sensory* or *non-mediated* knowledge. All sense is *representative—symbolic*—a medium. All sense perception is second-hand. The more peculiar and abstract, one might say, the representation, description, reproduction is, and the more dissimilar it is to the object, the stimulus, then the more independent, separate is the sense—if it did not even require an external cause, it would cease to be sense and would instead be a corresponding being. . . . Sense is a tool, a means. An absolute sense would be both means and end. Thus is every thing the *means itself* for getting to know that thing—to experience it or to have an effect on it. In order to feel and get to know a thing, I would have to make it both my sense and my object—I would have to *give it life*—make it absolute sense, according to the earlier meaning [*Bedeutung*].[29]

To a translator today, this sounds like a very modern meditation on the nature of meaning. "All meaning," it would read, "is representative—symbolic—a medium . . . Meaning is a tool, a means. An absolute meaning would be both means and end." But the title phrase of this fragment, in German, is "Von der unsinnlichen, oder unmittelbaren Erkenntniß" (the final word is in Novalis's now-archaic spelling). *Unsinnlich*, which contains the word *Sinn*, means "not based in the senses," and the first sentence begins with an observation about what can only mean "sense." What sort of logic would have prompted Novalis to lead off a discussion about non-sensory knowledge with the extremely odd comment that *meaning* is representative? No, the quasi-Kantian logic is this: (1) I'm about to discuss what knowledge would be if it did not come via the senses. (2) Knowledge that *does* come via the senses is a step removed, "secondhand." (3) This means that a sense perception is not the same thing as the object being perceived. (4) Rather it is a mere tool, a means. (5) If it were not a mere tool, it would be a hypothetical "absolute sense," that is, it would be coextensive with the object, and my concourse with the world would consist in an enlivening of objects as they came to be somehow identical with my "sense."

So what does *Sinn* mean here? That extremely long Grimm dictionary entry includes a number of closely related definitions of *Sinn* that make it essentially another word for "understanding" (in the Kantian sense of ordinary knowledge), "receptive faculty," "intellect," "consciousness"—all properties of the perceiving human subject, but also, by extension, "that which is thought," a property of *objects*. So *Sinn* here cannot mean *meaning*, as the published English translation has it, because the fragment becomes incoherent if meaning is the topic.[30] If, on the other hand, *Sinn* rather fluidly means something like "sensory receptive faculty" and also "what such a faculty receives, in the form of representations of objects" (modern psychology would perhaps use the term *percept* here), then we have a slightly adventurous speculation on what it would be like if we could directly perceive things in the world. If we could, Novalis claims paradoxically, my senses wouldn't be senses anymore; they'd *be* the objects and, as part of an animate being (me), would invest those objects with life.

Novalis's fragmentary attempt at a philosophical novel, *The Novices of Saïs*, includes a number of passages that would tempt, and that have tempted, modern translators to assume the author was issuing grand statements about meaning in connection with the world and nature. Once again, for the sake of consistency, I'll render *Sinn* as *sense*, before suggesting possible reasons for choosing a different English term. The novel, such as it is (Novalis died before finishing it, and his original manuscript was lost), consists of very little in the way of action and much in the way of lengthy contemplative declarations by members of a group gathered in the temple of Isis. We read this, for example: "What's the point in our wandering arduously through the murky world of visible things? The purer world lies within us, in this source. Here is where the true sense of the great, dappled, muddled spectacle reveals itself; and if, filled with these sights, we set forth into nature, then everything is well-known to us, and we know with certainty every form."[31] There are two widely available English translations of this work, one by British historian and biographer Una Birch (1875–1949), published in 1903, the other by Ralph Manheim (the renowned translator of Hitler's *Mein Kampf*), published in 1949. This is how Birch rendered the second sentence: "Here is revealed the true meaning of this great motley crazy Show, and if full of this revelation we traverse Nature again, everything appears familiar and with assurance we distinguish every form."[32] Here is Manheim: "Here lies the true meaning of the great, varicolored, confused pageant; and if full of these perceptions we go out into nature, everything is familiar to us, and with a certainty we know every shape."[33] In this instance, we might find some warrant for rendering *Sinn* as *meaning*, since Novalis appears to be suggesting that inside ourselves we come to *understand* "the great, dappled, muddled spectacle": it "makes sense." But, as in the last example, the focus is on how our senses fail us in "the murky world of visible things." Only within, Novalis seems to hint, do we have a *sense* that grasps the spectacle such that the spectacle has *sense*. *Sinn* once again seems to hesitate between indicating a human faculty and indicating the object of that faculty.

Finally, consider this passage from *The Novices of Saïs*: "The sense of the world is reason: it is for the sake of reason that the world exists, and if at first the world is the battleground of a childish, blooming reason, then one day it will become the divine image of reason's activity, an arena for a true church. . . . Let him who would attain to knowledge of nature practice his moral sense."[34] Both Birch and Manheim translate the opening phrase as "meaning of the world."[35] I am far from confident that I grasp what Novalis is trying to get across here. If, as earlier, *Sinn* means something lying between our perceptive faculty and what is rendered comprehensible by that faculty, then what is Novalis saying? Does *reason* mean *practical reason*, as Kant presented it in his second critique, that is, as the moral faculty—a faculty that is distinct from the *understanding*, by which we navigate our way through the physical world? If so, then perhaps Novalis is saying that reason is the faculty by which we gain a comprehension of the world superior to the one that we gain through ordinary understanding. Whatever Novalis meant by this odd turn of phrase, it cannot possibly be right to render *Sinn* as *meaning*. How can the *meaning* of the world be a human faculty? And yet that is how the passage has been presented to English-speaking readers.

So, how are we to understand "Nur ein Künstler kann den Sinn des Lebens errathen"? It contains, after all, the exact phrase that appears to have given rise to speculation, in a variety of languages, on the "meaning," sense, direction, purpose, value of life, a phrase that for over two centuries has almost invariably been translated into English as "the meaning of life." Since this fragment appears in complete isolation, there are no contextual clues about what was on Novalis's mind when he wrote it. Can we write "the meaning of life"? If so, what might Novalis have understood by this phrase?

It's not entirely impossible that he did have something like this in mind. Elsewhere in *The Novices of Saïs*, he wrote, "Thus arise multifarious views of nature, and if, at one end, our feeling for nature becomes a merry inspiration, a feast, then we see that feeling transformed into the most devout religion, giving to an entire life direction, position, and meaning."[36] But here Novalis uses *Bedeutung*, which unquestionably must be translated as *meaning* (both Birch and Manheim translated it this way). If the word *Sinn* had begun to bleed over into the semantic space of *Bedeutung*, then it is possible that Novalis might have used the two words roughly synonymously. *Der Sinn des Lebens*, understood in this way, would suggest that life is something we interpret in order to discover, as in a word or story, what lies behind it—its meaning. It would also indicate that life *does* something: it *means* (*bedeutet*).[37]

Bleeding over into the semantic space of *Bedeutung* is what definition 22 in the Grimm dictionary entry for *Sinn* is all about. With only a handful of exceptions, the earliest literary examples cited in the entry date from Novalis's era (though, strangely, there are no examples from Novalis himself). Many feature *Sinn* in what has since become a routinely used definition, as in the meaning of a word or story. Others, as I mentioned a moment ago, present situations in which understanding is not achieved, that is, where a speaker fails to convey, or a listener fails to receive, the correct sense or meaning. But, for purposes of our discussion here, one sub-category in definition 22 really stands out. The category is "Sinn haben, *etwas Bedeuten*" ("to make sense, *to mean something*"). The examples cited under this category show *Sinn* functioning not just as *meaning* in the simplest sense but as something grander, something that can be characterized as "big," "deep," or "secret." In Goethe's *Wilhelm Meister's Apprenticeship* (1795–1796), for example, we find at one point the eponymous hero and an acquaintance engaged in a conversation about the relation between fate and chance. To bolster his claim that chance seldom carries out what fate has decreed, the acquaintance says, "Most of what happens in the world confirms my opinion. Don't many incidents show, in the beginning, a great sense, and don't most end up being something trivial?"[38] In his essay on the great archaeologist Johann Winckelmann (1805), Goethe drew a contrast between the modern age and the "antique" age of ancient Greece. In the antique age, he writes, "man [*der Mensch*] and the human [*das Menschliche*, "that which is human"] were esteemed as being of the greatest value, and all man's internal as well as external relations with the world were represented and perceived as having great sense."[39]

We find similar usages in Novalis, and it is here in particular that we see *Sinn* and *Bedeutung* overlap, such that *Sinn* might properly be rendered as *meaning* in English. "Morality and philosophy," he writes in a fragment, "are arts. The former is the art of making one's choice, among the [possible] motives for actions, according to a moral idea, an a priori artistic idea, thereby investing all actions with a great, deep sense/meaning [*Sinn*]— giving life a higher meaning [*Bedeutung*]."[40] Another particularly striking passage shows Novalis reverting to the old "book of nature" trope, using *Sinn* (metaphorically, to be sure), as per Grimm definition 22, in connection with the interpretation of words and texts. "Everything we experience," he writes, "is a *communication*. Thus is the world in fact a *communication*, revelation of the spirit. The time is no longer when God's spirit was intelligible. The sense/meaning [*Sinn*] of the world has gone missing. We're stuck at the letters [of the alphabet]."[41] And a further reflection on the lost sense/meaning of the world as we try to decipher its script: "In olden days, everything was spirit-appearance [*Geistererscheinung*]. Nowadays we see nothing but dead repetition, which we don't comprehend. The meaning [*Bedeutung*] of the hieroglyphs is missing. We yet live off the fruit of better times."[42]

This feeling of loss appears to be what prompted one of Novalis's most dramatic fragments, where once again we find *Sinn* as a lofty quality that combines the ideas of sense and meaning. "The world," he writes, "must be romanticized. In this way we find the original sense/meaning again. Romanticizing is nothing but a qualitative potentiation. In this operation, the lower self comes to be identified with a better self. Just as we ourselves are such a qualitative power series [a type of mathematical infinite series]. This operation is still completely unknown. To the extent that I give to the general a lofty sense/meaning, to the ordinary a secret respect, to the known the dignity of the unknown, to the finite an infinite glow, I am romanticizing it."[43] To trust what Novalis has written in these fragments, the world originally possessed a sense/meaning that exalted it above what it has become today. That the sense/meaning is, at least in principle, subject to retrieval by interpretation is clear from the author's claim that nowadays we're stuck on the mere letters, that we've lost our power to "read." Romanticization is thus a process, an "operation," by which we could either reinvest the world with a lofty sense/meaning ("give to the general a lofty sense/meaning") or rediscover the world's original, already lofty sense/meaning.

The world as language and a lost sense/meaning are in fact the theme of the opening paragraphs of *The Novices of Saïs*, and here too *Sinn* (in the plural) doubles as *sense* and *meaning*:

> Many are the paths that men travel. Whoever follows and compares them will see peculiar figures arise; figures that appear to belong to that great cipher-script [*Chiffernschrift*] that one sees everywhere, on wings, eggshells, in clouds, in the snow. . . . In them we suspect we will find the key to this wonder-script [*Wunderschrift*], its grammar; except our suspicion

does not want to arrange itself in any fixed forms and appears not to want to become any higher key. An alcahest appears to have been poured over the senses of men. Only momentarily do their wishes, their thoughts, appear to consolidate. . . .

From afar I heard someone say that incomprehensibility is the consequence only of incomprehension, that incomprehension seeks what it has and therefore could never find anything further. That we do not understand language because language does not understand itself and does not wish to understand itself; that the true Sanskrit speaks in order to speak, because speaking is its joy and its essence.

Not long thereafter someone spoke: holy scripture [*die heilige Schrift*] needs no explanation. Whoever speaks truthfully is filled with eternal life, and his writing [*Schrift*] appears to us wonderfully related to true mysteries, for it is a chord from the symphony of the universe.[44]

Alcahest is the alchemists' name for a putative universal solvent. William Arctander O'Brien, author of one of the few book-length studies of Novalis in English, writes that Novalis's reference to this imaginary substance, as it is "poured over the senses," "suggests a dissolution of 'meanings' as well as of the 'sensory faculties.'"[45] If O'Brien is right, then we see once again the blurring of the boundary between the five senses and the sense/meaning of a thing in the world.

Novalis's reference to "the true Sanskrit" evokes the mania of the German Romantic era for finding the earliest sources not only of German and other European languages but of language in general. The eighteenth century had seen the rise of Sanskrit studies inspired, early on, by the belief (erroneous, it turned out) that the ancient Indian language was related to ancient Egyptian and, later, by the sense that it enjoyed the status of a virtual, if not literal, *Ursprache* ("original language"; the German word was coined in precisely this era). After the death of Novalis, his friend Friedrich Schlegel would do much of the pioneering philological work on the relationship of Sanskrit to the Indo-European language family. Novalis appears to have first heard about the allegedly primeval language, and the literature written in it, in the mid-1790s, for as early as 1795 he was referring to his teenage fiancée as "Sakontala," after the work of that title (today generally spelled *Shakuntala*) by the classical Sanskrit writer Kālidāsa (fourth-fifth centuries CE) appeared in German translation (1791). Given that much of what was written about language and its origins in the second half of the eighteenth century was, certainly by modern standards, fanciful in the extreme, "the true Sanskrit" as a phrase encapsulates perfectly the blend of the mythical (Romantic speculation about an original language that somehow provided an unmediated form of communication) and the scholarly (actual philological studies into the origins of words and the relations among existing modern languages). Into the suggestion that the world is a text of some sort and that our challenge is to decipher it, that is, to discover its meaning(s), Novalis has incorporated the myth of an *Ursprache* that sprang up in an Edenic era when there was no barrier to understanding, when we were not frozen, uncomprehending, in the face of mere letters and ciphers, when, as a consequence, *Sinn* (our senses) and *Sinn* (the meaning of something) actually were (almost) the same thing.[46]

O'Brien writes some brilliant pages on Novalis's conception of language. Central to that conception is the unbridgeable gap separating a transcendent absolute from the world of experience, which is a world of mere representations. "On the one extreme," O'Brien writes, "Hardenberg's works are metaphysical, pious, and theological: they rest secure in a *faith* in an essence, being, or God that grounds all appearance. Yet the ground of presentation, the totality (*das All*), remains itself unpresentable; and although one may *feel* an awe or reverence for essence, being, or God, none of them presents itself as such. . . . All signs are fragments of a totality of whose everpresent absence, of whose un(re)presentability, they continually remind us. . . . [T]he failure of signification incessantly points to an Absolute that hovers right there or right here, always transcendently and tantalizingly out of reach."[47] The conception of language is thus inseparable from an overarching worldview, which, in its own peculiar way (Novalis was not a systematic philosopher, in the conventional sense of the term), is idealist to the core. The dream of a lost, mythical Eden, where God's spirit was intelligible, where the sense of the world had not yet gone missing, where external things were directly accessible and language was not just a collection of mute ciphers, serves as an acknowledgment that today's *actual* world is one in which we *do* stand frozen before mere representations and ciphers, where, in other words, experience, which exists at the mercy of our *senses*, consists of a perpetual quest for the *sense*/meaning that lies behind mere representations. And, given the extraordinary powers that the Romantic generation attributed to artists, we can hardly be surprised to see Novalis claim that only an artist can guess—just *guess*, not actually *retrieve*—the sense/meaning of life itself. And, if it's true that the revival of the "book of nature" theme was a principal weapon in the arsenal of anti-Enlightenment sentiment, what could be more anti-Enlightenment than the assertion that artists enjoy some sort of superior access to the secrets of life?

That's Novalis. It would be a mistake to suggest that his use of *Sinn*, in the often confusing array of meanings and nuances it enjoyed in his writings, was directly and solely responsible for the proliferation of its use in German letters during and after his lifetime. And yet he surely played an important role. The last few years of the eighteenth century mark the birth of what shortly afterward came to be officially known as Romanticism, and key figures in that birth were Novalis himself, Friedrich Schlegel (1772–1829), and Friedrich Daniel Schleiermacher (1768–1834), who would go on to become one of Germany's most prominent Protestant theologians. In Schlegel's writing, we see something curious happen in the last years of the century. The document that is credited with introducing the word *romantisch*, and thereby naming the fledgling movement, is a fragment (Schlegel, together with Novalis, helped establish the new vogue for fragments) that appears in a collection published in 1798 by Schlegel and his elder brother, August Wilhelm, under the title *Athenaeum Fragments* (*Athenäums-Fragmente*).[48] Though Novalis, August Wilhelm, and Schleiermacher contributed a small portion of the content, the younger Schlegel was responsible for the vast bulk of it. The word *Sinn* appears dozens of times. Apart from its casual use in such phrases as "the words in their original sense," it occurs repeatedly in the phrase "sense for" (*Sinn für*), where it appears to mean something like "proclivity for," "inclination toward," "feeling for," "appreciation of," "understanding of"—for example, "sense for the infinite," "sense for art history," "sense for representative value," even "sense for fragments." *Sinn* in these phrases denotes a mental faculty or ability of some sort. Not once is the word used in the way Novalis had begun to use it in the same year that the *Athenaeum* volume came out, when he wrote about guessing the sense/meaning of life. Then, in 1799, Schlegel wrote a novel. *Lucinde* is a love story, utterly lacking in any sort of plot interest (apart from some scandalously racy passages) but filled with the sort of florid language that in Schlegel's eyes captured the spirit of the new cultural moment (a novel, *Roman* in German, was a fit vehicle for the *romantisch* in literature). The final pages present a description of the culminating stage of the love between the hero and Lucinde. Here is the fourth-to-last paragraph: "Now the soul understands the lamentation of the nightingale and the smile of the newborn, and it understands that which reveals itself significantly [*bedeutsam*] in the secret hieroglyphs on flowers and in the stars: the holy sense/meaning of life [*Sinn des Lebens*] as well as the beautiful language of nature. All things speak to it [the soul], and it sees everywhere the lovely spirit through the delicate covering."[49]

Novalis died before the movement he helped initiate would fully blossom. But he certainly helped establish a language and a literary style for Romanticism, and though an important component of that language was the word *Sinn* with the peculiar set of sub-definitions that it bore in his writings, it was his companion Schleiermacher who, no doubt unwittingly (for it is extremely unlikely that he was conscious of "doing" something to the word *Sinn*), took the word and its accompanying concepts to the next historical and semantic level. His use can be divided into three stages, each corresponding to a phase of his intellectual, philosophical, and theological development.

Schleiermacher is probably best known today for the work, published in 1799, that is credited with originating the modern comparative study of religion, together with the generic concept of *religion* that lies at the foundation of such study. The title of the work, *Über die Religion: Reden an die Gebildeten unter ihren Verächtern*, might be most accurately (though not elegantly) translated as "On religion: speeches to the educated/cultivated among its despisers." The idea in the title is that religion has its despisers and among them are some highly educated and cultivated people; these speeches are directed at them. Here, grossly simplified, is the argument (ordered somewhat differently from the presentation that the author gives) of the five "speeches." To begin with, we must distinguish between *religion* as an overarching concept and "positive religions," or the actual, existing religions in the world. What we're after is that overarching concept, which would serve as the factor or set of factors common to all religions. The phrase that encapsulates the common factor(s) is *Sinn und Geschmak* [in Schleiermacher's spelling] *fürs Unendliche*: "sense and taste for the infinite."[50] As in Schlegel's *Athenäum* fragments, *Sinn für* suggests a faculty or inclination of the mind—not one of the senses, which are receptive, but rather something that propels us in a particular direction or toward a particular thing. It occurs dozens of times in *Über die Religion*. "The infinite" was a major obsession in German Romanticism, where it appears to have meant, in an informal way, "something very, very big." Schleiermacher's phrase accomplishes two important and closely related goals: (1) It divorces *religion* from the particular content of actual, "positive" *religions*, with the consequent leveling effect (if they're all just an expression of this tendency, why should any one of them presume to supersede all the others?), and (2) it reduces religion not to a particular conception of a particular deity but to human subjectivity, that is, what we feel and appreciate. *Sinn* serves to denote this most central idea in *Über die Religion*. At one point, Schleiermacher expands on the function of *Sinn*, which can take three directions: (1) "inward, toward the self," (2) "outward, toward the indeterminate in one's worldview [*Weltanschauung*, literally "intuition of the world"]," and (3) both together, for, as he explains at the beginning of the third speech, "The range and the truth of the intuition depends on the acuity and breadth of the sense, and the wisest man who is without sense is no nearer to religion than the most foolish who possesses an accurate view."[51] Though Schleiermacher would go on later to produce one of the most important works of Protestant theology ever written, there is in this conception of religion a stunning implicit agnosticism, one that will help to lay the groundwork for the historical-critical approach to religion that Germans will champion in the new century. That approach, in which the investigator steps outside whatever faith, if any, he or she embraces, will in turn lead to a climate in which conventional religious terms come to be replaced by a variety of attenuated, secularized terms. Among those terms is *meaning*.

The second stage is represented by a fleeting phrase that appears in a set of "monologues" that Schleiermacher published in 1800, as a "New Year's gift" to a lady friend. Like *Über die Religion*, the new work is filled with instances of *Sinn* as a faculty or propensity of mind. But at one point Schleiermacher introduces the thought that mankind finds itself confronting two paths, one of which leads in the direction of moral virtue (not his phrase) while the other leads in the direction of artistic expression. This thought inspires the author to offer us a characterization of the artistic impulse in humanity:

How could there be any doubt as to which of the two I have chosen? So decisively have I always avoided troubling myself over what the artist does, so yearningly have I seized on everything that serves my own cultivation and speeds and strengthens the determination of that cultivation, that no doubt remains. The artist hunts for anything that can become a sign and symbol of mankind . . . he rummages through the treasury of languages, he takes the chaos of sounds and forms it into a world; he seeks secret sense/meaning and harmony in the beautiful color-play of nature; artists, in every work that presents itself to them, explore the impression of all its parts, the composition and law of the whole, and take pleasure in the artistic vessel more often than in the delightful content that it presents.[52]

That Schleiermacher, close as he was to Schlegel and Novalis in the couple of years leading up to the composition of the monologues, should have exalted the power of artists and attributed to them the capacity to "read" nature and discover its sense or meaning is not surprising. But the third stage in his use of this richly polyvalent German word represents a pivotal moment both in Schleiermacher's philosophical journey and in the evolution of *Sinn* in the direction it would take in the nineteenth and twentieth centuries, when it becomes formally associated with interpretation and the discovery of meaning (as we use the word in English), when (in German) it increasingly finds itself in a kind of semantic companionship with *Bedeutung*. In the first decade of the nineteenth century, after he had published his book on religion and his monologues, Schleiermacher turned his attention to hermeneutics, the science of interpretation. The discipline under that name has a long and complicated history, much of which is not important for our purposes here. As late as Schleiermacher's student days, in the 1780s, hermeneutics was almost exclusively a discipline concerned with biblical interpretation and, in the version that he encountered during those years, was referred to specifically as "theological hermeneutics."[53] Also long and complicated is the history of Schleiermacher's own contributions to the field, because almost none of his writings on the topic, spanning roughly three decades, were published during his lifetime in any sort of finished form. What is important here is Schleiermacher's contribution to the evolution of the word *Sinn*, which, later on, would carry the heavy burden that characterized its use in the twentieth century.

Underlying Schleiermacher's hermeneutics and his use of *Sinn* is a highly influential conception of language and the origin of language that emerged in the last decades of the eighteenth century, thanks largely to Johann Gottfried Herder (1744–1803), whose influential *Treatise on the Origin of Language* was published in 1772. The foundational assertion of the argument, controversial in its era, would turn no heads today: language is of human, not divine, origin. When you consider the properties that set us humans apart from other forms of animal life, the emergence of language practically explains itself, Herder believed. Two of these stand above all others. *Besinnung*, sometimes translated as simply "consciousness," is the property of being aware, *sinnvoll*, in possession of one's sensory apparatus. *Besonnenheit* suggests thoughtfulness and self-awareness. It is formed from the verb *besinnen*, "to know, reflect, consider, be self-aware."[54] As their names indicate, both properties stem from our possession of *Sinn* ("sense," "sense for") and *Sinne* (the five senses).

Sensory faculties are not unique to human beings, but the type of aware-ness that Herder has in mind is. His aim is to show a direct line from these uniquely human qualities to the emergence of language. Of the distinctively human, Herder writes this (I'll leave the two words untranslated): "One may name this entire disposition of [man's] powers what one will. *Understanding, reason, Besinnung* and so forth. It is all the same to me, as long as one does not accept these as names for distinct powers or just for a heightened level of an-imal powers. It is the whole arrangement of man's powers, the entire economy of his sensory [*sinnlich*] and cognitive, his cognitive and willing nature, or, rather, it is the singular positive power of thinking that, bound to a certain organization of the body, is called *reason* in men, *deftness* [*Kunstfähigkeit*] in animals, *freedom* in man, *instinct* in animals."[55] The human being is a creature that "not only cognizes, wills, and effects [*würke* in Herder's ar-chaic spelling] but *knows* that it cognizes, wills, and effects . . . This entire disposition of [the human being's nature]," he continues, "we would like to name *Besonnenheit*, in order to escape confusion with the peculiar powers of reason etc."[56] The aim is to demonstrate that man is *by nature* a "linguistic creature" (*Sprachgeschöpf*), and Herder builds his case by repeatedly drawing on the notion of *Sinn* (as proclivity) and *die Sinne* as the natural means by which language emerges. It is no surprise that, when it came to *interpreting* language, that is, to discovering *meanings* in it, Herder, ever the secularist, insisted that thought is dependent on human language and that word usages, rather than items independent of language, were the key to interpretation.[57]

In the somewhat unruly process by which he elaborated, or attempted to elaborate, a hermeneutics, Schleiermacher relied heavily on Herder's con-ception of language, in particular the relation between thought and language and the focus on word usages. In his hermeneutics manuscript of 1819, Schleiermacher includes a section titled "Grammatical interpretation" (*Die grammatische Auslegung*), to be followed later by a section on psychological interpretation. If the reader is seeking a crystal-clear terminological presen-tation, the opening of the section is likely to be disappointing, perhaps be-cause the discipline to a considerable extent defies clarity. In fact, the topic that begins this section is precisely the process of clarifying, or seeking "deter-mination" (*Bestimmung*) in a particular utterance. "Anything in a given utter-ance that requires still further determination," Schleiermacher begins, "may be determined only from the linguistic domain that is common to the author and his original readership. Everything," he continues, "requires further de-termination and acquires it only in the context. Every part of the utterance,

material as well as formal, is in and for itself undetermined. For a particular word in isolation, we can think to ourselves nothing more than a particular cycle of usages. Similarly with every linguistic form." Schleiermacher
then launches into a circuitous and inconclusive series of thoughts on the
relations among *Sinn, Bedeutung,* and *Verstand* (understanding). Here is an
abridged version (with the three German words untranslated)

> Some call what we think to ourselves in a word taken all by itself the
> *Bedeutung* and what we think to ourselves of the same word in a given con-
> text the *Sinn*. Others say that a word has only a *Bedeutung* and no *Sinn*,
> that a sentence taken all by itself has a *Sinn* but no *Verstand*, which only a
> fully closed utterance can have. . . . For *Sinn* in comparison with *Verstand*
> is entirely the same thing as *Bedeutung*. The truth of the matter is that the
> passage from the indeterminable to the determined in every interpretation
> undertaking is an endless task. Where an individual sentence constitutes a
> closed utterance unto itself alone, the difference between *Sinn* and *Verstand*
> seems to disappear as between an epigram and an aphorism.[58]

We might charitably say that this is not terribly lucid, but if it shows anything, it is that Schleiermacher has now unequivocally begun to use *Sinn*
to denote a property of interpretable things, of language and its constituent
parts. And as we move along in this section, we see that *Sinn* has now settled
into a definition that was largely missing in his earlier works. "The *Sinn* of
every word in a given location," he writes, "must be determined according
to how it stands together with other words that surround it."[59] *Sinn* has now
begun to resemble many of the functions of English *meaning*.

By the time of Schleiermacher's forays into hermeneutics, this key German
word has done the work necessary to make possible the use of its equivalents
in other European languages for expressing whatever it is that gets expressed
in such phrases as "the meaning of life." Above all, (1) it fits neatly within the
structure of an idealist epistemology that posits a separation between a cog-
nizing mind and the outside world, thus the concomitant need to "interpret"
or find "meaning," and (2) it nicely accommodates the anti-Enlightenment
sentiment that, to use Novalis's word, "romanticizes" the world by seeing that
world as invested with mysterious qualities lying behind phenomena available to our senses (*Sinne*).

But something else is happening here that cannot be overstated. Whatever
he understood by the word *Sinn*, Novalis has absolutized it. "Book of nature"

thinkers talked about reading the world, which was to say combing it for a multitude of meaning-bearing signs and symbols. Novalis, by contrast, spoke of *the* meaning/sense, *one* meaning/sense, of the world or of life and strongly suggested that this meaning cannot be retrieved by an act of interpretation. While the countless signs and symbols in the book of nature might have required some effort to interpret and might have given rise to considerable controversy regarding their meanings, the quest for those meanings was not doomed at the outset. Finding meanings was held to be entirely possible. But finding a *single* meaning/sense of life or of the world seems by its very nature to be an impossibility. What could it possibly be, when formulated in this way? But that appears to be the point, and it's part of the key to the mystique surrounding conversations about "the meaning of life." Artists have the best chance at finding it, but even they can do no more than guess. The mystery, consequently the mystique, is built in.

4

Thomas Carlyle and Ralph Waldo Emerson Bring the "Mystery of Existence" and the "Sense of Life" to the English-Speaking World

A Brief and Uneventful Stop in Copenhagen

In the first half of the nineteenth century, the most abundant use of *meaning*—or its equivalent in languages other than English—in connection with such concepts as "life" is no doubt to be found in the works of Søren Kierkegaard (1813–1855), who earns a place in a couple of the chronological studies, in German, of the *Sinn des Lebens* theme.[1] If you read lots of Kierkegaard in English or German translation, then indeed you're likely to find numerous instances of phrases that have been rendered as either *meaning* or *significance* in English, and either *Sinn* or *Bedeutung*, in German. *Either/Or* (1843), in the relatively recent translation by Alastair Hannay, contains quite a few instances of *meaning* in connection with life, including the exact phrase "the meaning of life." At one point, Kierkegaard complains about the *lack* of meaning in life: "How empty life is and without meaning [*betydningsløs*].—We bury a man, we follow him to the grave, we throw three spades of earth on him, we ride out in a coach, we ride home in a coach, we take comfort in the thought that a long life awaits us. But how long is threescore years and ten? Why not finish it at once?"[2] At another, he wonders, "Whatever can be the meaning of this life? [*Betydningen af dette Liv*] . . . But working for one's living can't be the meaning of life [*Livets Betydning*] . . . Usually the lives of the other class have no meaning [*Betydning*] either, beyond that of consuming the said conditions. To say that the meaning of life [*Livets Betydning*] is to die seems again to be a contradiction."[3] In *The Concept of Anxiety* (1844), Kierkegaard includes a breezy and ambiguous reference to meaning *in* (not *of*) life: "One may even become something great in the world, if then, on top

What Do We Mean When We Talk About Meaning? Steven Cassedy, Oxford University Press. © Oxford University Press 2022. DOI: 10.1093/oso/9780190936907.003.0005

of that, one attends church once in a while, then everything goes exceedingly well. This seems to suggest that for some individuals the religious is the absolute, for others not, and so 'Goodnight' to all meaning in life [*Mening i Livet*]."[4] And in *Repetition* (1843), Kierkegaard featured the notion in a jocular moment: "Praised be the coach horn! It is my symbol. Just as the ancient ascetics placed a skull on the table, the contemplation of which constituted their view of life, so the coach horn on my table always reminds me of the meaning of life [*hvad Livets Betydning er*, literally "what life's meaning is"]."[5]

Two problems immediately present themselves when we place Kierkegaard on a timeline showing occurrences of "the meaning of life" and similar expressions in various languages. First, outside Denmark, we couldn't really look for evidence that Kierkegaard's use of these expressions had any impact on other writers till much later, for his work did not begin to be translated till long after his death. A few German translations appeared as early as the 1860s, but the bulk of the major works first appeared in German between 1890 and 1922, thanks to the (lamentably uneven) efforts of German theologian Christoph Schrempf. English translations began to appear only in the 1930s, continuing into the 1960s. Second, while I've chosen English translations here that feature the word *meaning*, there are actually two Danish words that (sometimes) get translated as *meaning*, and it's safe to say that neither one exactly corresponds to the English word. *Mening* is certainly the etymological cognate of *meaning*, and, like the English word, it can carry the connotation of intention. It is used, like German *Sinn*, to suggest the "sense" of something and can also mean simply "opinion." *Meningen med Livet* (literally "meaning with life") is the modern Danish equivalent to the English "meaning of life" (it's the translated title, for example, of the Monty Python film *The Meaning of Life*). *Betydning* is cognate with, and fully equivalent to, German *Bedeutung*. When you speak of the meaning of a word in Danish, you're more likely to use *Betydning*, just as you would use *Bedeutung* in German. In the examples above, Kierkegaard has used *Betydning* everywhere except in " 'Goodnight' to all meaning in life," where he uses *Mening*. It's not clear that Kierkegaard gave much thought to the distinction, nor is it clear that he had anything in mind beyond something like "importance" (for *Betydning*) and "aim" or "purpose" (for *Mening*).[6]

Kierkegaard will play an enormous role much later on, once his work begins to be translated, especially into German and English, but it will not be because he used these rather imprecise phrases containing *Betydning* and *Mening*; rather, it will be because other aspects of his writing fed into theological and philosophical currents in which *meaning*, in English, and *Sinn*, in German, had already taken on a valence of their own. I will briefly take this up in a later chapter.

Thomas Carlyle Discovers Novalis

If we are looking for a conduit in the mid-nineteenth century through which German Romanticism, its idealism, its view of nature either as a book containing signifying objects or as a veil concealing such objects (and thus producing mystery), its consequent preoccupation with *meaning*, together with the implication of meaning in the *senses* (and our *sense* of things), passed into the English-speaking world, that conduit would be Thomas Carlyle. What to call the Scottish writer? Philosopher? Hardly, since despite his fascination with the work of many philosophers he never elaborated anything like a coherent body of thought on any of the questions that occupied philosophers in his era or earlier eras—though the work of such philosophers certainly guided Carlyle's thinking. Thinker? Yes, he did a great deal of thinking and set much of it down in writing. Historian? Yes, but not exclusively. Maybe we should leave it at *writer*.

Carlyle's life (1795–1881) spanned most of the nineteenth century, thus also most of the Victorian age (1837–1901). If biographers and commentators can agree on one thing about the sometimes confusing array of ideas that Carlyle entertained and embraced over his long career, it is that he remained what in largely Presbyterian Scotland he was raised to be—namely, a Calvinist. But even this label requires some qualification. Charles Frederick Harrold, a Carlyle scholar writing in the 1930s, helpfully reduced the complexity of Carlyle's Calvinism to, on one side, a familiar list of qualities and principles conventionally associated with that doctrine and, on the other, an important conflict within Calvinism that played out in Carlyle's life and thought. Calvinism's "affinity with the spirit of the Stoic," Harrold wrote, "its exaltation of the 'elect,' its emphasis on work, on order, and on submission to authority in a theocratic and corporate community," help us to understand Carlyle's social thinking, including what the author described as Carlyle's "Fascist-like emphasis upon social solidarity and leadership."[7] The conflict within Calvinism, as Harrold describes it, regards a conception of God as, at the same time, immanent, close to us, revealed in nature, and transcendent, forbidding, distant. Even the "immanent" side is double-edged, as Harrold described it. "To many a Calvinist," he wrote, "God's immanence was not so much cause for comfort as the ground for a constant shuddering awareness of being observed."[8] Harrold wrote of "the reassurance offered in the doctrine of divine immanence," something that emerges in Carlyle in "the Calvinist conception of nature as a direct revelation of the divine."[9]

This last conception, Harrold believed, exerted its greatest power over Carlyle during the period of his greatest infatuation with Germany and German Romanticism. And this is where we pick up the story from Chapter 3. For in his early twenties, in part because his curiosity had been aroused by the book that introduced "Germany" not only to the French but to the British as well, Madame de Staël's *De l'Allemagne* (1813, English edition the same year), Carlyle had learned German and had begun avidly reading Goethe and Schiller in the original language. He translated *Wilhelm Meisters Lehrjahre* and wrote a *Life of Schiller*. In addition, he read Jean Paul Richter, Fichte, Schelling, Friedrich Schlegel, and Kant (though, most agree, not very carefully and without really understanding him). In the late 1820s, he read Novalis, in the two-volume edition of the poet's works edited by Ludwig Tieck and Friedrich Schlegel. Then, in 1829, in a review essay titled simply "Novalis," he introduced the English reading public to this intriguing figure from the German Romantic era. Charles Frederick Harrold somehow acquired Carlyle's personal copy of Novalis's *Schriften* for his own library and surmised from the almost complete absence of marginal notes that the Scottish writer drew his knowledge of Novalis from Tieck's foreword and did not otherwise closely study the writings themselves. That may well be true, but it makes little difference for our purposes. For one thing, if he didn't *study* the writings closely, he translated some extended passages into English, giving non-readers of German a glimpse into the poet's mind. For another, Carlyle clearly formed some strong opinions about Novalis and his worldview, and whether or not a careful scholar deems these opinions to be responsibly supported, they clearly demonstrate the flow of German culture at the beginning of the nineteenth century—as filtered through Carlyle—to British culture several decades later.

It's easy to conclude, along with many of Carlyle's academic readers, that the essay serves as a perfect example of the author's tendency to project his own views onto his subject. Responsible Novalis scholars might understandably differ with Carlyle's characterization of the German poet. But it's equally easy to conclude that Carlyle found the elements that reflected the highest degree of resemblance to his own thinking, perhaps featuring those elements at the expense of some others. Whatever we might think is Novalis's actual worldview, here is what Carlyle thought: Novalis was a mystic, and his writing is pervaded with idealism. What does Carlyle mean by these terms? His thinking is admittedly a bit jumbled. He quotes Tieck as claiming that Novalis had sought "to unite Philosophy with Religion," which leads to this rather puzzling sequence of thoughts: Novalis is a follower of "Kantism," which is to say idealism. For Kant, Carlyle thought, idealism meant the annihilation of matter and, further, that "Time and Space have no absolute existence."[10] Hence, "when we say that the Deity is omnipresent and eternal, that with Him it is a universal Here and Now, we say nothing wonderful; nothing but that He also created Time and Space . . . and the black Spectre, Atheism, 'with all its sickly dews,' melts into nothingness forever."[11] Further, Carlyle characterizes the Kantian distinction between understanding and reason in this startling way: "We allude to the recognition, by these Transcendentalists [among whom Carlyle classes Kant], of a higher faculty in man than Understanding; of Reason (*Vernunft*), the pure, ultimate light of our nature; wherein, as they assert, lies the foundation of all Poetry, Virtue, Religion."[12]

Had Kant lived to the age of 105, he might have been a bit surprised to read this account of his critical philosophy. But if Carlyle thought that Novalis's mysticism was "exemplified in some shape among our own Puritan [that is, Calvinist] Divines,"[13] why not claim that Kant provided a basis for an "omnipresent and eternal" deity, the immanent deity of Calvinism? Why not also make him the champion of the sort of anti-Enlightenment thinking that we do in fact find in Novalis as well as in Carlyle's version of Calvinism? And what could be more Calvinist than this remarkable description of Novalis: "Naturally a deep, religious, contemplative spirit; purified also, as we have seen, by harsh Affliction, and familiar in the 'Sanctuary of Sorrow,' he comes before us as the most ideal of all Idealists. For him the material Creation is but an Appearance, a typical shadow in which the Deity manifests himself to man. Not only has the unseen world a reality, but the only reality: the rest being not metaphorically, but literally and in scientific strictness, 'a show.' "[14]

Given this understanding of the "mystical" German poet, it's easy to see the rationale for Carlyle's choice of illustrative passages in Novalis's collected writings. In Chapter 3, I quoted at some length from the opening of *The Novices of Saïs*, where the unnamed novice delivers an extended fantasy on the theme of language and writing, referring, for example, to "that great cipher-script," the "wonder-script" (apparently of nature), and "the true Sanskrit." Carlyle was so fascinated by the opening of Novalis's peculiar little prose work that he included in the essay his own translation of fully a dozen pages from the very beginning and from the second chapter (titled "Nature"). And understandably so, for this is where we find the theme of reading nature, using our *senses*, and discovering *meaning* and *sense* in nature. This is Carlyle's translation of the passage that I translated using the phrase "the true sense of the great, dappled, muddled spectacle":[15] "Here discloses itself the true meaning of the great, many-coloured, complected Scene." This is his translation of the passage that in my translation begins, "The sense of the world is reason": "The significance of the World is Reason; for her sake is the World here." And two sentences later, we find this: "Let him, therefore, who would arrive at knowledge of Nature, train his moral sense [*seinen sittlichen Sinn*], let him act and conceive in accordance with the novel Essence of his Soul."[16] If Novalis, in the space of three sentences, speaks of a moral sense and a "sense of the world" that he names "reason," it's quite possible he's referring to the same thing, namely, that practical reason is our "moral sense" (*der sittliche Sinn*) and, consequently, the sense that has to do with the world (*der Sinn der Welt*). Carlyle, prompted by Novalis's context, which is filled with evocations of the "book of nature" theme, and by his view of nature as presenting a veil, behind which lies the unseen, mysterious world that alone is real (and that needs to be discovered, or "read"), reflexively reaches for the translation that suggests recovery by interpretation: "the *significance* of the World." He even distorted a passage from Tieck's foreword, in order (it appears) to give it the gravity that the word *meaning* might confer upon it. Tieck is likening Novalis to Dante, and, literally translated, the beginning of the long passage reads, "Thus did he [Novalis] invent, uncorrupted by examples, a new way of description, in the many-sidedness of the relationship [*Beziehung*], in the view of love and the belief in it, love that is at once his instructress, wisdom, and religion."[17] Here's what Carlyle has done with the passage: "Thus did he, uncorrupted by examples, find out for himself a new method of delineation: and, in his multiplicity of meaning, in his view of Love, and his belief in Love, is at once his Instructor, his Wisdom, his Religion."[18] While I'm not sure I understand what Tieck had in mind when he used the word *Beziehung*, nothing in the passage (as best I can tell) suggests that the English word *meaning*, with any of its possible connotations, should have been chosen to render it. But Carlyle, who elsewhere in the essay refers to the "wise and deep meaning" in some of Novalis's passages, clearly not thinking of the meaning of the words, is on to something.

Two years after the Novalis essay was published, Carlyle set to work on what is likely his most bizarre creation and one of the more bizarre creations in the history of the genre in which he chose to write: the novel. *Sartor Resartus* (The tailor re-tailored) is almost unreadable today. To the reader unacquainted with Carlyle and his era, it comes across as a thicket of complicated, pretentious, mock-erudite inside jokes about Germany and (then-) recent German philosophy and literature, written in a deliberately turgid and antiquated English style. The hero, Diogenes Teufelsdröckh ("devil's drek," a name reminiscent of Voltaire's consonant-rich, Germano-phobic invention "Thunder-ten-Tronckh" in *Candide*), is a professor of *Allerley Wissenschaft* ("Science of Things in General") at the New University of Weissnichtwo (Know-not-where), and he has written a book titled *Die Kleider, ihr Werden und Wirken* (Clothes, their origin and influence), hence the novel's title. There is little in the way of a plot, no doubt because this is an idea book. But the ideas in it, to the extent that one can penetrate through layers of irony to reach them, are completely serious.

Clothes: a covering, a veil, a wrapper, a disguise. It's the perfect metaphor for a worldview focused on revelation, for revelation is not a truth or reality plain to see from the outset but the disclosure of what it at first actually or apparently concealed. To say that nature is a book that we have the ability to "read" is still to say that we must *read* it; it is *not* to say that we are in constant, unmediated contact with its truths. We "read," and we interpret—hence the centrality of *meaning* (or *signification* or *significance*). So, Carlyle's plot conceit, that a cartoonish German professor writes a book about as silly a topic as clothes, allows him to explore the *serious* topic of meaning and interpretation in a *serious* exposition of Carlyle's (for want of a better term) theology. Here, for example, is an early statement of what might pass for the fictional German professor's philosophy:

All visible things are Emblems; what thou seest is not there on its own account; strictly taken, is not there at all: Matter exists only spiritually, and to represent some Idea, and *body* it forth. Hence Clothes, as despicable as we think them, are so unspeakably significant. Clothes, from the King's-mantle downwards, are Emblematic, not of want only, but of a manifold cunning Victory over Want. On the other hand, all Emblematic things are properly Clothes, thought-woven or hand-woven: must not the Imagination weave Garments, visible Bodies, wherein the else invisible creations and inspirations of our Reason are, like Spirits, revealed, and first become all-powerful?[19]

Visible things are emblems; emblems, metaphorically speaking, are clothes. Not surprisingly, the "book of nature" image occurs and recurs in *Sartor Resartus*. Teufelsdröckh's childhood prepared him to be a "reader": "Thus encircled by the mystery of Existence; under the deep heavenly Firmament; waited on by the four golden Seasons, with their vicissitudes of contribution . . . did the Child sit and learn. These things were the Alphabet, whereby in after-time he was to syllable and partly read the grand Volume of the World."[20]

Teufelsdröckh has speculated at length on symbols, so Carlyle includes a chapter containing extended passages from the professor's work on the subject. One can almost hear the voice of Novalis, who is mentioned only a few pages earlier, for the theory of symbols is a theory of concealment, revelation, and signification tied to "the Infinite." "In a Symbol," writes Teufelsdröckh,

> there is concealment and yet revelation; here therefore, by Silence and by Speech acting together, comes a double significance. And if both the Speech be itself high, and the Silence fit and noble, how expressive will their union be! Thus in many a painted Device, or simple Seal-emblem, the commonest Truth stands out to us proclaimed with quite new emphasis.
>
> For it is here that Fantasy with her mystic wonderland plays into the small prose domain of Sense, and becomes incorporated therewith. In the Symbol proper, what we can call a Symbol, there is ever, more or less distinctly and directly, some embodyment and revelation of the Infinite; the Infinite is made to blend itself with the Finite, to stand visible, and as it were, attainable there. By Symbols, accordingly, is man guided and commanded, made happy, made wretched: He every where finds himself encompassed with Symbols, recognised as such or not recognised: the Universe is but one vast Symbol of God; nay if thou wilt have it, what is man himself but a Symbol of God; is not all that he does symbolical; a revelation to Sense of the mystic god-given force that is in him.[21]

Highest of all symbols are the religious ones, in particular the highest of *these*: "If thou ask to what height man has carried it in this matter, look on our divinest Symbol: on Jesus of Nazareth, and his Life, and his Biography, and what followed therefrom. Higher has the human Thought not yet reached: this is Christianity and Christendom; a Symbol of quite perennial, infinite character; whose significance will ever demand to be anew inquired into, and anew made manifest."[22] And so we find ourselves once again in the presence of the book of nature, or in Carlyle's case the "Volume of Nature." Here is how Teufelsdröckh puts it: "We speak of the Volume of Nature: and truly a Volume it is,—whose Author and Writer is God. To read it! Dost thou, does man, so much as well know the Alphabet thereof? With its Words, Sentences, and grand descriptive Pages, poetical and philosophical, spread out through Solar Systems, and Thousands of Years, we shall not try thee. It is a Volume written in celestial hieroglyphs, in the true Sacred-writing; of which even Prophets are happy that they can read here a line and there a line."[23] Teufelsdröckh appears to have read his Novalis. To read the Volume of Nature is to interpret it and find meaning therein.

Teufelsdröckh's creator thought deeply about meaning, and his specula-tion on symbols, first in the basic sense and then in a cosmic sense, easily led him to the same place as his German precursor Novalis, for in *Sartor Resartus* we find, possibly for the first time in the English language, the phrase "the meaning of life" (where the phrase refers not to the meaning, or definition, of the word *life* but to the meaning of life itself). At the beginning of the chapter titled "The Everlasting Yea," in which we read of Teufelsdröckh's emergence from despair (as recounted in the earlier chapter "The Everlasting No"), appears this statement, from the professor himself: "Our Life is compassed round with Necessity; yet is the meaning of Life itself no other than Freedom, than Voluntary Force: thus have we a warfare; in the beginning, especially, a hard-fought Battle. For the God-given mandate, *Work thou in Welldoing*, lies mysteriously written, in Promethean, Prophetic Characters, in our hearts; and leaves us no rest, night or day, till it be deciphered and obeyed; till it burn forth, in our conduct, a visible, acted Gospel of Freedom."[24] What does *meaning* mean in this sentence? One clue lies in "The Everlasting No," where Teufelsdröckh, recalling his period of despondency, says, "To me the Universe was all void of Life, of Purpose, of Volition, even of Hostility: it was one huge, dead, immeasurable Steam-engine, rolling on, in its dead indif-ference, to grind me limb from limb."[25] If the depths of negation are char-acterized by a lack of purpose and volition, the heights of affirmation are conversely characterized by freedom as expressed in morally commendable conduct. In Carlyle's reading of Kant and "the Transcendentalists" (presum-ably his favorite German Romantic thinkers and poets, including Novalis), such conduct is the province of (practical) reason, "the foundation of all

Poetry, Virtue, Religion" but also the faculty that asserts our freedom, that is, not our civic or political freedom but our capacity to act in accordance with our will (hence not only the word *freedom* but also the words *voluntary, volition*, and *purpose*).

It's tempting to equate *meaning* in Carlyle/Teufelsdröckh's declaration with "purpose." In fact, the *Oxford English Dictionary*, in the sub-entry under *meaning* that includes as an example the phrase "the meaning of life" and in which the earliest occurrence of that phrase is listed as precisely the one in this sentence from *Sartor Resartus*, offers this definition: "Something which gives one a sense of purpose, value, etc., esp. of a metaphysical or spiritual kind; the (perceived) purpose of existence or of a person's life." But I don't think this is what Carlyle had in mind. For one thing, the *OED* definition fits only contexts where *meaning* suggests some sort of ineffable quality that life (or something else) either has or lacks but that is not defined—as if, between speaker and listener, there were a winking understanding of what *meaning* is. The last of the five illustrative passages that accompany this sub-entry, a *Time* magazine account of a speech, not identified as such, by then First Lady Hillary Clinton in 1993, on Michael Lerner's "politics of meaning," is an example of such a context: "America, she [Clinton] said, suffers from a 'sleeping sickness of the soul' . . . that we lack, at some core level, meaning in our individual lives and meaning collectively." Michael Lerner never paused to define *meaning* in any of his writings on the topic, including the full-length book *The Politics of Meaning*, published in 1996, and neither did Hillary Clinton in her speech. *Meaning* here functions in much the same way as, say, *faith* or *honor*. If you're arguing that our society needs to restore honor to the public square, you might give examples of behavior that's honorable, but you don't necessarily need to offer a technical definition of the term. The same seems to be true of *meaning* in Lerner's and Clinton's usage. Everyone presumably already pretty much understands what it means. That's the usage the *OED* writer appears to have had in mind.

But the definition does not really apply to statements that suggest the possibility of, or that explicitly tender, an answer to the question "What is the meaning of life?" It's possible that in such instances the word *meaning* in the question (expressed or implied) means "purpose," as in numerous statements by Tolstoy beginning with "The meaning of life is . . . " followed by a phrase such as "to love one's fellow man." In such a case, the statement can accurately be rephrased as "The purpose of life is to love one's fellow man." But that's different from saying that meaning, the thing that life is said to possess, *is* purpose. Now, Carlyle's character is telling us what the meaning of life is: it is "Freedom," "Voluntary Force." So, what does *meaning* mean here, and why use this word, especially if it's true that Carlyle is using it in this sense for the first time in the English language? It's important to know this, because the author is establishing an apparently fundamental connection between life and freedom/voluntary force.

Can we rephrase the statement without using the word *meaning*? The immediate context suggests that *meaning* could be replaced with something as mundane as "most important thing about," though that certainly lacks the gravity of "meaning of." But I think the larger context matters. In a work that has offered up a theological worldview built on the notion that nature, including "Life," is a book we read in order to recover meanings, that the universe is a vast symbol of God and so is "man himself," that matter bodies forth, which is to say *incarnates*, an idea, what we have is a theology of incarnation that equates revelation with semiosis. Discovering whatever it is that lies behind appearances is, figuratively speaking, a form of reading and interpretation by which we retrieve, again figuratively speaking, a meaning from a sign or symbol. Carlyle has a number of grand words and expressions for what lies behind appearances, including the German Romantic standby, "the Infinite." The phrase *meaning of* in "the meaning of Life" appears to mean something like "the essence of," "the essential quality in," "the idea incarnated in." That essence or essential quality is, Carlyle's character believes, freedom, with all the resonance that the word carries in Carlyle's German Romanticism- and transcendentalism-infused world.

In subsequent years, Carlyle would use *meaning* in an array of senses that fit under the category of the somewhat misleadingly worded sub-entry in the *OED*. We need look no farther than his 1840 lecture series on "Great Men," published in book form as *On Heroes, Hero-Worship, and the Heroic in History* (1841). The sixth and final lecture is titled "The Hero as King. Cromwell, Napoleon: Modern Revolutionism." There we find that a human being can have a meaning and that this meaning is equivalent to *worth*. "In the age which directly followed that of the Puritans," Carlyle wrote, "their cause or themselves were little likely to have justice done them. Charles Second and his Rochesters [a reference to Henry, Viscount Wilmot, Earl of Rochester, and his son, John Wilmot, 2nd Earl of Rochester, both supporters of Charles II in the second half of the seventeenth century] were not the kind of men you would set to judge what the worth or meaning of such men [that is, the Puritans] might have been. That there could be any faith or truth in the life of a man, was what these poor Rochesters, and the age they ushered in, had forgotten."[26] Of Oliver Cromwell, Carlyle wrote this: "What could gilt carriages do for this man? From of old, was there not in his life a weight of meaning, a terror and a splendour as of Heaven itself? His existence there as man set him beyond the need of gilding. Death, Judgment and Eternity: these already lay as the background of whatsoever he thought or did. All his life lay begirt as in a sea of nameless Thoughts, which no speech of a mortal could name. God's Word, as the Puritan prophets of that time had read it: this was great, and all else was little to him."[27] In this capsule description of Calvinism, *meaning* appears to mean something like "dread-inspiring religious truth," and it's no surprise that it appears in a context rich with references to symbols, reading, and interpretation. And, once again in the context of the life of Cromwell, Carlyle wrote, "And yet, I say, there is an irrepressible tendency in every man to develop himself according to the magnitude which Nature has made him of; to speak out, to act out, what Nature has laid in him. This is proper, fit, inevitable; nay it is a duty, and even the summary of duties for a man. The meaning of life here on earth might be defined as consisting in this: To unfold your *self*, to work what thing you have the faculty for. It is a necessity for the human being, the first law of our existence."[28] Here, *meaning* means (as it frequently will later, for Tolstoy) "purpose" or "aim."

Emerson as Emissary to the United States

In August 1833, when Carlyle and his wife were living in Craigenputtoch, the family estate nestled in the hills sixteen miles from Dumfries in southwest Scotland, they received an unannounced visit from a gentleman, unknown to them, who had found his way to this desolate site all the way from Concord, Massachusetts. His name was Ralph Waldo Emerson. Carlyle was so captivated by his visitor that he asked him to stay the night. The conversation the two men enjoyed over the two days marked the beginning of a long transatlantic friendship, most of it conducted by mail. The American writer had first discovered Carlyle three years earlier, reading, among other things, his translation of Goethe's *Wilhelm Meister* and his essay on Novalis.[29] Carlyle would catch on in America more than in his native land, and it was Emerson who, almost single-handedly, boosted his Scottish friend's reputation by arranging for the publication in Boston of *Sartor Resartus* in 1835. Carlyle's strange novel had garnered little acclaim in Great Britain; in the

United States, it found a substantial and enthusiastic readership, as did his subsequent history of the French Revolution, for whose publication in the United States Emerson personally advanced the funds.[30]

To judge from the Novalis- and Carlyle-inflected language of one very early American response to *Sartor*, the mystique of the book of nature and its metaphysically understood *meaning* appears to have caught on right away. Unitarian minister Convers Francis wrote to Emerson, "The book is a study, & the more I read it, the more my mind struggles after the higher truths of our wonderful being. There are parts of Sartor, which are so full fraught with the great meaning of the invisible and the infinite, that each sentence may become a text for a whole volume to one to whom it is given to unfold." Leon Jackson has written about the reception of *Sartor* in the United States, which can be described as encompassing a wide range of attitudes, from the awestruck admiration expressed by Francis to the charge that the book was a hoax. As Jackson documents, contemporary observers, characterizing the Carlyle enthusiasts, described the Scottish writer's influence as a contagion or infection, images that, while unfavorable, certainly convey the strength of the public's admiration. Among those who received *Sartor* favorably, as Jackson classes them, two groups stand out: one, comprising Calvinist and liberal Congregationalists, for whom "*Sartor* provided a template for spiritual conversion," and another for whom *Sartor* "pointed to a dualistic world in which the clothing of spiritual life changed, but the body of truth remained the same."[31] To the extent that the American Transcendentalists, a group that included not only Emerson but his friend Henry David Thoreau, Convers Francis, Bronson Alcott, and others, represented something like a unified worldview, it's worth noting, as Jackson points out, that their society, the Transcendental Club, was organized in the almost immediate aftermath of the Boston publication of *Sartor*. "In this charged context," Jackson writes, "the vogue for Carlyle's work took on a whole new light. Almost overnight, Carlyle became a cause célèbre."[32]

It would be a gross simplification, of course, to suggest a clear, direct line running from Novalis (and other German Romantic figures) through Carlyle to Emerson and leading to the introduction in the United States of the new, metaphysically tinged senses of the word *meaning*. The situation is certainly more complicated than that. For one thing, to the extent that Emerson's writings are infused with ideas originally derived from the Romantic era in Germany, Carlyle was not his lone source. Emerson knew enough German and read enough German material in English translation to find some of these ideas on his own, and he also drew on the work of an additional British figure who adapted and transmitted German Romanticism, Samuel Taylor Coleridge. For another, Emerson was very much the product of his New England upbringing, complete with a religious tradition—one, to be sure, that he would rebel against—alien both to the Calvinism of Carlyle and to the sometimes heterodox, often ambivalently regarded Lutheranism of the late eighteenth- and early nineteenth-century German philosophers and poets.

But if what we're looking for is some version of the idealism (loosely defined) that we found in Novalis and Carlyle, a worldview predicated on the existence of a figurative veil separating the world of appearances from a truer, sacred, even divine world that is revealed to us when we exert upon it our powers of interpretation (when we "read" it), we will find this plentifully in Emerson, though eventually in a form rather different from what we saw in his German and British predecessors. Emerson had discovered Carlyle well before he arranged for the publication of *Sartor*. Among the first essays he read was "The State of German Literature" (1827), where he encountered not only an astonishingly compendious account and defense of that national tradition (before *Germany* denoted an officially established nation) but an introduction to the type of thinking that would become a hallmark of Transcendentalism. The most cogent passage in Carlyle's essay is his summary of the philosophy of Fichte. "According to Fichte," Carlyle wrote,

> there is a "Divine Idea" pervading the visible Universe; which visible Universe is indeed but its symbol and sensible manifestation, having in itself no meaning, or even true existence independent of it. To the mass of men this Divine Idea of the world lies hidden: yet to discern it, to seize it, and live wholly in it, is the condition of all genuine virtue, knowledge, freedom; and the end, therefore, of all spiritual effort in every age. Literary Men are the appointed interpreters of this Divine Idea; a perpetual priesthood, we might say, standing forth, generation after generation, as the dispensers and living types of God's everlasting wisdom, to show it and imbody it in their writings and actions, in such particular form as their own particular times require it in. . . . It may throw some light on this question, if we remind our readers of the following fact. In the field of human investigation, there are objects of two sorts: First, the visible, including not only such as are material, and may be seen by the bodily eye; but all such, likewise, as may be represented in a shape, before the mind's eye, or in any way pictured there: And, secondly, the invisible, or such as are not only unseen

by human eyes, but as cannot be seen by any eye; not objects of sense at all; not capable, in short, of being pictured or imaged in the mind, or in any way represented by a shape either without the mind or within it. If any man shall here turn upon us, and assert that there are no such invisible objects; that whatever cannot be so pictured or imagined (meaning imaged) is nothing, and the science that relates to it nothing; we shall regret the circumstance. We shall request him, however, to consider seriously and deeply within himself what he means simply by these two words, God and his own Soul; and whether he finds that visible shape and true existence are here also one and the same?[33]

On his first trip to Europe, before his meeting with Carlyle, Emerson visited the Jardin des Plantes in Paris and the Hunterian Museum (of anatomical specimens) in London. It was here, apparently, that Emerson resolved to become a "naturalist." As one Emerson scholar explained, the Hunterian Museum in particular embodied for the American writer the "book of nature" idea, which he had found in Coleridge.[34] Whether the idea stemmed primarily from Coleridge or from Carlyle, by the time Emerson wrote "The Uses of Natural History" (1833–1835), his first essay on his newfound profession, he was fully in the grip of the book metaphor, complete with a reference to the discovery of *meaning* in nature. Here we read, for example, that "the whole of Nature is a metaphor or image of the human Mind." He quotes from an article about Swedenborg what, as we have seen, had become a central article of Romantic orthodoxy and what Carlyle had enunciated in his essay on German literature: "The visible world and the relations of its parts is the dial plate of the invisible one."[35] But the core statement of his dedication to the naturalist's outlook is in the concluding sentences of the essay:

Nature is a language and every new fact we learn is a new word, but it is not a language taken to pieces and dead in the dictionary, but the language put together into a most *significant* and universal *sense*. I wish to learn this language—not that I may know a new grammar but that I may read the great book which is written in that tongue. A man should feel that the time is not lost and the efforts not misspent that are devoted to the elucidation of these laws; for herein is writ by the Creator his own history. If the opportunity is afforded him he may study the leaves of the lightest flower that opens upon the breast of Summer, in the faith that there is a *meaning* therein before whose truth and beauty all external grace must vanish, as it may be, that all this outward universe shall one day disappear, when its whole *sense* hath been comprehended and engraved forever in the eternal thoughts of the human mind.[36]

The "book of nature" trope, in slightly varied forms, will run through Emerson's work to the end of his life. If there is one piece of writing that has served as a manifesto for his Transcendentalist thought, containing a catalogue of the major themes of his life's work, while also revealing the possible impact of his reading of *Sartor*, it is undoubtedly the essay *Nature* (first published as a book). Emerson composed it during the winter of 1835–1836, when he was busy arranging for the publication of *Sartor* and while he was reading Coleridge and Swedenborg, among others. Consider the opening of the chapter titled "Language," where Emerson advances the three claims that he will argue in what follows:

1. Words are signs of natural facts.
2. Particular natural facts are symbols of particular spiritual facts.
3. Nature is the symbol of spirit.[37]

Let's leave to one side any dispute over whether this counts as a serious, consistently argued philosophy. What is clear is the easy transition from the largely uncontroversial claim that words are (or let's say *can be*) signs of natural facts to the much more extravagant claim that natural facts not only are symbols of something but are symbols of "spiritual facts" (whatever those might be) and that, as a consequence, all nature not only is a symbol of something but is *the* symbol of "spirit" (whatever *that* might be). And from there it is but a small jump to reading, meaning, signifying, clothing, garments, emblems, ciphers—the entire apparatus of the book of nature in a passage that reads for all the world like a mash-up of Novalis and Carlyle:

We are thus assisted by natural objects in the expression of particular meanings. But how great a language to convey such pepper-corn informations! Did it need such noble races of creatures, this profusion of forms, this host of orbs in heaven, to furnish man with the dictionary and grammar of his municipal speech? Whilst we use this grand cipher to expedite the affairs of our pot and kettle, we feel that we have not yet put it to its use, neither are able. We are like travellers using the cinders of a volcano to roast their eggs. Whilst we see that it always stands ready to clothe what we would say, we cannot avoid the question whether the characters are not significant of themselves. Have mountains, and waves, and skies, no significance but what we consciously give them when we employ them as emblems of our thoughts? The world is emblematic. Parts of speech are metaphors, because the whole of nature is a metaphor of the human mind. . . . A Fact is the end or last issue of spirit. The visible creation is the terminus or the circumference of the invisible world. "Material objects," said a French philosopher, "are necessarily kinds of *scoriæ* of the substantial thoughts of the Creator, which must always preserve an exact relation to their first origin; in other words, visible nature must have a spiritual and moral side."

This doctrine is abstruse, and though the images of "garment," "scoriæ," "mirror," etc., may stimulate the fancy, we must summon the aid of subtler and more vital expositors to make it plain. "Every scripture is to be interpreted by the same spirit which gave it forth,"—is the fundamental law of criticism. A life in harmony with Nature, the love of truth and of virtue, will purge the eyes to understand her text. By degrees we may come to know the primitive sense of the permanent objects of nature, so that the world shall be to us an open book, and every form significant of its hidden life and final cause.[38]

The "French philosopher," incidentally, is Swedenborg devotee Guillaume Oegger, whose *The True Messiah; or The Old and New Testaments, Examined According to The Principles of the Language of Nature* (originally published in French in 1829) Emerson read, in English translation, in 1835.[39]

Scholars of Emerson will be able to explain better than I how what lies behind the symbols or emblems of nature can be all at once "the human mind," "spirit," "the invisible world," "the substantial thoughts of the Creator," and a "hidden life and final cause"—unless these are all expressions for the same thing, in which case we are to imagine the human mind and nature as continuous with the Creator's creation and therefore mutually pervasive. But for our purposes, these niceties don't really matter. What does matter is that Emerson envisages a world in which we "read" (metaphorically speaking) and interpret not just actual books but, well, that world itself, which he implicitly represents as yielding up *meaning, significance, sense* to our acts of interpretation.

And this is because, once again, with due allowance for considerable fluidity, polyvalence, and ambiguity in the usage of the term, we are looking at a form of idealism. Emerson, in fact, devotes a chapter of *Nature* to the topic, which he presents in a manner reminiscent of Berkeley (whom he mentions here), though in his own literary style.

> A noble doubt perpetually suggests itself,—whether this end be not the Final Cause of the Universe; and whether nature outwardly exists. It is a sufficient account of that Appearance we call the World, that God will teach a human mind, and so makes it the receiver of a certain number of congruent sensations, which we call sun and moon, man and woman, house and trade. In my utter impotence to test the authenticity of the report of my senses, to know whether the impressions they make on me correspond with outlying objects, what difference does it make, whether Orion is up there in heaven, or some god paints the image in the firmament of the soul? . . . Whether nature enjoy a substantial existence without, or is only in the apocalypse of the mind, it is alike useful and alike venerable to me. Be it what it may, it is ideal to me so long as I cannot try the accuracy of my senses. . . . But whilst we acquiesce entirely in the permanence of natural laws, the question of the absolute existence of nature still remains open.[40]

As in Berkeley, there is doubt about "whether nature outwardly exists," but there are natural laws that can reliably characterize and predict the behavior of objects in nature. Emerson spends the chapter refining his conception of how we are to approach nature—neither as definitively sustaining our conviction that it truly exists nor as meriting our disdain for its insubstantiality. And, while Berkeley's thinking with respect to the "volume of nature" follows a logic somewhat different from what we see in *Nature*, Emerson apparently considered the theme a natural fit for the topic of idealism.

In the previous chapter, titled "Discipline," he hinted at the "book of nature" theme (from his earlier discussion of language) by referring to *significance* and *meaning*: "In view of the significance of nature," he writes, "we arrive at once at a new fact, that nature is a discipline. . . . Space, time, society, labor, climate, food, locomotion, the animals, the mechanical forces, give us sincerest lessons, day by day, whose meaning is unlimited."[41] It must then have seemed natural to begin the chapter "Idealism" like this: "Thus is the unspeakable but intelligible and practicable meaning of the world conveyed to man, the immortal pupil, in every object of sense. To this one end of Discipline, all parts of nature conspire."[42] It would certainly be a great stretch to claim that Emerson had in mind Novalis's *Sinn der Welt* ("sense of the world," as alternately having "gone missing" and being the same thing as reason), but the impulse seems similar—namely, to interpret something as grand as "the world" and to discover sense or meaning within it.

In an essay titled "The Transcendentalist" (1842), intended as a kind of retrospective manifesto for the New England movement of which he was a member, Emerson flatly states that Transcendentalism *is* idealism but presents this term with what had become and would remain, for him, a characteristic ambiguity: "The idealist, in speaking of events, sees them as spirits. He does not deny the sensuous fact: by no means; but he will not see that alone. He does not deny the presence of this table, this chair, and the walls of this room, but he looks at these things as the reverse side of the tapestry, as the *other end*, each being a sequel or completion of a spiritual fact which nearly concerns him. . . . In the order of thought, the materialist takes his departure from the external world, and esteems a man as one product of that. The idealist takes his departure from his consciousness, and reckons the world an appearance."[43] Yes, indeed, one sub-definition of *idealism* presents the term as centering experience in the mind or consciousness rather than in the material world. But for Emerson, the mind or consciousness always bleeds over into a mysterious spiritual realm that appears to be simultaneously coextensive with and hidden from it—hidden, in this case, by "tapestry," a Carlylean image if ever there was one. In future writings, Emerson will return again and again to the idea that the mind, while being somehow one with nature, nonetheless, in a way characteristic of an idealism that emphasizes the *gap between* mind and nature, reaches across the gap to uncover hidden meanings.

One of Emerson's last writings was "Poetry and Imagination" (1872), revised and enlarged from a lecture he had written almost twenty years earlier. The essay is shot through with the themes he had elaborated over the years: the suggested coextensivity of nature and the mind, the superior power of the poet to "read" and interpret nature, and nature's status as a book, a system of symbols, emblems, or (figuratively speaking) words. As in the past, *meaning* and *significance* are what the superior intellect uncovers in nature. A few examples: "Natural objects, if individually described and out of connection, are not yet known, since they are really parts of a symmetrical universe, like words of a sentence; and if their true order is found, the poet can read their divine significance orderly as in a Bible. . . . The world is an immense picture-book of every passage in human life."[44] In a probable reference to Swedenborg's notion of correspondences (which I mentioned in Chapter 3): "Every correspondence we observe in mind and matter suggests a substance older and deeper than either of these old nobilities."[45] "Seas, forests, metals, diamonds and fossils interest the eye, but 't is only with some preparatory or predicting charm. Their value to the intellect appears only when I hear their meaning made plain in the spiritual truth they cover. The mind, penetrated with its sentiment or its thought, projects it outward on whatever it beholds."[46] "The poet accounts all productions and changes of Nature as the nouns of language, uses them representatively, too well pleased with their ulterior to value much their primary meaning."[47]

If part of the story I'm telling is how *meaning* accumulated an array of sub-senses, so that in the future it could wink suggestively at us and invite us to choose among those sub-senses—or let them all float around at once— then we might say that Carlyle and Emerson, perhaps more than any other English-language writers, asserted the mystical, "book of nature" dimension of the word. *Meaning* could thus function not only as a near-synonym of *purpose*, *aim*, and *goal* but also as something to be retrieved from behind a sign or a metaphorical suit of clothes. For, as we'll see, *meaning* will never be simply a substitute for *purpose*, and the reason is that it hauls around its primitive association with recovery (through interpretation), hiddenness, mystery.

5

Two Russian Titans Weigh In

Tolstoy Actually Answers the Question

Vladimir Chertkov (1854–1936) was an extremely wealthy Tolstoy devotee and hanger-on who devoted the better part of his adult life to disseminating the ideas and publishing the work of the great Russian writer and thinker (Russian had "thinkers" before it had professional, academic philosophers in the conventional Western European sense of the word). He was notorious for the role he played in a successful bid to wrest from Tolstoy's wife control over her husband's literary works, whose monetary proceeds helped pay the considerable expenses of the family and the huge Tolstoy estate. It was said that Chertkov was partly responsible for Tolstoy's decision to leave his family and set out on the journey that led him in 1910 to that most famous of literary deaths, in a tiny provincial railroad station.[1] In 1901, while living in England, Chertkov published a pamphlet in Russian, bearing the title *O smysle zhizni. Mysli L. N. Tolstogo* (On the meaning of life. Thoughts of L. N. Tolstoy). In the preface, Chertkov explained that the booklet consisted of material gathered from "diaries, private letters, notebooks, unfinished drafts, and similar private, as yet unpublished papers of L. N. Tolstoy." While it seems clear from his correspondence with Tolstoy that Chertkov was acting with his master's permission and blessing, it also seems clear that the master had virtually nothing to do with the choice of material. It is also quite possible that Chertkov took liberties well beyond simply selecting passages, given his habit of freely editing and outright composing material that he attributed to Tolstoy. Even on the dubious assumption that all the contents of *On the Meaning of Life* are genuine, Chertkov offers nothing in the way of context for any of the pithy statements that we read in this collection. Are they recent? To whom are the letters addressed from which Chertkov has excerpted passages? What was happening in Tolstoy's life when he wrote a particular diary entry? We don't know. As I'll explain in a moment, it matters, because it's possible to see a shift in thinking about the question of meaning following the crisis of faith Tolstoy underwent after the publication of *Anna Karenina*, in 1877.

What Do We Mean When We Talk About Meaning? Steven Cassedy, Oxford University Press. © Oxford University Press 2022. DOI: 10.1093/oso/9780190936907.003.0006

What impact did the pamphlet have? Chertkov, it turns out, was living in England for a good reason: he was in exile, having been banished from his homeland at a time when Tolstoy's ideas were very much out of favor with the Russian authorities. So, *O smysle zhizni* did not become a bestseller in Russia, for the good and simple reason that it was not published there. It was, however, quickly translated into English (first as part of Chertkov's own publishing series, possibly by Chertkov himself, later by the American Slavist Leo Wiener), French, and German, so that readers of those languages could now gain access to the thinking of Tolstoy on the weightiest of questions: What is the meaning of life? Nor would readers of any of the four languages in which the collection was published have been disappointed, for, unlike so many great writers and thinkers before him, both inside and especially outside Russia, Tolstoy did not hesitate to furnish actual answers to the question. Who before him had dared to write a sentence that began with the words "The meaning of life is . . ." and to end with a phrase that stated what that meaning was?

Chertkov's pamphlet contained a number of such sentences. For example, there are many variants of this statement: "The meaning of our life, the only rational and joyful one, [consists] in this: to serve, and to feel oneself as serving, God's work, the establishment of His Kingdom."[2] Elsewhere we read, "Briefly expressed, the meaning of life is this: that every living person is an instrument of God—an instrument through which the highest power does its work. And thus the meaning of life [consists] in this: to do as best you can the work that this highest power requires of you."[3]

But first I should say something about the Russian word. *Smysl* is formed from a prefix (*s-*) plus the root *mysl'*, which means "thought." Unlike German *Sinn*, it is not connected specifically with the senses or sensory experience, and yet, to the extent that sensory experience and thought are related, because both have to do with the mind, *Sinn* and *smysl* are both able to point to mental content in the way that the English *sense* and German *Sinn* do and in the way that English *meaning* (except when it means "intention") and German *Bedeutung* generally do not. In fact, Russian has a word that functions almost identically to *Bedeutung*: *znachenie*, which, like the German word, is a verbal noun built on a word that means "to signify." A Russian is much more likely to say *smysl zhizni* (meaning/sense of life) than *znachenie zhizni* (meaning/signification of life), though, as we'll see, this latter phrase does occur from time to time. Unlike *Sinn*, *smysl* has no original association with the idea of *direction*. And yet it comes to assemble a range of sub-definitions that partly resemble the ones we find in the Grimm German dictionary. The closest Russian equivalent to that work of linguistic nationalism is the four-volume dictionary compiled by Russian lexicographer Vladimir Dal' in the 1860s. The entry for *smysl* includes the following sub-definitions: "capacity of understanding," "comprehension," "reason," "capacity to judge correctly, to draw inferences," "force," "meaning," "sense" (*tolk*, the result of *tolkovat'*, to interpret, as in the *sense* of a word or utterance), "reason," "essence."[4] With relatively few exceptions, the Russian word when used in connection with *life* is translated into English as *meaning*, so English-speakers who were reading Count Tolstoy in the flood of translations that began to appear in the final decades of the nineteenth century encountered dozens and dozens of instances of the phrase "the meaning of life" (or closely related variants, such as "the meaning of our life").

What did Tolstoy mean by the word *smysl* in such phrases? If we look only at the examples I cited a moment ago from Chertkov's pamphlet, we find two rather different usages.

What the "meaning of life" is can be expressed with a verb in the infinitive ("to serve," "to do"), and here the Russian word appears to mean "aim," "purpose," or "goal"; that is, the aim of life is (or, rather, *should be*) to serve God's work, to do God's work. But it can also be expressed with something that Tolstoy regards as an important truth (in this instance, about being "an instrument of God"), and here the Russian word appears to denote something that either is discovered through an act of interpretation or is revealed by some unnamed means. Tolstoy himself explicitly acknowledged the equivalence between "aim" and "meaning/sense" in the pamphlet's very first excerpt. He is apparently writing a letter to someone who had asked him what the *goal* (*tsel'*) of life is and who had suggested that the answer was to be found in religion. Here is what Tolstoy wrote in response:

> You are right that religion alone can answer this question. Religion—true religion—is nothing but an answer to this question. And the religion that I profess, the Christian teaching in its true meaning [*smysl*], gives to this question the same simple and clear answer as the question itself, provided only that we substitute the word *smysl* ["meaning"] for the word *goal* [*tsel'*].
>
> The goal [*tsel'*], the ultimate [or "finite"] goal of human life in a world that is infinite in time and space, obviously cannot be accessible to man in his limitedness. But the meaning [*smysl*] of man's life, that is, what he lives

for and what he ought to do, must surely be comprehensible to man, just as comprehensible as a worker's function in a big factory is to that worker.

Tolstoy then goes on, as elsewhere, to explain that the meaning of life is to establish the Kingdom of God on earth.[5]

The use of a single word to mean both "meaning/sense" and "aim/goal" is something we've already seen in the German *Sinn* and something that becomes more and more common with the increasingly frequent use of *Sinn* in connection with "life," "history," and similar concepts. And, as we've already seen, *Sinn*, given its primeval association with direction, is naturally drawn to the suggestion of "direction toward," therefore *goal* or *aim*. (So is the French *sens*, which has continued down to the present day to mean both "meaning" and "direction"—"one-way" in French is *sens unique*.) Tolstoy did us a favor by making the association explicit in the undated letter that Chertkov excerpted (accurately, let's hope) in his pamphlet.

From an early age, Tolstoy was obsessed with the notion of a "goal of life." We find the phrase in diary entries written when he was in his late teens and early twenties. One long entry, written immediately after he quit his university studies in order to head home and devote himself to the management of his estate, is almost entirely devoted to "the goal of life"—primarily the goal of his own life (an understandable concern at this moment) but also the goal of life in general. "Now," he wrote, "the question presents itself: what is the goal of life for a person?" He answered his question with youthful grandiosity: "Whatever the point of departure might be for my reasoning, whatever I might accept as its source, I always come to one conclusion: the goal of life for a person is the promotion, to the extent possible, of the comprehensive development of everything that exists." With all the wisdom of an eighteen-year-old university dropout, he surveys nature, history, theology, and the history of philosophy and determines that everything points in the same direction, that is, toward "the comprehensive development of humankind." Following this sequence of thoughts, he poses the question "What will be the goal of my life in the country over the next two years?" The answer is a long list of absurdly ambitious prospective accomplishments (one item among many, for example, is "To study languages: French, Russian, German, English, Italian, and Latin").[6]

This is not the place for an exhaustive analysis of Tolstoy's use of the word *smysl*, in connection with "life," over his entire career. But it's possible to see a pattern and a development over time. The slightest acquaintance with Tolstoy's fictional work will reveal the author's fondness for creating characters modeled on himself, which is to say that they are what might be described as "seekers" and that, almost pathologically self-conscious and self-absorbed, they are perpetually tormented by what they regard as the essential questions of human existence. Correspondingly, the slightest acquaintance with the non-fictional writings will reveal the consistent presence of these traits in the author himself. Tolstoy himself and the fictional characters who resemble him, when it comes time to ponder those essential questions, invariably start out thinking about themselves and then broaden their perspective in an attempt to arrive at truths that are universal. In the early diary entry I quoted a moment ago, even though the order is reversed (the young Tolstoy speaks first about the universal goal of life in general and then about his personal goals), the driving force is the urgent need to establish a personal agenda: What am I going to do all day long, now that I've moved back home?

As best I can see, if there is a pattern and a development over Tolstoy's career, it is the tendency over time to answer questions concerning "the meaning of life" and "the goal of life" more and more frequently in the absolute and universal form and less frequently with reference to *me* (Tolstoy himself or the Tolstoy-like hero of a fictional work). When the reference is primarily to *me*, meaning and goal are usually mentioned only because they are yet to be found.

Consider, for example, the central male figures in Tolstoy's best-known works of fiction, *War and Peace* and *Anna Karenina*: Pierre Bezukhov in the former and Konstantin Levin in the latter. Book Two of *War and Peace* presents a pair of crises in Pierre's life that drive him to speculate on the big questions: he has fought a duel in which he unexpectedly wounded an opponent who was clearly the more accomplished gunman, and he has left his wife, whom he has quite reasonably suspected of infidelity. The solution? Join the Freemasons. At a certain moment in the initiation ritual, the "rhetor" (that is, as the narrator explains, a Freemason who initiates a "seeker" into the brotherhood), having explained that death is "no longer a fearsome enemy, but rather a friend who frees from this disastrous life a soul languishing in the labors of virtue, in order to lead it into a place of reward and solace," leaves Pierre to a few moments of solitary contemplation. Here is what Pierre contemplates: "It must be so, but I am still so weak that I love my life, whose meaning [*smysl*] is just now, little by little, being revealed to me."[7] What does *meaning* mean here? Since it is being gradually revealed, we know neither what the meaning is nor precisely what the word for it (*smysl*) means. The verb "being revealed" is the same one that is used in connection with Christian revelation, suggesting not a goal but a metaphysical "meaning" that is disclosed to the privileged believer or interpreter. Needless to say, as anyone familiar with Tolstoy's fiction will guess, what follows is anything but an emerging understanding of "the meaning of life." Rather, there is confusion and muddled thinking, as Pierre struggles to remember (let alone to understand) the seven virtues of Freemasonry, as just presented to him by the rhetor. But also typical of Pierre's thinking is that it is centered entirely in himself (I love *my* life), so he cannot draw any sort of overarching conclusion about life in general.

A bit later, in despair upon learning that the woman he loves is engaged to another man, Pierre returns to the standard questions and responds to them with the same feckless uncertainty that we find in all of Tolstoy's seekers (before they finally come to think they've chanced upon the ultimate truth): " 'For what? To what avail? What is going on in the world?' he asked himself with perplexity several times a day, involuntarily beginning to ponder the meaning [*smysl*] of the phenomena of life; but knowing from experience that there were no answers to these questions, he would quickly seek to turn away from them, take up a book, or hurry off to the club or to Apollon Nikolaevich's to catch up on the latest gossip about town."[8] Once again, because the thing that the word denotes eludes Pierre, we can do no more than speculate that it stands for whatever the answers might be to the three questions he asks himself.

Toward the end of the novel, there is a passage that shows the logical connection between the word *smysl* as applied to words and language and the word as applied to "life." Pierre has been taken prisoner and has seen the French execute five fellow Russians. Among the surviving prisoners is an elderly peasant named Platon Karataev, who speaks in the folksy idiom that so many aristocratic Russian authors gave to characters from this class. Platon says something that catches Pierre's attention, and Pierre asks the peasant to repeat the remark. Platon can't remember the words he pronounced only moments ago, nor can he remember the words to his own favorite song. As it turns out (who knew?), for peasants, individual words apparently lose their meaning when detached from their context. This observation leads Pierre to draw an analogy between the individual words in their context (in this instance, a song) and an individual life in *its* context (some larger whole). Here is how Tolstoy presents Pierre's thoughts:

When Pierre, sometimes struck by the meaning [*smyslom*] of his [Platon's] speech, asked him to repeat what he had said, Platon could not remember what he had said a minute earlier, just as he could never tell Pierre the words to his own favorite song. [The words] *Rodimaia* [my dear], *berezan'ka* [birch tree], and *toshnen'ko* [my heart aches] were all in there, but [when these sentiments were] put into words, no meaning [*smysl*] came out. [Platon] did not understand, nor could he understand, the meanings [*znacheniia*] of the words taken separately from speech. Each word of his and each action was the manifestation of a reality unknown to him, which was his life. But his life, as he looked at it, had no meaning [*smysla*] as a separate life. It had meaning [*smysl*] only as a part of a whole, which he constantly felt. His words and actions poured out of him as evenly, necessarily, and immediately as a scent detaches itself from a flower. He could understand neither the value nor the significance [*znachenie*] of a separately considered action or word.[9]

Whatever Pierre understands by the "whole" of which the peasant Platon is a part, he never quite seems to find it for himself. When he is finally to be united with Natasha, we read that "the entire meaning of life, not for him alone but for the entire world, seemed to him to lie solely in his love and in the possibility of her love for him."[10] But the obvious irony in this description makes it clear that Pierre is simply mistaking his own happiness for something bigger than it really is.

At the very end of *Anna Karenina*, published almost ten years after *War and Peace*, there is a scene remarkably similar to the one with Platon Karataev. The unwitting source of truth is once again a peasant, also named Platon. Another peasant, Fedor, informs Levin that Platon "lives for the soul. He remembers God."[11] These seemingly inconsequential words strike Levin like a divine revelation, leading him to think about the meaning of life. But here, that meaning fails to emerge. "And I was amazed," Levin thinks, "that, despite the greatest exertion of thought along this path, the meaning of life [*smysl zhizni*], the meaning of my motives and aspirations, did not reveal itself to me. But the meaning of my motives [now] is so clear to me that I live constantly according to it, and I was amazed and overjoyed when the peasant expressed it: to live for God, for the soul."[12] He reverts to a Tolstoyan truism regarding philosophers and men of science: that methods employed by a learned intellect turn up nothing of value—or nothing that simpler feelings could not turn up. "And is this not what all philosophical theories do, by the

TWO RUSSIAN TITANS WEIGH IN   101

path of thought, alien and extrinsic to man, leading him to knowledge of what he already knows, and knows so surely that he would not be able to live without it? Is it not clearly evident in the development of the theory of every philosopher that he knows in advance just as indubitably as the peasant Fedor, and no more clearly than he, the main meaning of life and only by a doubtful, intellectual path wants to return to what was already known to him?"[13] The ultimate result is the final sentence of *Anna Karenina*, in which Levin expresses yet another new outlook on life, following so many earlier ones that he had adopted, only subsequently to reject them: "I shall continue to get angry at Ivan the coachman, I shall continue to quarrel, I shall continue to express my thoughts inappropriately, there will continue to be a wall between the holy of holies of my soul and others, even my wife, I shall continue to blame her for my own fears and regret it, I shall continue not to understand with my reason why I pray and yet shall continue to pray—but my life now, my entire life, independently of what might happen to me, every minute of it not only is not meaningless, as it used to be, but has the indubitable meaning of good, with which I have the power to invest it."[14]

What in heaven's name does the end of this sentence mean? Saying that one's life is not meaningless is quite different from saying affirmatively that it has a meaning and also saying what that meaning is. But what is the "meaning of good"? Is it vaguely "the sense of good," that is, a hint or flavor of goodness? Or does Levin's life have the same thing as the meaning (definition) of the word *good*? Or does *smysl* here mean "goal," suggesting that Levin now aspires to goodness in his life? And why does he finish off the sentence with the extremely confusing statement that he has "the power to invest" his life with this "meaning of good"? If Levin's life must wait around for him to invest it with the "meaning of good," then how can he say it already has that meaning? If we can draw one conclusion from this ambiguity, it is that neither Levin nor Tolstoy himself by this point has formulated a compelling statement of what "the meaning of life" is, apparently because that meaning is always missing or because those seeking it cannot divorce it, whatever it is, from their own selfish interests. This is perhaps why neither Levin nor Tolstoy at this point seems even to have settled on what the meaning of the word *smysl* is.

Following the publication of *Anna Karenina* came Tolstoy's famous crisis, which led to the list of renunciations that would dominate the final thirty years of his life: no longer would he write fiction, for example, accept royalties from his publications, enjoy sexual relations, exploit his peasants, use money, toe the Russian Orthodox Church's dogmatic line, support the use of armed force, or treat his fellow human beings with anything but love and compassion. That he fell far short of honoring most of the items on this list is perhaps testimony more to their uncompromising stringency, their status as pure ideals, than to weakness and raw hypocrisy on his part (what human being would have the strength to carry out all of these ideals?). The written work that related the story of the crisis and its results was *Confession*, written from 1879 to 1882 and published in Geneva in 1884 (it was initially banned by Russian censors). It would hardly be an exaggeration to say that "the meaning of life" (*smysl zhizni*), or the author's quest for it, is the very topic of this short book, so frequently does the phrase (or the single word *smysl*) occur and so central is it to the story. In fact, one might say that *Confession* validates the understanding of *smysl* as "meaning" by telling the story of a quest of interpretation that finally yields a result, or several results, in a form that could be described as "a meaning" in the same way that one receives a meaning from an oracle.

Tolstoy depicts the meaning-of-life quest in *Confession* as having been especially urgent because of the finality of death. Here is how he presents his thinking early in the book, in a way that foreshadows such twentieth-century thinkers as Camus and Sartre, for the immediate issue is to find a good reason not to commit suicide: "The question consists in this: 'What will come of what I do today, what I shall do tomorrow—what will come of my entire life?' Differently expressed, the question is this: 'Why should I live, why should I desire anything, why should I do anything?' One might express the question yet differently: 'Is there in my life some meaning [*smysl*] that would not be inevitably annihilated by the death that awaits me?' "[15]

There's no point in carrying out a detailed review of the many, many instances of *meaning* (*smysl*), for *Confession* follows a fairly simple logic: (1) my many unsuccessful attempts to discover the meaning of life (unsuccessful because of my immorality and impiety), (2) my discovery of the meaning of life from (predictably) "simple working folk." I'll give just one example of the first. It's a restatement of Tolstoy's classic (for him) delegitimization of "science" or any sort of formal, academic knowledge:

Well, I said to myself, I know all that science so obstinately desires to know, but, as for an answer to the question of the meaning of my life, there was none on this path. In the speculative field, however, I understood that, notwithstanding, or precisely because of, the fact that the goal of knowledge

was directly aimed at the answer to my question, there was no answer
other than the one I gave myself: What is the meaning of my life? —None.
Or: What issues from my life? —Nothing. Or: Why does everything exist
that exists, and why do I exist? —Because it exists . . . With an answer such
as this [from the physical and biological sciences], it turns out that the answer does not answer the question. I needed to know the meaning of my
life, and the claim that it is a particle of the infinite not only does not give it
any meaning, it annihilates every possible meaning.[16]

And, as for the second, later in the book, we finally get the statement we've
been waiting for:

I renounced the life of our circle, having recognized that this is not life but
only a semblance of life, that the conditions of excess in which we live de-
prive us of the possibility of understanding life and that in order to understand life I must understand a life not of exceptions, not of us the parasites
of life, but the life of the simple working folk, that which makes life, and
the meaning that it gives to life. This meaning, if one can express it, was the
following: every human being has arrived in this world by the will of God.
And God created man in such a way that everyone may destroy his soul or
save it. The task of man in life is to save his soul; in order to save one's soul,
one must live in a godly way, and in order to live in a godly way, one must
renounce all the comforts of life, one must labor, humble oneself, suffer, and
be merciful. This meaning the people have derived from an entire creed,
transmitted to them in the past and in the present by pastors and by tradition that lives among the people and that is expressed in legends, proverbs,
stories. This meaning was clear to me and near to my heart.[17]

As usual in Tolstoy, a sudden revelation, together with the resulting oblig-
atory renunciations, is not the end of the story. What is left for him is to sort
out the extent to which conventional Christian teachings are consonant
with his new understanding of the meaning of life. Is meaning to be found
in the general and purely ecumenical precept that one must save one's soul
by living "in a godly way," or is there content in that meaning that is peculiar
to Christianity and, specifically, to Russian Orthodox Christianity? "Earlier,"
he tells us, "life itself had seemed to me to be the fulfillment of meaning, and
faith had appeared to be an arbitrary assertion of certain propositions that
were, to me, completely unnecessary, irrational, and unconnected with life.

I had asked myself back then what meaning these propositions could have, and, convinced that they could not have any, I had rejected them. Now, however, by contrast, I firmly knew that my life [unto itself] did not and could not have any meaning, and not only did the propositions of faith not seem to me unnecessary but by indubitable experience I was led to the conviction that only these propositions of faith gave life meaning."[18] Where do we find such propositions? A bit closer to the end of *Confession* Tolstoy relates an experience that, oddly, appears to have been lifted from his own earlier fiction. "I was listening," he writes, "to the conversation of an illiterate peasant about God, faith, life, salvation, and the knowledge of faith was revealed to me. I drew closer to the peasantry, listening to their judgments on life, faith, and I began more and more to understand the truth. The same thing happened when I read *Chet'i Minei* and the *Prologues* [Russian Orthodox collections primarily of lives of saints]; this became my favorite reading matter. Excepting the miracles, which I regarded merely as fables expressing a thought, this reading revealed to me the meaning of life."[19]

And finally, at the end of *Confession*, relating how for a time he had turned his back on the teachings of Russian Orthodoxy and then had reconsidered, Tolstoy writes this: "I turned to the study of the very same theology that at one time I had rejected with such contempt as unnecessary. Back then it had seemed to be a series of unnecessary absurdities, back when the phenomena of life surrounded me from all sides, seeming to me clear and filled with meaning; now, however, I would have gladly rejected everything [within these teachings] that would not enter a healthy mind, but there was nowhere to turn. On this creed is founded—or at least it is inextricably connected with it—the only knowledge of the meaning of life, which was revealed to me."[20]

Are these *the* definitive statements? Tolstoy concludes with a vague promise to revisit the truth and falsity of the teachings he has just mentioned and to publish his thoughts "sometime and someplace" in the future.[21] Some three years after he finished writing the main text of *Confession*, he decided for some reason to tack on a final couple of pages relating a bizarre dream in which he is suspended in a bed over a bottomless abyss. But he did not mention any further thinking on the truth and falsity of the teachings. Two observations are worth making. First, though Tolstoy repeatedly identifies sources for his new understanding of the meaning of life, he offers, apart from the precept about living in a godly way, precious little about the content of that understanding. Second, the sources are primarily scriptural, both in

the sense of sacred writings and in the sense of material derived from and illustrative of such writings (for example, saints' lives, proverbs, propositions
about faith). This appears to suggest a connection, or at least an analogy, between the meaning that we extract from texts, by interpreting them, and the
meaning that Tolstoy claims to see in life. And yet, oddly, the meaning of life
that he is prepared to state explicitly (about living in a godly way) is something whose source he does not identify. It appears simply to emerge, un-
bidden, from the realization (hardly new, it must be said, to Tolstoy in the late
1870s) that members of the landowning class are parasites whose lives are
inauthentic and detached from the true lives that peasants lead (of course, in
the way that such members of the landowning class as Lev Tolstoy envision
those lives).

Confession as a genre, on the model of such illustrious predecessors as
Augustine and Rousseau, suggests a story that at the very least begins on a
deeply personal and individual level and perhaps moves into universal con-
siderations later on. Augustine's *Confessions* followed this model, concluding
in the final chapters with a turn from the author's personal life to larger
questions regarding God and humankind. Tolstoy's *Confession* similarly
tells the personal, autobiographical story of Tolstoy's spiritual journey and
concludes with his reformulated version of Christianity, something intended
for his fellow human beings.[22] The meaning of life that is revealed to Tolstoy
toward the end of his story is a private meaning for himself alone but something presumably valid for all humankind.

A few years later, in a work titled simply *On Life*, we run into an odd twist in
the story of Tolstoy's relationship with "the meaning of life." For a significant
portion of the new work is actually about *life*, not in the sense of *my life* (or
anyone else's life) as the totality of one person's lived experience from birth
to death; not in the sense of a spiritual "journey," including a person's self-
conscious reflections on why, whence, and to what end; and not in the sense
of the events that constitute a biographical account of someone. If only to
reemphasize the importance of the first two of these senses, Tolstoy decided
to address the question of life in its most basic sense. The result is a piece
of writing in which, first, the two Russian words for "meaning" (*znachenie*
and *smysl*) come to be used alternatively and, at times, interchangeably and,
second, the meaning of these two words shifts, sometimes within a single
paragraph, between "definition," that is, of the *concept* of life as a phenomenon investigable in biological science, and the collection of other senses we
have encountered in Tolstoy and elsewhere ("goal," "list of actions you should

take," "consummate spiritual or religious truth"). Here's how he presents the problem of definition:

> The word *life* is very short and very clear, and everyone understands what it means. But precisely because everyone understands what it means, we are obliged always to use it in this meaning [*znachenie*] that is understandable to all. After all, this word is understandable to all, not because it is exactly determined by other words and concepts but, on the contrary, because this word designates a basic concept from which many, if not all, other concepts are derived, and therefore, in order to draw inferences from this concept, we are obliged above all to take this concept in its central meaning [*znachenie*] that is indisputable for everyone. But this is the very thing, it seems to me, that is left out by the parties to the dispute regarding the concept of life. What happened was that the basic concept of life, taken at first not in its central meaning [*znachenie*], as a consequence of the debates over it, distancing itself more and more from the basic, central meaning [*znachenie*] recognized by everyone, finally lost its basic meaning [*smysl*] and took on another meaning [*znachenie*] inappropriate to it.[23]

Here the Russian words for "meaning" denote a definition of, or our understanding of, a *concept*, and that concept is life in the sense of living matter and its origins. There follows, predictably, an effort to discredit science and scientists, in order to make the also predictable assertion that science and scientists miss the essential point. But the topic, what they miss the point *about*, is still life as a phenomenon that we study (but that those of us who are scientists somehow misunderstand). "Debates concerning what life is all about, where life comes from, whether it's animism, or vitalism, or the concept of yet some other special force, have concealed from people the important question of life—the question without which the concept of life loses its meaning [*smysl*]—and have put them in the position of a man who is walking along in tremendous haste but has forgotten exactly where he's going."[24]

The polyvalence particularly of the word *smysl* allows Tolstoy to make the almost seamless transition from the meaning of the *concept* of life to the meaning of life as he appears to have understood that phrase in his earlier writings. In fact, the mandatory discrediting of science, where the meaning (definition, intellectual understanding) of the *concept* of life is precisely the topic, leads irresistibly to the observation that the meaning of life—where *life* is now our lived, spiritual experience, from birth to death, and *meaning* is "goal," "consummate spiritual/religious truth"—lies beyond the ken of the spiritually unenlightened scientists. We can see the sequence of thoughts in a passage where Tolstoy speaks with disdain of people who "have lived and still do live solely an animal life." "And there have always been and are today, among those people, yet such people who, thanks to their external, exclusive position, consider themselves called to lead mankind and who, not understanding the meaning [*smysl*] of human life, have taught and still teach other people, concerning life, which they don't understand, that human life is nothing but individual existence."[25]

Later in the essay, Tolstoy explicitly completes the logic that connects his thoughts on animal life, as understood by scientists and as lived by unenlightened people, with his thoughts on the affirmative meaning of life, understood in the spiritual and metaphysical sense. For example: "A man cannot help seeing that his existence as an individual, from birth and childhood to old age and death, is nothing other than a constant loss and diminution of his animal individuality, ending in inevitable death; and thus the consciousness of his life in individuality, including within it the desire for the augmentation and indestructibility of that individuality, cannot help being a ceaseless contradiction and suffering, cannot help being evil, whereas the sole meaning [*smysl*] of his life is a striving for the good."[26] We might say that a sentiment such as this completes a larger double process: from the meaning (definition) of life (as a scientifically investigable phenomenon) to the meaning of life (in the spiritual and metaphysical sense) and from the meaning of *my* life (in the spiritual and metaphysical sense) to the *universal* meaning of life (also in the spiritual and metaphysical sense).

For English-speaking readers, the niceties in Tolstoy's fluid definition of "life" were probably not an issue at all. What is certain is that beginning in the 1880s, the publishing market was flooded with English translations of Tolstoy's works, and the ones that initially captured the most attention were not *War and Peace* and *Anna Karenina* (first published in distinctly inferior translations) but the religious and philosophical writings I've been discussing. English-speaking readers were thus treated to the dozens and dozens of passages in which Tolstoy commented on what was almost always translated into English as "the meaning of life." To take just one example: in 1894, Constance Garnett, who, next to Aylmer and Louise Maude, produced the most respected early English translations of Tolstoy (despite whatever criticism has been leveled at her in more recent times), brought out an edition of *The Kingdom of God Is Within You: Christianity Not as a Mystic*

Religion but as a New Theory of Life (written 1890–1893). Tolstoy concluded this book with the verse from Luke (17:21) that includes the words in his title. The previous sentence, that is, the final one that Tolstoy himself wrote, was this, in Garnett's translation: "The sole meaning of life is to serve humanity by contributing to the establishment of the kingdom of God, which can only be done by the recognition and profession of the truth by every man."[27] The similarity of this sentiment to those expressed in the passages that Chertkov included in *On the Meaning of Life* suggests that those passages (assuming they were actually written by Tolstoy himself) were of relatively recent authorship.

Even though Tolstoy was probably the world's writer most widely read in translation at the beginning of the twentieth century, one did not even have to read actual works by him to encounter his thinking on the meaning of life.[28] He was extensively, obsessively covered in the American press, particularly in the last decade of the nineteenth century and the first two decades of the twentieth. During that period, *The New York Times*, to take only one example, printed hundreds of articles on Tolstoy and mentioned his name thousands of times. During the height of Tolstoy fever, the years leading up to and immediately following his death, there were repeated references to "the meaning of life" in the Count's thinking. In 1909, for example, the *Times* published an article *by* Tolstoy (translator not listed), under the title "Tolstoy Arraigns the Ways of the Nations." "The cause of the wretched condition of the Christian nations," Tolstoy wrote, "is the absence of a supreme conception, common to them all, of the meaning of life, of faith, and of the guidance for conduct resulting from faith."[29] A few months later, a *Times* reader would see the title "Tolstoy's Plea for the Liberation of Man. The Great Russian Inveighs Against 'Pseudo-Christianity' and Government and Calls on Every Man to Be Master of Himself'" and read these words: "Here is all I wished to say. I wished to say that we in our day have reached a position in which we can no longer stay: and that whether we like it or not we must enter a new path of life, and that in order to enter that path we must not invent a new faith, nor any new scientific theories to explain the meaning of life and to guide it; above all, we do not require any particular kind of activity, but we only require one thing: to liberate ourselves from the superstitions of pseudo-Christianity and of governmental organization."[30] In fact, if you do a digital search of the phrase "meaning of life" in *The New York Times* for the thirty-year period 1887–1917, you will find that fully one in five of the

articles that come up includes Tolstoy—and in nearly all of those cases because he was the actual topic of the article.

It would be almost impossible to determine in broad terms how Tolstoy's
English-speaking readers in this period construed the word *meaning* as it
appeared in translations of his works. Then as now, few writers who themselves used it in such expressions as "the meaning of life" paused to define
the word, and commentators who referred to the views of such important
users of the expression "meaning of life" as Tolstoy tended simply to quote it,
highlighting its tremendous gravitas, but without attempting to explain what
it meant. What I think we can say is that Tolstoy contributed significantly to
the expression's frequency of appearance in English.

One small measure of Tolstoy's impact may be found in William James's
classic exploration of the psychology of religion, *The Varieties of Religious
Experience*, published in 1902 as an edited version of a lecture series. In
Lectures VI and VII, titled "The Sick Soul," James found an instructive example in Tolstoy's *Confession*, and, not surprisingly, "the meaning of life" was
central to his understanding of the Russian author's "sick soul." "In Tolstoy's
case," James writes,

> the sense that life had any meaning whatever was for a time wholly with-
> drawn. . . . At about the age of fifty, Tolstoy relates that he began to have
> moments of perplexity, of what he calls arrest, as if he knew not "how to
> live," or what to do. It is obvious that these were moments in which the ex-
> citement and interest which our functions naturally bring had ceased. Life
> had been enchanting, it was now flat sober, more than sober, dead. Things
> were meaningless whose meaning had always been self-evident. The
> questions "Why?" and "What next?" began to beset him more and more
> frequently. At first it seemed as if such questions must be answerable, and as
> if he could easily find the answers if he would take the time; but as they ever
> became more urgent, he perceived that it was like those first discomforts of
> a sick man, to which he pays but little attention till they run into one contin-
> uous suffering, and then he realizes that what he took for a passing disorder
> means the most momentous thing in the world for him, means his death.[31]

It's hard to know what James understood by *meaning* here—or, rather,
what he understood Tolstoy to have understood by the term. James appears
to have read *Confession* in the early French translation, where the original
Russian *smysl* is consistently translated as *sens*, which James has rendered

as *meaning*.[32] In the first lecture of the series, where he defines his topic, he distinguishes between two "orders of inquiry" that might be brought to bear on the topic of religious experience, the first inquiring into the "constitution, origin, and history" of the matter, the second into its "importance, meaning, or significance."[33] Here, *meaning* appears to be roughly synonymous with its two accompanying nouns. In the following lecture, he discusses the possible meanings, in the sense of definitions, of the word *religion*.[34] But in his presentation of Tolstoy's crisis, James clearly means something other than "importance" or "definition." Whether he was taking his cue directly from Tolstoy, by simply translating into English (via French) the Russian word and letting his readers infer for themselves what it meant, or whether readers in 1902 were already familiar with this metaphysical sense of *meaning* and required no further clarification, James certainly joined the trend at the beginning of the twentieth century that consisted in the increasingly frequent use of the word *meaning* by itself, in an undefined metaphysical sense or set of senses, and the phrase "meaning of life."

What to make of all this? At first glance, we have the odd spectacle of a writer who appears to have puzzled mightily over "the meaning of life" before arriving at a moment where he can blithely answer the question "What is the meaning of life?" And yet the era when Tolstoy composes sentences beginning with the phrase "The meaning of life is . . ." does not end the sense that a mystery continues to surround that meaning. A facile explanation would be that he simply understood the word *smysl* in two rough senses, "purpose" and "mysterious essence," thus lending it its own peculiar form of ambiguity. So, while it was easy to complete a sentence whose actual import was "The real aim in life is to do such-and-such," it was never possible to complete the one whose actual import was "The mystery that lies behind the veil of life is such-and-such." The former statement is never a plausible answer to the what-is-the-meaning-of-life question that aims at a mysterious, metaphysical essence or truth of some sort. No one, Tolstoy included, has ever answered that question, no doubt because it's designed to be unanswerable.

Dostoevsky, Without Admitting It, Takes the Secular Side

Tolstoy's slightly older contemporary and rival appears to have discovered "the meaning of life" as a concept a bit later in his own life, and here the phrase takes a rather different turn, one that points ahead to the resonance it adopted in the second half of the twentieth century. It makes a dramatic appearance in Dostoevsky's final novel, *The Brothers Karamazov*, in Book V, "Pro and Contra."[35] This is the section of the novel that includes what are undoubtedly its most stunning and noteworthy ideas, as expressed by Ivan Karamazov, the rational skeptic and sometime atheist, to his younger brother Alesha, the monk-in-training. Here is where we hear Ivan's cogent argument for the incomprehensibility of the concept of justice in a world where children, defined in his eyes as innocent by nature, suffer. Ivan's argument turns on an implicit epistemological distinction. What does *not* allow him to comprehend the suffering of children, in a world created by a good and just God, is what he calls his "Euclidean understanding," by which he appears to mean a faculty roughly equivalent to Kant's understanding (*Verstand*), with its innate set of ordering "concepts." What *would* allow him to understand the suffering of children is a power that Ivan does not name but that would, no doubt, be equivalent to Kant's *faith*, which, unlike the understanding, allows us to grasp the grand metaphysical ideas: God, freedom (that is, of will), and immortality. Posing the problem in this way makes the quest for truth an interpretive one, one whose result would be a *meaning* (even if that meaning proves always to be elusive).

This is in fact how Dostoevsky described his work-in-progress in the letter he wrote to his editor accompanying the manuscript of Book V. And, for reasons pertinent to the political scene in Russia, Dostoevsky represents this tormented quest and the extravagant inferences to which it leads as lying at the heart of contemporary socialism and anarchism. "In this text, which I have now sent you," he writes, "I simply portray the character of one of the most important figures in the novel as he expresses his fundamental convictions. These convictions are what I recognize as the *synthesis* of contemporary Russian anarchism. A denial not of God but of the meaning [*smysla*] of his creation. All socialism issued from and started with the denial of the meaning [*smysla*] of historical reality and proceeded to a program of destruction and anarchism. The founding anarchists were, in many cases, people sincere in their convictions. My hero takes a theme that, *in my opinion*, is irrefutable: the senselessness of the suffering of children and deduces from it the absurdity of all historical reality."[36] The word that I have translated as "senselessness" is *bessmyslitsa*, "without *smysl*."

Ivan's argument about the suffering of children is presented in the chapter titled "Rebellion." We encounter "the meaning of life" in the chapter immediately preceding that one. As if in anticipation of the reaction that his "rebellion" will elicit from his brother, who embodies religious faith of the sort we always find in Dostoevsky—conflicted and challenged by doubt, but faith nonetheless—Ivan purposefully proclaims his wholehearted, irrational love of life:

> "The sticky springtime leaves, the blue sky—I love them! There, I've said it! It's not intellect, it's not logic, it's with your gut, with your belly that you love, you love your earliest youthful forces. Do you understand anything in my rant, Alesha, or no?" Ivan said, suddenly laughing.
>
> "I understand all too well, Ivan: one wants to love with one's gut and belly, you've said it beautifully, and I'm frightfully glad that you want to live so," exclaimed Alesha. "I think everyone should love life above all else in the world."
>
> "Love life more than its meaning [*smysl*]?"
>
> "Certainly, love it before logic, as you say. Certainly, it has to come before logic, and only then will I understand the meaning [*smysl*]."[37]

The actual phrase "meaning of life" comes a few pages later. Ivan is in the middle of an extended harangue that sounds for all the world like the rantings of a confirmed atheist, but an atheist wrestling with his own faithlessness. Ivan wonders, did man invent God (as Voltaire had suggested man would have to do if God didn't exist)? "But surely man invented God," he exclaims. "And what would be strange, what would be a marvel would be not that God existed in actual fact; what would be a marvel would be that such an idea—the idea of the necessity of God—should enter the head of such a savage and evil creature as man, so holy is that idea, so moving, so wise, lending so much honor to man." Then, clearly hoping to stun his younger brother with a maximally paradoxical sequence of thoughts, he says, "And therefore I announce that I accept God directly and simply. Still, however, I must note: if God exists and if he really created the earth, then, as is completely known to us, he created it according to Euclidean geometry, and he created the human mind with the concept of only three dimensions in space." What does it mean to "accept God" if you follow your announcement of acceptance with a conditional statement ("If God exists . . .") that in no way confirms a *belief* in God? The definitive statement, which hardly clears the matter up, is where we find the reference to the meaning of life. Here it is:

> "And so, I accept God and not only willingly but, what's more, I accept his wisdom too and his purpose [*tsel'*], completely unknown to us; I believe in

order, in the meaning of life; I believe in the eternal harmony in which we will apparently merge together; I believe in the Word toward which the universe is tending and that 'was with God' and that is God, and so on and so on, etc., to infinity. There are many words made for this point. So, it seems I am on the right path, yes? But just imagine: in the final result it is this world of God that I don't accept, and though I know that it exists, I will not admit it at all. It's not God that I don't accept, please understand that; it is the world created by him, God's world that I do not accept and cannot agree to accept."[38]

Shortly after these remarks, in order to justify his refusal to accept the world that God created, Ivan will launch into his speech on the necessarily unjust sufferings of children. He thus claims to *accept* God, whatever that means, but not to accept God's world; he does not, however, say that he *believes in* God, yet he *does* believe in "the meaning of life." So, what does he mean by "the meaning of life"? Is it the same thing he referred to a few minutes earlier in the conversation, when he drew a distinction between loving life itself (the better choice) and loving the meaning of life? What did he mean by it then?

I can find very little guidance in the text of *The Brothers Karamazov* itself. But this was not the first time Dostoevsky had been drawn to the phrase. During the 1870s, he published a periodical journal whose contents were written exclusively by himself. He called it *Diary of a Writer*, and, having established himself, initially through his fictional works, as a kind of national prophet, he used it as a forum for the expression of his views on a range of social, political, and religious issues. For much of his adult life, Dostoevsky had been preoccupied, not to say obsessed, with the loss of religious faith he witnessed among members of the intellectual classes in Russia, as well as with the scientific-materialist worldview that he viewed as responsible for that loss. In fact, it would be no exaggeration at all to claim that the conflict between conventional religious faith and the opposing worldview lay at the center of his best-known literary works. But in 1876, something new arose in Russian life that appeared to confirm the worst about the conflict and that inspired in Dostoevsky a particularly disturbing sense of doom.

The story began in June 1876, when he received a letter from a total stranger who signed himself N. N. The correspondent detailed the process by which he had lost all religious faith and come to embrace a purely scientific, materialist view of the world. He gave a list of writers who had helped inspire the process, among them positivist historian Henry Thomas Buckle, who taught him "the meaning of history" (*smysl istorii*); Charles Darwin, thanks to whom he had become "a different man"; and Ludwig Feuerbach, author of *Das Wesen des Christentums* (*The Essence of Christianity*, 1841), the scandalously atheistic book that reduced religion to purely human drives and feelings. But, as N. N. wrote, the starting point lay in his childhood: "An abominable upbringing and school discipline bore their fruit: flippancy, absence of principles, tasks, incomprehension both of myself and generally of the meaning of life!"[39] At the end of the intellectual process, he wrote, stood atheism. "*The Great Mystery*," he proclaims. "But the mystery remains a mystery, and it is in just this that the entire meaning of our existence consists, the entire cycle of conditions in which the world stands. You see, it is atheism."[40] At the end of the *entire* process, presumably (we don't know for certain), was the writer's own death, for this letter to Dostoevsky was a suicide note.

From October through December of the same year, Dostoevsky returned obsessively in his *Diary of a Writer* to the theme of suicide, as if it were a true epidemic in Russia. In October, in an article titled "Sentence" (*prigovor*, the legal term), he printed what appeared to be a letter to himself from someone identified as "N. N.," just like the author of the extended suicide note, except that this "N. N." and his letter were entirely fictional. In December, in an article titled "Empty Assertions," he commented on "Sentence," as if in response to "N. N.," and reflected generally on suicide in his era. Curiously, he now takes up the phrase "meaning of life," qualified with the adjective "highest," as if in response to the *real* N. N. who had written him back in June:

> Those who, having taken away from man his faith in his own immortality, want to replace this faith, in the sense of the highest goal [*tseli*] of life, "love for mankind," those, I say, are the ones who raise their hand against themselves; for, instead of love for mankind they merely plant in the heart of one who has lost his faith the seed of hatred for mankind.... And there emerges precisely the opposite, for only with faith in his own immortality can man grasp his entire reasonable goal on earth. Without conviction in his own immortality, man's ties to the earth are severed, become thinner and rotten, and the loss of the highest meaning of life [*smysla zhizni*] ... without doubt brings in its wake suicide.[41]

Dostoevsky returned repeatedly that December to "the highest meaning of life" (or equivalent phrases) and its connection with scientific materialism and suicide. "The highest meaning of life" is now firmly equated with belief in the immortality of the soul, and the ills of the younger generation—ills that lead even to suicide—are all owing either to a loss of "the highest meaning of life" or to a perversion of it. In an article about today's youth, he laments the number of people who pray from time to time and even go to church but give no thought to—let alone believe in—the immortality of their souls. "And meanwhile," he writes, "it is only from this faith, as I was saying above, that the highest meaning [*smysl*] and significance [*znachenie*] of life emerges, that the desire and urge to live emerges. Oh, I repeat, there are many who are eager to live, lacking all ideas and the entire highest meaning of life, to live simply the life of an animal." Many of these even yearn for "the highest goals [*tseliam*] and significance [*zhacheniiu*] of life," he goes on, and some will shoot themselves precisely from having yearned for and not found "the highest meaning of life."[42]

What to say about a seventeen-year-old girl who committed suicide for no apparent reason? Dostoevsky had written about her in the October issue, and now, in December, responding to a critic, he echoes the language of the original letter from N. N.: "I expressed the supposition that she died from melancholy [*ot toski*] (much too early melancholy) and from the purposelessness of life—but as a consequence of an upbringing, in her parents' home, perverted by a theory, an upbringing with an erroneous concept of the highest meaning and purposes of life, with the intentional extermination in her soul of its [the soul's] immortality."[43] Having a *correct* concept of the highest meaning and purposes of life appears to be equivalent to believing in the immortality of the soul.

There's a fascinating episode in Dostoevsky's life that, at least chronologically, might serve as a link between his reflections on the suicide/meaning of life/immortality nexus in the late 1870s and the central arguments in *The Brothers Karamazov*. Arkadii Kovner was an impoverished Russian Jew who in 1875 embezzled a large sum of money from the bank where he was employed, allegedly in order both to strike a political blow against big business and to help provide for his family. After his almost immediate and completely predictable arrest, Kovner wrote two letters to Dostoevsky from prison, the second one in response to "Empty Assertions." He quotes back at Dostoevsky this line: "But there is only one highest idea on earth, namely the idea of the immortality of man's soul, for all the other 'highest' ideas of life by which man might be alive flow only from this one." A self-proclaimed atheist, Kovner decides to attack this assertion on logical grounds, correcting it to something that he himself, of course, couldn't possibly believe (at least, if his statements about his own beliefs were sincere). "It seems to me," he writes, "that all the 'highest' ideas of life must flow not from the idea of the immortality of the soul but from the idea of the existence of God, that is, of a being who consciously creates the universe, *consciously* directs and *consciously* takes an interest in *all* the actions of all living things, or at least of people."[44] Kovner then, gleefully goading Dostoevsky, lists all the things that, thanks to science and a materialist worldview, he *knows* to be true, including "Darwin's hypothesis about the origin of species." A few paragraphs later he comes to this: "You observe with complete justice that without the idea of immortality (or, in my opinion, God) there is no meaning or logic in life . . . and yet in the very existence of the soul, immortality, a God who punishes and rewards (in whatever philosophical interpretation of this you like), there is even less meaning and logic."[45] Unable to embrace the notion of immortality or, for that matter, God, this confirmed atheist connects "meaning" with "logic," as if "meaning" were nothing more than a scientific, logic-based explanation, and then craftily attempts to enlist both to cast doubt on immortality (by disingenuously claiming that it lacks them), for Kovner cannot grasp immortality on its own terms.

As Irina Paperno correctly observes, these thoughts, particularly about immortality, will find their way, with relatively little modification, into *The Brothers Karamazov*. Kovner even uses the phrase "pro and contra," which Dostoevsky chose as the title of Book V.[46] And this brings us back to the conversation between Ivan and Alesha. If the articles in *Diary of a Writer* offer any clue to what Ivan has in mind in his conversation with Alesha when he refers, twice, to the meaning of life, then what can we say about the concept? In the *Diary*, the "highest meaning of life" (or any closely related phrase) appears to be something you seek, find, lose, or misconstrue. We can see, too, that its loss (1) easily comes about through the acceptance of a scientific/materialist worldview and (2) can thereby lead to suicide. But the very phrasing appears to capture that worldview perfectly, since in this case *meaning* (*smysl*), with all its vagueness but at the same time its ability to convey the idea of a quest for something that is never found, appears to have been brought in precisely so as to allow the observer to avoid the appearance of embracing the scientifically incoherent idea of immortality. For, in the *Diary* articles, "the highest meaning of life" is never presented as something that anyone actually has or has found. It's there as the thing whose absence, along with the absence of belief in immortality, helps explain suicide.

Once again, the phrase enters the scene when conventional faith is the object of doubt. So, what does "the meaning of life" mean in the conversation between Ivan and Alesha? According to Alesha, it's what you find after you've abandoned logic and, presumably, the scientific, materialist worldview. But Ivan, not Alesha, is the one who supplies the word *meaning*. Why not just say *immortality* or *God*? Because we've adopted Ivan's perspective, the perspective of one who has recently denied the existence of both. Why *meaning* specifically? Because, to Ivan, the inaccessible something can be only the object of a faculty of understanding, *Euclidean* understanding, as if we are reading the world from a scientific perspective—for he cannot construe the problem in other than epistemological terms, where epistemology covers ordinary knowledge. True, the phrase shows up in the list of what Ivan now, for the sake of his circuitous argument, claims *not* to grasp through ordinary knowledge but to *believe*, as it keeps company with a set of conventional metaphysical ideas: God, God's wisdom and purpose, eternal harmony, and the Word of God. And of course, to someone like Ivan, the meaning in question is unrecoverable, for his "Euclidean understanding" cannot gain access to it. "The meaning of life" is an expression that belongs to someone who stands outside true faith.

And why did Dostoevsky himself use it in his *Diary* articles? Once again, the source of the phrase appears to be his thoroughly skeptical correspondents, N. N. and Kovner. To *them*, such a phrase safely avoids any indication that they themselves actually believe in the thing that the phrase appears to suggest, whether it is immortality or some other metaphysical quality. This puts Dostoevsky himself in the characteristic (for him) position of the vacillating believer in, and defender of, Orthodox Christianity. It's immortality, he'd like us to think, that he truly believes in, yet he adopts the secular-sounding term of the doubters and deniers against whom he constantly inveighs. If "the meaning of life" is merely a placeholder for "immortality," then how apt that Ivan should choose the phrase for something he claims implausibly to believe in, as if to say, in modern colloquial English, "or whatever." And how apt that Dostoevsky himself, the creator of Ivan, should fall back on the secular phrase when he laments the rise of suicide in his native land. What's missing among the despairing members of society is what they can regard only as an inaccessible object of knowledge, an elusive "meaning," and the fact of its inaccessibility *to them* is precisely what drives them to take their own lives.

It's no surprise that Albert Camus, writing three-quarters of a century later, noticed Dostoevsky's attention to "the meaning of life." In *The Myth of Sisyphus* (1942), the French thinker famously declares early on that "the meaning of life is the most pressing of questions," and the opening sentences of the book explain why: "There is only one philosophical problem that is truly serious, and that is suicide. To judge that life is or is not worth living is to answer the fundamental question of philosophy."[47] He devotes an entire chapter to Kirilov, one of a slew of darkly comical atheists in *The Devils*. This is how he leads off: "All of Dostoevsky's heroes wonder about the meaning of life. This is what makes them modern: they do not fear ridicule. What distinguishes the modern sensibility from the classical sensibility is that the latter feeds on moral problems and the former on metaphysical problems. In the novels of Dostoevsky, the question is posed with such intensity that it can invite only extreme solutions. Either existence is mendacious or it is eternal." For evidence to support his claim about Dostoevsky's heroes, Camus amusingly quotes from the letter to Dostoevsky by the fictitious "N. N.," specifically the highly secular language about the imaginary correspondent's incapacity for happiness in this world: "Since, to my questions about happiness, I receive from nature via my consciousness only the answer that I cannot be happy otherwise than in a harmony with the whole that I do not understand [and from which stem what he calls "proclamations of religion"] and, for me, that I will obviously never be capable of understanding . . . this nature, which has so unceremoniously and brazenly made me for suffering, I condemn to annihilation, along with myself."[48] This "letter" includes no instances of the phrase "meaning of life," and for some reason Camus does not quote from "Empty Assertions," which (in reference to the letter) does.

I mention Camus's comments on Dostoevsky to show how easily subsequent readers found in the Russian novelist's works support for purely secular claims that are completely at odds with his *professed* metaphysical outlook, including his apparent faith in immortality.[49] Camus does not neglect to mention that to the prospective suicide N. N. (as professedly to Dostoevsky himself), "human existence is a perfect absurdity for anyone who lacks faith in immortality," and yet to him (Camus) the question of "the meaning of life" can be posed only in a godless and "absurd" world. While it would be wildly inaccurate to claim that Dostoevsky completely embraced a secular worldview, his use of the phrase "(highest) meaning of life" is, to me, clear evidence that in his contemplation of the bases of religious faith in the *Diary* and in *Brothers Karamazov* he was adopting the secular perspective. "The meaning of life," with its enormous potential for ambiguity, is a phrase that allows the secularist to form at least a partial understanding of what a person of putatively pure religious faith actually believes.

6

Paul Tillich

Bridge to the Twentieth Century and the "Age of Anxiety"

An Initially Obscure German Theologian Makes the Cover of *Time* Magazine

I'm guessing that relatively few readers today remember much of anything about Paul Tillich and that a majority under a certain age have never even heard the name. It might come as a surprise that Tillich (1886–1965), a Protestant theologian who immigrated to the United States from Germany in 1933, was practically a household name in the late 1950s and early 1960s. *Time* magazine featured him on the cover of the March 16, 1959, issue. A painted image shows the white-haired, bespectacled Tillich, a row of bookshelves behind him and a small human skull model on the side table next to him. He stares intently, unsmilingly at an object a few feet to your left. On a diagonal yellow band at the top right corner of the cover you read "A Theology for Protestants" (though the cover article, in the "Religion" section, was unimaginatively titled "To Be or Not to Be"). Six years later, he was centrally featured in what is quite possibly, in the history of American popular periodical literature, the most famous article that no one actually read—or *remembers* having read. It's the cover article for the April 8, 1966, issue of *Time*, sensationally bearing, in stark red on black, the question that left Americans truly *shocked, shocked*: "Is God Dead?" The article was titled "Toward a Hidden God," and it was written by John T. Elson, a reporter whose name will arouse recognition from virtually no one today—not even from those old enough to remember the cover. Elson was *Time*'s religion reporter, and he conscientiously did his homework for what reads a little bit like an honors thesis by a talented Ivy League undergraduate. *Meaning* appears at the very beginning, as lying at the heart of the quandary that Elson believes Americans are facing. "Is God dead?" he begins. "It is a question that tantalizes both believers, who perhaps secretly fear that he is, and atheists, who possibly suspect that the

What Do We Mean When We Talk About Meaning? Steven Cassedy, Oxford University Press. © Oxford University Press 2022. DOI: 10.1093/oso/9780190936907.003.0007

answer is no. Is God dead? The three words represent a summons to reflect on the meaning of existence." Tillich, who had died two years earlier, appears only twice in the article, but it is clear that he is a driving force in the movement that Elson sees in American religious life. I'll return to that movement shortly.

Two decades earlier, Tillich had published an article in the academic *Journal of the History of Ideas*. The topic was "existential philosophy," which in its broadest sense, as he describes it, is about a move from the focus on essence in a philosophy that identifies reality with mind, that is, with "reality-as-known," to an "existential" focus on reality as immediately experienced in actual living. In 1944, Tillich knew nothing of Sartre or Camus, who in the following years would be widely associated with the term "existentialism" (and both of whom used the French equivalent of the phrase "meaning of life").[1] One of the key twentieth-century figures Tillich discusses, Martin Heidegger, famously began his best-known work, *Being and Time* (1927), by addressing the question of "the meaning of being" ("Sinn von Sein").[2]

That existential philosophy in the twentieth century, as Tillich sees it, is concerned with *meaning* is clear from statements he makes toward the end of the article. "The Existential philosophers," he writes, "were trying to discover an ultimate meaning of life beyond the reach of reinterpretation, revived theologies, or positivism. . . . Existential philosophy can be called the attempt to reconquer the meaning of life in 'mystical' terms after it had been lost in ecclesiastical as well as in positivistic terms. . . . It is the desperate struggle to find a new meaning of life in a reality from which men have been estranged, in a cultural situation in which two great traditions, the Christian and the humanistic, have lost their comprehensive character and their convincing power."[3] These claims would probably come as a big surprise to scholars of existential philosophy today, but that's not really our concern. The interest of Tillich's article lies less in whether we think he has accurately characterized existential philosophy than in the light it shines on his own relationship to the concept of meaning.

Among the precursors to twentieth-century "existential philosophy," Tillich counts especially Kierkegaard, Nietzsche, and Wilhelm Dilthey (Marx much less convincingly). As we've seen, the works of Kierkegaard are shot through with references to the meaning of life—more, to the best of my knowledge, than in the works of any predecessor in Europe or the United States. It's difficult to say whether or not Tillich was familiar with any of them; he does not cite any in this article. The one work by Dilthey

that Tillich mentions is *Introduction to the Human Sciences*, which is positively brimming with references to the *Sinn* not of life but of history. As for
Nietzsche, Tillich quotes a passage that actually includes the word *Sinn* used
in a sense resembling the ones I've been exploring. The passage appears in
the volumes published posthumously under the title *Wille zur Macht* (*Will to
Power*).[4] Here is Tillich's English translation of the passage: "When we have
reached the inevitable universal economic administration of the earth, then
mankind as a machine can find its meaning in the service of this monstrous
mechanism of smaller and smaller cogs adapted to the whole." In the original German, the phrase that Tillich translated as "find its meaning" is "ihren
besten Sinn finden." Nietzsche's works include a number of instances of the
phrase "Sinn des Lebens," in most of which *Sinn* appears to mean "purpose"
or "aim." We can hardly be certain about what Nietzsche intended in this passage, which does not include the word *Leben*, but the context, where mankind is represented as "machinery," suggests strongly that *Sinn* is "direction"
rather than "meaning."[5] Nonetheless, Tillich, writing in English, gives this
gloss on the passage: "No one any longer knows the significance of this huge
process. Mankind demands a new aim, a new meaning for life."[6] *Aim* fits the
German; *meaning* does not, nor does Nietzsche's original contain any reference to the meaning—or aim—of *life*.

Tillich in German

Whatever Tillich's sources might have been for the development of his own
thinking in his youth, by the time he was in his early thirties, the word *Sinn*
had become such an obsession that his writing was filled with instances of
it almost to the point of absurdity. For example, in 1917 and 1918, when he
was serving at the front in the Great War, Tillich wrote to a friend about a
philosophical crisis he was undergoing and the new way of thinking it
had produced. This is how he described the crisis (I leave *Sinn* untranslated): "Precisely this is now my way of thinking [*Meinung*]. Spiritual life is
life in *Sinn* or incessant creative *Sinn*-giving. . . . The divine is *Sinn*, not being
[*Sein*]. . . . I am therefore teaching the monism of *Sinn*." What in heaven's
name does this mean? German theologian and philosopher of religion Ulrich
Barth devoted a scholarly article to what he calls the *sinntheoretisch* bases of
Tillich's early concept of religion (presumably, how that concept was based in
a theory of *Sinn*), and here we run into the recurrent problem of translating

Sinn, not only for purposes of understanding Barth's article but, above all, for purposes of understanding what Tillich meant. For the moment, let's leave it untranslated.

The claim that Barth advances about the concept of *Sinn* in Tillich is extraordinarily expansive. We can safely set aside the philosophical genealogy of the concept (it stems from Edmund Husserl and an obscure philosopher named Emil Lask), whose details need not concern us. As Barth sees it, by the time Tillich passes through his crisis, *Sinn* has come to denote "the universal medium of the understanding of the world."[7] What to do with a definition so broad and consequently so vague? What certainly does *not* offer guidance is Tillich's own use of the word in his writings from this period. I'll give just one example, though there are many. In 1925, Tillich published a work under the boldly ambitious title *Religionsphilosophie* ("philosophy of religion"). After a lengthy introductory section, the opening chapter of Part I is titled "Die Sinnelemente und ihre Relationen" (The *Sinn* elements and their relations). In the space of two and a half pages, the word *Sinn*, alone and in compound words, occurs no fewer than seventy-three times. Consider, for example, this passage (again I leave *Sinn* untranslated):

> Every consciousness of *Sinn* [*Sinnbewußtsein*] comprises three elements: first, consciousness of *Sinn*-connection [*Sinnzusammenhang*], in which every individual *Sinn* exists and without which it would be *Sinn*-less [*sinnlos*]; second, consciousness of the *Sinn*-fulness [*Sinnhaftigkeit*] of the *Sinn*-connection [*Sinnzusammenhang*] and, together with it, of every individual *Sinn*, that is, the consciousness of an unconditional *Sinn* that is present in each individual *Sinn* [*Einzelsinn*]; third, consciousness of a requirement for every individual *Sinn* [*Einzelsinn*] to fulfill the unconditional *Sinn*.[8]

How are we to understand this? Presumably a native speaker of German, reading this in the original language, would bring to bear an appreciation of the various nuances that the word *Sinn* has featured in that language for several centuries. Ulrich Barth would implausibly ask such a speaker to add "the universal medium of the understanding of the world" to the list. As for English-speakers, we can see the difficulty they face when we read how Unitarian theologian James Luther Adams, in his introduction to the English translation of this work, explained Tillich's concept of meaning. To begin with, Adams chose simply to render *Sinn* as *meaning*. Having made this choice, he explains that Tillich's philosophy of religion "is a philosophy of meaning, and of relatedness to the Unconditional in terms of meaning." What, we ask, is *meaning*? Meaning for Tillich "is threefold," Adams explains. "It is an awareness of a universal interconnection of meaning, an awareness of the ultimate meaningfulness of the interconnection of meaning, and an awareness of a demand to fulfill, to be obedient to, the ultimate, unconditional meaning-reality."[9] To say the least, this is unhelpful. Not only has Adams defined *meaning* in terms of *meaning* itself, but he has not paused to tell us what *meaning* means when he invokes it to define, well, *meaning* itself. Given the centrality of *meaning* here and given that, as we have seen, English *meaning* and German *Sinn* function differently from each other, the reader can hardly help being more than a little confused.

But the German original does not readily yield to interpretation. Tillich begins the section in which these statements appear with this claim: "Every act of mind/spirit [*Geist*] is a *Sinn* act [*Sinnakt*]." He goes on to write about various theories of knowledge and about how all of them share the premise that "the mind/spirit [*Geist*] is always a carrying-out of *Sinn* [*Sinnvollzug*] and that-which-is-intended in the mind/spirit [*das im Geist Gemeinte*] is always *Sinn*-connection [*Sinnzusammenhang*]."[10] He writes about a "ground of *Sinn*" (*Sinngrund*), by which term he defines "the unconditionality of *Sinn*." I wouldn't presume to say that I understand these statements, but let's say, for the sake of argument, that Barth's "universal medium of the understanding of the world" is at play in the passages I have just quoted in translation. It might make sense to speak of "consciousness of *Sinn*" or "*Sinn*-connection," if we are talking about an awareness of that medium or some notion of interconnectedness within, and thanks to, that medium. But what are we to understand by "individual *Sinn*," "unconditional *Sinn*," and "ground of *Sinn*"? If *Sinn* is a "universal medium," then how can there be an individual one, why is "unconditional *Sinn*" not a redundancy, and how can there be a ground of something that already appears to be the ground (or "medium") of all understanding? If "universal medium" is not what *Sinn* refers to in some or all of these instances, then what does it refer to? Is it something like the English *meaning*, as when *Sinn* refers to the meaning of a word—thus something that gets expressed? Is *Sinn* a term for some sort of grand metaphysical quality that is never quite defined? What appears clear is that *Sinn* functions in more than one way in these passages and that substituting "universal medium" for each and every instance of it would make the passages even more difficult to interpret than they are to begin with.

Tillich in English

When Tillich left Germany for the United States, he was lucky enough to have a position waiting for him, thanks to Reinhold Niebuhr (about whom more in Chapter 7), at Union Theological Seminary, right next to Barnard College and across the street from both Columbia University and the Jewish Theological Seminary. He knew not a word of English upon arrival, and like any forty-seven-year-old attempting to learn a new language, he had to work hard at it. After all, he would have classes to teach, once he was able, and a scholarly career to continue. He surely could not have known, disembarking from the steamer in New York Harbor in 1933, that some years hence he would be publishing, in English, not only widely respected scholarly books but bestselling popular books on religion as well.

The process by which Tillich wrote his works in English was almost comically helter-skelter. The great theologian, working with a band of American assistants, would introduce German words and expressions, which would be unsystematically translated by the assistants, or he would attempt to come up with proper English words and expressions, which would be unsystematically vetted by the same assistants. But clearly at some point, whether as the result of careful reflection or simply because Tillich's new assistants never suggested otherwise, *Sinn* in its adopted homeland metamorphosed into *meaning* in all but a very few cases, thus shedding any of its sub-senses that do not overlap with the English word. *Meaning* became almost as frequent in occurrence as *Sinn* had been in German. It also became slippery and polyvalent, just as *Sinn* had been in German. And yet, because of the peculiarities of the English word, including its own sub-senses that do not overlap with its German near-equivalent, Tillich would often necessarily be saying something new in his newly acquired language, something that was missing in his German writings.

But Tillich's thinking overall would undergo a number of changes during his American period, and what is difficult if not impossible for scholars of his work is to determine the degree to which these changes were attributable to the new language. Did the English language, that is to say, merely present challenges to Tillich as he sought to find suitable equivalents for concepts formed in German and quite possibly best expressed in German? Or did the new language, thanks to features that simply do not match up with German—for example, the word *meaning* when it has to do with *signification* and *interpretation*—push Tillich toward thoughts that would not have occurred to him when he was functioning exclusively in his native linguistic medium?

Tillich's American writing is voluminous, complicated, and often difficult, especially for readers lacking a background in Protestant or, for that matter, any Christian theology—the vast majority, no doubt, of the large number who purchased his books in the 1950s and 1960s. It is also representative of a key moment in American religion, one that is easy to overlook because it is so much at odds with the popular image of the era in question. I'll have much more to say about that era in Chapter 7. For now, let me focus on Tillich's contributions to the conversation about religion and on the role that *meaning* played in them. I am not attempting to give a thorough account of Tillich's theology, something both beyond the scope of this book and beyond my own competence. But I'll start with the feature of his religious thinking that must have aroused surprise, if not shock, among his contemporary American readers.

The words you expect to encounter in Christian religious writing, such words as *God, Jesus, Christ, spirit*, and *soul*, are continually replaced in Tillich's work with substitute terms and phrases or with accompanying language that modifies what we might regard as the conventional understanding of these words. Tillich scholars tell us that the move to America coincided with a shift in thinking, entirely independent of the shift from native tongue to English, that resulted in a new emphasis on the concept of *being*, thus a focus on *ontology*. Again, we need not concern ourselves with the details or the defensibility of Tillich's new theological position. Instead, let's look at the forms of expression in which it resulted.

Tillich's most important purely scholarly work of this era was his three-volume *Systematic Theology*, published between 1951 and 1963. Early in the first volume of this work we find the phrase "ultimate concern," apparently an English rendering of the rather ungainly German phrase "das, was uns unbedingt angeht" ("that which unconditionally concerns us"). Tillich defines "ultimate concern" variously and confusingly, including with this puzzling statement (italics in the original): "*Our ultimate concern is that which determines our being or not-being. Only those statements are theological which deal with their object in so far as it can become a matter of being or not-being for us.*"[11] What is *being*? It is "the whole of human reality, the structure, the meaning, and the aim of existence," he writes. "All this is threatened; it can be lost or saved. Man is ultimately concerned about his being and meaning."[12] If this sequence of thoughts is not puzzling enough,

Tillich moves on to introduce the "New Being," something that will occur and recur through all three volumes of *Systematic Theology*. The "New Being" will turn out to be another name for Jesus, and the "ground of being," one of Tillich's best-known phrases, together with "being-itself," will be alternative expressions for God. Why use these expressions, instead of simply saying "Jesus" and "God"? Because those expressions appear to denote external objects—a real Jesus of Nazareth who was the Son of God and a real God as an externally existing deity—and are thus misleading. Instead, Jesus Christ becomes "Jesus as the Christ," reflecting a daring agnosticism on the historical reality and divine paternity of the more conventional Jesus. And God becomes the "ground of being."

It is in a tortuous passage at the end of the first volume of *Systematic Theology* that Tillich makes his strongest and most explicit case against God and in favor of a theology that has replaced essence with existence, just as, in his own account, a major strain of European philosophy had done in the nineteenth century (as he had discussed in the journal article on existential philosophy). "However it is defined," he writes, "the 'existence of God' contradicts the idea of a creative ground of essence and existence. The ground of being cannot be found within the totality of beings, nor can the ground of essence and existence participate in the tensions and disruptions characteristic of the transition from essence to existence. . . . God does not exist. He is being-itself beyond essence and existence. Therefore, to argue that God exists is to deny him."[13] Similar language appears a year later in *The Courage to Be*, under the heading "Theism Transcended." There, "ground of being" is presented as synonymous with "absolute faith," and the content of absolute faith is presented as synonymous with "the 'God above God.'"[14] Tillich refers here to the conventional God as "the God of theism," *theism* being his disdainful term for the archaic conception of God as an externally existing something.[15] My goodness, this is a Protestant theologian.

It is also in *The Courage to Be* that we find the full blossoming of *meaning*, where it now keeps company with a set of terms very much in vogue at the time, thanks both to the recent appearance of Kierkegaard in English translation and (quite probably) to the emergence of Sartre and Camus as influential postwar thinkers. They are *anxiety, ultimate concern, faith, being,* and *freedom*. I'll have more to say about anxiety in Chapter 7. For Tillich, the concept is indissolubly linked with *meaning*, which, as in Sartre and Camus (both briefly mentioned in *The Courage to Be*), arises in connection with its negative, *meaninglessness*. Tillich explains:

We use the term meaninglessness for the absolute threat of nonbeing to spiritual self-affirmation. . . . The anxiety of meaninglessness is anxiety about the loss of an ultimate concern, of a meaning which gives meaning to all meanings. . . . Anxiously one turns away from all concrete contents and looks for an ultimate meaning, only to discover that it was precisely the loss of a spiritual center which took away the meaning from the special contents of the spiritual life. . . . The anxiety of emptiness drives us to the abyss of meaninglessness. . . . Man's being includes his relation to meanings. He is human only by understanding and shaping reality, both his world and himself, according to meanings and values.[16]

As "meaninglessness" is placed in apposition to "loss of an ultimate concern," "meaning" and "ultimate concern" come to be equivalents, together with "meaning which gives meaning to all meanings" and "ultimate meaning." *Ultimate*, which till now in Tillich had chiefly modified *concern*, has now come to modify *meaning*, and "ultimate meaning" appears to be yet another substitute expression for *God*.

Tillich generally doesn't trouble to define *meaning* any more than he defined *Sinn* in the writings of his pre-American period. But one usage stands out for its clear and obvious association with *signification*. In another popular book titled *Dynamics of Faith* (1957), Tillich elaborated a theory of symbols, specifically religious symbols, that fuses a conventional notion of signifying with an elaborate and (to my mind) not entirely coherent theology. Symbols of any sort, he claims, bear six characteristics: (1) They "point beyond themselves to something else." (2) A symbol "participates in that to which it points." (3) A symbol "opens up levels of reality which otherwise are closed for us." (4) A symbol "unlocks dimensions and elements of our soul which correspond to the dimensions and elements of reality." (5) "Symbols cannot be produced intentionally." (6) Symbols "cannot be invented."[17] Whether or not this is clear, one can certainly say that Tillich, without expressly so far using the word *meaning*, is giving a fairly standard account of signification: symbols "point beyond themselves to something else."

Then the word *meaning* makes its appearance, with thoroughly confusing results. "Whatever we say about that which concerns us ultimately," Tillich writes, "whether or not we call it God, has a symbolic meaning. It points beyond itself while participating in that to which it points." To what does it point? Ultimate concern? God? Are they the same? "The fundamental symbol of our ultimate concern is God," Tillich then writes. "Ultimate concern cannot deny its own character as ultimate. Therefore, it affirms what is meant by the word 'God.' " Now, however, we are speaking of the word *God* and what it *means*, or points to, in its signifying function, but presumably we are not speaking of God, that is, what the word *God* means, or points to. Tillich then moves on to speak about God by referring to atheism, which, in denying God, "can only mean the attempt to remove any ultimate concern—to remain unconcerned about the meaning of one's existence."[18] But this is not the same *meaning* as in the phrase "symbolic meaning"; this is something grander, something metaphysical but undefined. Thus *meaning* (and *to mean*) in this brief passage alone carries more than one sense: (1) Religious symbols appear to *mean*, that is, to *point to* the ultimate, namely God. (2) But God *is* a symbol and thus must point to, or *mean*, something ultimate. (3) Another equivalent for "ultimate concern" is "the meaning of one's existence," where *meaning* no longer has to do with symbolic pointing but clearly serves as an equivalent to "ultimate concern." Even if we can make little sense of this, here is a clear instance where the English word, a verbal noun from the verb *to mean*, affords nuances that German *Sinn* lacks entirely.

There's no way to know what Americans who picked up Tillich's popular books understood when they read the word *meaning*. A studious reader would certainly have paused to wonder what to make of such phrases as "a meaning which gives meaning to all meanings," "ultimate meaning," and (at least as Tillich uses it) "symbolic meaning." And almost any reader might have noticed that *meaning* occurred with greater frequency in Tillich's religious writing than the terms I listed a moment ago: *God, Jesus, Christ, spirit,* and *soul* (even though it generally does not earn a place in the indexes of his books). So, what can we say about *meaning* in the English-language works of Paul Tillich?

Meaning carries a number of sometimes overlapping senses: "ultimate concern," metaphysical essence, explanation, what a sign or symbol points to, intention, God. What Tillich refers to as the theistic God has been cast aside in favor of a set of notions ambiguously suggested in the word *meaning*, which helps point to our human situation as a quest for something that may or may not end up winking at, and revealing itself to, us.

By the time the word lands in Tillich's popular books and in journalistic accounts of his ideas (such as the *Time* magazine article), it has traveled a winding path, in its guise as the German *Sinn*, from the nineteenth-century German philosophy and theology that we've examined so far, through such twentieth-century German and French thinkers as Martin Heidegger, Karl

Jaspers, Camus, and Sartre, to its new incarnation in the United States as *meaning*, with the lexical nuances that attended that new incarnation. This certainly does not suggest that when John T. Elson writes about "the meaning of existence" in *Time* magazine and goes on to discuss Paul Tillich, the word *meaning* is packed full of all the sub-senses and nuances it gathered in its earlier, German incarnation and accrued in English. But it does suggest that we can regard Tillich as a kind of bridge from the earlier German history to mid-twentieth-century America. It is thanks to the polyvalence and resulting ambiguity of *meaning* that the word slipped so easily both into popular writing in the 1950s and 1960s and into the receptive minds of American who read those writings. The polyvalence and ambiguity must have been a huge advantage for the word, since it allowed readers in part to supply their own possibly vague notions of the meaning of *meaning* when they read the word in a book or magazine article about religious faith.

In that midcentury era, *anxiety* was a guiding motif in popular writing about religious faith, and it was inextricably tied up with *meaning*. That is the subject of Chapter 7.

7

Meaning in the Age of Anxiety and Well Beyond

The Age of Anxiety

From the end of the 1940s through the 1960s, few phrases were more gravely and more uncritically circulated in the press and on the airwaves than "The Age of Anxiety." W. H. Auden's book-length poem, published in the United States in 1947, launched the phrase. Leonard Bernstein's symphony of the same title (premiering in 1949), together with the Jerome Robbins ballet set to that symphony (1950), helped to keep the phrase in the newspapers for a number of years, if only on the cultural pages. I wish I could state with confidence, in a few sentences, what Auden meant by his title and how it applied to the age in which he composed his "baroque eclogue," as the poem is subtitled. I don't think I'm alone in this respect. In the introduction to a critical edition of *The Age of Anxiety* published in 2011, Auden scholar Alan Jacobs states it honestly: "But given the poem's difficulty, few [cultural critics] have managed to figure out precisely *why* [Auden] thinks our age is characterized primarily by anxiety—or even whether he is really saying that at all." And that's not even to comment on what the word *anxiety* means in the title of this poem (it occurs only once in the text of the poem—in an entirely mundane sense—though *anxious* is sprinkled about here and there). Jacobs tells us that *The Age of Anxiety* reflects the poet's interest in Jung, so we might think, *anxiety*, *Angst*, a sometimes pathological condition treated on the psychiatrist's couch. But then the poem introduces us to four lost souls who come together in a bar in New York City during World War II, so we might think, *anxiety*, existential doubt, a profound sense of disorientation in deeply uncertain times. In Auden's own words, the setting of the work is "war-time, when everybody is reduced to the anxious status of a shady character or a displaced person." So, the Age of Anxiety is just a period when people are justifiably nervous, a bit . . . anxious?

What Do We Mean When We Talk About Meaning? Steven Cassedy, Oxford University Press. © Oxford University Press 2022. DOI: 10.1093/oso/9780190936907.003.0008

But, no matter how we end up understanding the title of Auden's poem, over the next couple of decades the phrase was hardly used exclusively to refer to a sense of unease and apprehension. Countless people picked it up and used it, always as if its import were completely self-evident—and to denote a remarkably wide range of things. In fact, the year before Auden's book was even published, Alfred Kazin, writing in the *New York Times*, reviewed a recently published collection of short novels by Dostoevsky. The piece was less a conventional book review than a commentary on the Russian writer as one whose works were peculiarly suited to the era, which Kazin referred to as an "Age of Anxiety." What did "Age of Anxiety" mean in 1946? From today's vantage point, the answer would appear obvious; not surprisingly, given the events of the previous year, it meant, among other things, "this age when man can no longer tell in his atomic insecurity how much his inner conflicts, human-duplicated, contribute to the social disorder and how much they are made by it." Kazin uses Auden's name, the year before *The Age of Anxiety* was published, as if these words could have been lifted from the pages of that book (a review of Auden's *For the Time Being* in 1944 mentioned the name of the work in progress).[1] A few years later, just as the phrase was hitting the cultural pages, Alan W. Watts, the British-born early champion of Zen in the United States, opened his *Wisdom of Insecurity* (1951) with a chapter titled "The Age of Anxiety." Anxiety, or insecurity, in 1951 had to do with the loss of traditions, including those of religious belief, which had now been replaced by "the authority of science."[2] "Atomic insecurity," as frightening as that was in those days, did not appear to be the only source of anxiety.

One place where these various elements come together vividly is the cover article of *Newsweek* magazine's Christmas issue for 1957.[3] The title is from Luke: "And the angel said unto them, Fear not . . ." To an American looking back at the magazine today, there's something stunning not only about the article but about the entire issue. American life at Christmastime is represented as decidedly and unapologetically Christian (and, of course, white). In the midst of dozens of ads for popular brands of distilled spirits, the Norfolk and Western Railway has taken a full page to show a line of well-dressed white middle-aged couples, plus a few children, filing into a warmly lighted church (Episcopal, no doubt) in the evening. "Let's Keep Christ in Christmas," the ad reads. On another page, hotelier Conrad N. Hilton offers a Christmas prayer, in which he asks our Father in heaven "to save us from *ourselves*." You think: of course, this is the high point of conventional religiosity in American history, when polls show the greatest percentage of Americans professing a belief in God. It's also the Age of Anxiety, as the cover article clearly shows. And so we read, as if no one needed to be told, that Americans are "beset with feelings of fear and anxiety," the cause being certain unspecified "international and domestic uncertainties." The unnamed author then goes on to cite the views of the reigning theologians of the day. The "dean" of these was Reinhold Niebuhr, just then finishing his third decade as professor of practical theology at Union Theological Seminary. Here's what Niebuhr is quoted as saying to his fellow anxious Americans: "[The church] should teach that men always have a dignity beyond nature, but that they are also miserable creatures. It's not hope, but faith that keeps us going—faith that God has given a meaning to existence no matter what comes." One would hardly characterize this as a cheerful message, especially given the explicit denial of hope in favor of pure faith. But the prize that faith will bring us in the face of hopelessness, not surprisingly, is *meaning*. Of possibly greater authority is Paul Tillich, now of Harvard University (where he was hired in 1955), described here as "a religious philosopher of great stature." If other theologians in some way sought to allay the anxiety of the age, Tillich told us to grow up and get used to it. "Anxiety is a state of man," he's quoted as saying, before urging on us "the courage of the human being who feels all the riddles and all the meaninglessness of life, and who, nevertheless, is able to say 'yes' to life."[4]

By 1962, when CBS television's Sunday evening documentary show *The Twentieth Century* ran a two-part program titled "The Age of Anxiety," the writers were no doubt so convinced of the phrase's omnipresence in its general gloomy and forbidding connotation that they could count on their audience to get the double entendre. If you're old enough, you'll remember that *The Twentieth Century* usually served up a diet of horrific scenes from very recent history—dazed Londoners looking at the smoking ruins of their apartment buildings after a German bombing campaign, grisly scenes of combat in the South Pacific—over the mesmerizingly solemn and paternal voice of the show's narrator, Walter Cronkite. So the viewer who consulted *TV Guide* that February naturally expected a commentary on a world trembling in daily fear at the very real prospect of nuclear annihilation. But no—it was actually about *anxiety*, of the sort that brothers Karl and William Menninger, two celebrated American psychiatrists (both of German extraction), treated with the latest surprising techniques in their Topeka, Kansas, clinic. The patients you saw on those two consecutive Sunday evenings were just patients, and if they suffered more acutely from anxiety than average members of the population, it wasn't necessarily because they were spending more time thinking about the Soviet menace (though at the end of the second installment of "The Age of Anxiety" we hear about the divorce rate, "the tragic situation in Berlin," and conflict among races and creeds as signs of the uncertain times).

But by 1962, *anxiety* had firmly established itself in American culture as a token of the era. It's just that it carried several slightly different senses, though these senses frequently bled into one another. Literary critic Cleanth Brooks, speaking at the University of Virginia in 1947, listed a few of the factors that made the title of Auden's recently published poem peculiarly appropriate to the times: "the current publication of the works of Kierkegaard, the just ending furore over the Existentialists, the stream of articles on Kafka."[5] Kierkegaard fever officially took hold in the late 1930s, when the first English translations of his works began to appear, first in England and then in the United States. From then into the 1960s, thanks to the efforts of a devoted band of translators and a few publishing houses, a steady succession of English translations emerged.[6] A striking consensus in the period, in fact, assigned cultural authority to Kierkegaard, "the existentialists," and a short list of additional intellectuals, including Freud, Jung, and, once again, Protestant theologians Paul Tillich and Reinhold Niebuhr. A common theme was *anxiety*—expressed with this word or related words. *Anxiety* naturally had its place in clinical psychology and psychiatry (as at the Menninger brothers' Topeka clinic), and, as we'll see in Chapter 8, so did *meaning*. The same was true for theology, as it was presented to the public. And, as it turned out, here too *anxiety* was inextricably tied to *meaning*, which came to form its own peculiarly twentieth-century gospel.

The Gospel of Meaning

If you were looking for a list of the most influential proponents of that new gospel, you could do worse than to consult the cover article from the "Is God Dead?" issue of *Time*, for Elson provided a list of names. Most prominent among them, in addition to Tillich, were Thomas J. J. Altizer, author of *The Gospel of Christian Atheism* (1966); Langdon Gilkey, author of *Maker of Heaven and Earth* (1965); Gabriel Vahanian, author of *The Death of God: The Culture of Our Post-Christian Era* (1961); Harvey Cox, author of *The Secular City* (1965); Paul Van Buren, author of *The Secular Meaning of the Gospel* (1963); Jesuit theologian John Courtney Murray, author of *The Problem of God: Yesterday and Today* (1964); and Rabbi Abraham Joshua Heschel, author of numerous popular works on his own mystically inflected strain of Judaism.

And Elson accurately captured the era's themes too. For us today, the article is a trenchant expression of the astonishment that Elson and apparently many of his fellow Americans felt in the face of an odd paradox: while polls at the time claimed to show that 97 percent of Americans believed in God, there seemed to be a widespread winking consensus that this figure was wildly out of kilter with a less obvious reality, namely, that conventional faith (whatever one understood by that) was very much on the wane. Sure, 97 percent of poll respondents checked "yes" to the question "Do you believe in God?" But that virtually unanimous answer to a troublingly ambiguous question masked the presence both of respondents who were simply dishonest and of others whose actual beliefs were clearly more complicated and nuanced than what might be conveyed in the statement "Yes, I believe in God."

Meaning, as I said in Chapter 6, makes its entrance from the moment the curtain goes up. And where there is *meaning*, it turns out, *anxiety* can't be very far behind. Some theologians, Elson writes, are "concentrating on an exploration of the ultimate and unconditional in modern life. Their basic point is that while modern men have rejected God as a solution to life, they cannot evade a questioning anxiety about its meaning." On the meaning of life, Elson quotes liberal theologian Langdon Gilkey: "When we ask, 'Why am I?', 'What should I become and be?', 'What is the meaning of my life?'—then we are exploring or encountering that region of experience where language about the ultimate becomes useful and intelligible." Elson himself immediately follows this with what might initially appear to be a non-sequitur: "That is not to say that God is necessarily found in the depths of anxiety." Who suggested that God *would* be "found in the depths of anxiety"? Part of the answer lies in the sentence preceding the passage quoted from Gilkey, as well as a few paragraphs before: Paul Tillich, who, as we saw in Chapter 6, closely linked anxiety with "ultimate concern," which is to say God.

It's amazing how the salient features of Tillich's cosmology were shared across denominational and even broad religious lines. A casual observer, on witnessing the extent to which certain leading Protestant, Jewish, and Catholic thinkers and writers in this era spoke with and even admired one another, might think, "What an extraordinary display of interfaith dialogue!" and assume it was born of a high-minded desire to overcome age-old animosities and, at the very least, keep faith—any faith—alive at a time when, despite what polling data purported to show, conventional faith seemed to be very much under a cloud. But clearly there was much more to it than this. After all, religious leaders from different denominations and faiths found themselves speaking very much the same language and drawing on very much the same sources. *Meaning, anxiety, ultimate concern* (or *ultimate* and *concern* used separately), *ground of being* (or *ground of existence*)—these terms and phrases had come along either to replace or to qualify radically the terms and phrases that had populated theological language for centuries. *Those* terms and phrases continued to appear, of course, but, as often as not, with language seemingly crafted to show an ironic wink at the reader or listener, as if to say, "No one really, literally, believes in God, the Son of God, or the Holy Spirit, from the naive and primitive understanding of an earlier and simpler era, but we can dress them up in existentialist garb and find a plausible stage for their new outfits in this Age of Anxiety." It's as if the central modern religious thinkers of the day had all studied at the feet of Tillich.

Some actually had.

The other towering figure from this era, at least in terms of popular exposure and appeal, was Reinhold Niebuhr, born to a pastor who, like Tillich, had immigrated from Germany. In 1948, *Time* had placed Niebuhr's aquiline features on the cover of an issue that presented an article titled "Faith for a Lenten Age." The unnamed author was Whittaker Chambers, only months before the Alger Hiss case broke. Chambers had been writing for *Time* since 1939, having contributed cover stories on a number of cultural figures, from James Joyce to Marian Anderson. Perhaps in order to sustain his claim to have rediscovered Christianity on the way to renouncing his commitment to Communism, Chambers turned his attention to Reinhold Niebuhr. And perhaps the suppleness of mind that had allowed him to navigate the shoals of Soviet Marxism, apparent disillusionment with it, *Finnegan's Wake*, and conversion to Quakerism allowed him to tackle the liberal theology of Niebuhr.

To a casual reader of popular magazines, Niebuhr would have appeared indistinguishable from Tillich. Chambers drew almost all his material from just one source, a handful of pages in the first volume of *The Nature and Destiny of Man* (1941), and yet the essential elements were there, including the genealogy of the new Protestantism. It began with Kierkegaard (how frequently the American public was suddenly encountering this previously unfamiliar name!), *anxiety* as both "the internal precondition of sin" and "the dizziness of freedom," and the omnipresence of *paradox* in Christian faith. The title phrase, "Faith for a Lenten Age," acknowledged the cataclysmic shifts in religious belief that lay at the heart of Tillich's theology.

It's not surprising that the two men should have come through as speaking roughly the same language. When they became colleagues at Union, Niebuhr's writings quickly began to show the impact, as he adopted a recognizably existentialist vocabulary and positions strongly resembling those of Tillich. He wrote repeatedly about *meaning*. Like Tillich, he used the word in a sometimes baffling array of senses, and, again as with Tillich, among these senses was one that appeared to be close to, or at least to draw on, the primary sense of the word.

"The problem of meaning," Niebuhr wrote in *The Nature and Destiny of Man*, "is the basic problem of religion."[7] It's not entirely clear how Niebuhr is using the word here. Nor are we helped along by this: "Implicit in the human situation of freedom and in man's capacity to transcend himself and his world is his inability to construct a world of meaning without finding a source and key to the structure of meaning which transcends the world beyond his own capacity to transcend it."[8] Grand metaphysical essence of some sort? Something having to do with interpretation and comprehensibility?

And like Tillich, Niebuhr developed a theory of symbols that (1) bespoke an adventurously modern theological orientation and (2) offered a use of *meaning* plausibly grounded in the historically fundamental sense of the word. The clearest statement came in a sermon titled "Mystery and Meaning" (1946). What do we do, Niebuhr asks, with a religion that features both mystery and revelation? Does the mystery disappear when what was hidden is revealed? God, after all, is hidden, and yet he makes himself known. That's easy to grasp, and Niebuhr was certainly not the first person to ask these questions. Then why not title the sermon "Mystery and Revelation"? What's *meaning* got to do with it, and what does it mean? At first, it appears that Niebuhr has come up with a plausible theory where *meaning* actually has its primitive sense. The created world, he says, "points beyond itself to a mysterious ground of existence, to an enigmatic power beyond all discernible vitalities, and to a 'first cause' beyond all known causes."[9] "Pointing beyond" is what signs and symbols do when they *mean* something. Niebuhr pursues the thought: "All known existence points beyond itself. To realize that it points beyond itself to God is to assert that the mystery of life does not dissolve life into meaninglessness. Faith in God is faith in some ultimate unity of life, in some final comprehensive purpose which holds all the various, and frequently contradictory, realms of coherence and meaning together."[10] In this model, "all known existence" functions as a *symbol* and points beyond itself to God, who becomes the *meaning* of that symbol. Warrant for the term *meaning* thus stems from an implicit act of *signifying* carried out by "all known existence" and interpreted by us, the faithful, presumably just as we interpret signs and symbols of a more mundane sort: a stop sign points beyond itself to (or *means*) the need to apply the brake (which is the *meaning* of the sign). Existence means (signifies) God (who is thus the *meaning* of existence).

But even within this short piece, Niebuhr is inconsistent in his use of *meaning*. At one point, he's classifying people according to the level of per- plexity they experience in the face of mystery. "Those who are not perplexed," he writes, "have dissolved all the mysteries and perplexities of life by some simple scheme of meaning." As for those who are overly perplexed: "A faith which is overwhelmed by mystery denies the clues of divine meaning which shine through the perplexities of life."[11] But here *meaning* is no longer a re- placement expression for *God* (or "ground of existence"). Instead it appar- ently has to do with interpretation, explanation, and comprehension. "Those who are not perplexed" are undoubtedly the materialists, for whom a mystery remains a mystery till it succumbs to scientific explanation, which reveals the *meaning* (explanation) they seek. The overly perplexed fail to see "clues" that presumably are revelatory of some sort of truth, or "divine meaning." But here too, *meaning* cannot be a replacement for *God*, because if it were, it wouldn't be redundantly qualified with *divine*.

In fact, mystery appears to be completely intrinsic to meaning regardless of our worldview. Perplexity in the face of mystery is a necessary and unavoid- able condition of those who have not succumbed to simplicity; the only task is to find the appropriate degree of perplexity. And this suggests that if the target is something called *meaning*, that something, confronted by a meas- ured and appropriate level of perplexity, will never cease to be mysterious. It suggests too that the word *meaning* itself, the generic term for whatever-it-is- that-we-discover-in-our-perplexity, is mysterious. What do we even mean by the word *meaning*? Best not to specify, for the entire project—attempting to discover a mysterious something lying beyond ordinary perception and attempting to assign a generic term to that type of something—needs to be enveloped in a haze of uncertainty and indeterminacy. Niebuhr's inconsist- ency is not a sign of incompetence on his part; it's unavoidable.

Niebuhr was not the only one to drink from the fount of Tillich. In fact, when you look through the writings of the "death of God" theologians that Elson mentioned in his article, you quickly see that almost all either identify Tillich as a teacher or cite him as a seminal influence. And that's no surprise.

Despite differences from one thinker to another, differences that no doubt loomed larger in that era than they do many years later, there is an astonishing uniformity and consistency in concepts and terms. Everyone was speaking much the same language. Kierkegaard is mentioned, as is anxiety. God is "the ground of being." *Ultimate* turns up with nouns to form phrases that connote metaphysical grandeur. *Meaning* is everywhere and now, by contrast with earlier eras, often without "of life" or "of existence."

One of the big shockers of this Age of Anxiety was a book with the aggressively impious title, *The Gospel of Christian Atheism*. Christian atheism: think about that. The author, Thomas J. J. Altizer, tells us in his preface that the work of Paul Tillich was what led him to the Christian faith in the first place. If the use of the term *atheism* seems like a step or two beyond such suggestively ambiguous formulations as "ground of being" and "ultimate concern," it's because Altizer considered the master's work to be insufficiently radical. Here is how he described the situation of humanity in then-modern times: "If there is one clear portal to the twentieth century, it is a passage through the death of God, the collapse of any meaning or reality lying beyond the newly discovered radical immanence of modern man, an immanence dissolving even the memory or the shadow of transcendence."[12] If this is truly where we now stand, if it's truly all about "radical immanence," why are we bothering to talk about Christian faith in the first place? But that's where *meaning* steps in to fill the void left by the disappearance of all the conventional metaphysical qualities. God is dead, we're told. Now, instead, we talk about a "source of meaning," insisting that, whatever that might be, it must lie not beyond but within "the life and movement of humanity."[13] Existence over essence, as Tillich had observed. But what exactly is *meaning*? Of course Altizer doesn't say.

One of the most stunning examples of a relationship that was not only interfaith but inter-theological was the one between Paul Tillich and Rabbi Abraham Joshua Heschel, who arrived in the United States in 1940, another refugee from Nazi Germany. Widely celebrated by Jews and non-Jews alike for his passionate devotion to progressive social causes (there's a famous photograph of him with Martin Luther King Jr. in the front row of the Selma civil rights march in 1965), Heschel held a faculty position at the Jewish Theological Seminary, a two-minute walk up Broadway from Tillich (before Tillich left for Harvard) and Niebuhr at Union. Heschel quickly became sufficiently well known in his adopted homeland that an essay by him appeared, in 1958, in a collection titled *Religion in America*. His fellow contributors included John Courtney Murray, Reinhold Niebuhr, Will Herberg (author of the 1955 classic *Protestant—Catholic—Jew*), and Paul Tillich—all members of the Age of Anxiety community and all, except Herberg, mentioned in Elson's *Time* magazine article. Heschel certainly knew Tillich's work, for he quoted from it in "No Religion Is an Island," the inaugural lecture he delivered in 1965, when he was beginning his academic year as (imagine this) Henry Emerson Fosdick Visiting Professor at Union Theological Seminary (Fosdick was the liberal pastor at the interdenominational Riverside Church, right behind the seminary). Heschel certainly followed a conventional path to Jewish theology and rabbinical life, at least as such a path existed in Germany before the rise of Hitler, and yet when you look at the work he produced after he came to the United States, you'd almost be inclined to conclude he had immersed himself in the work of Tillich and simply adapted it to Judaism (despite, to be sure, some clear differences). To a certain extent, the similarities are not surprising. Both men were products of the German university system, and both had an intimate connection with existential philosophy. And yet what other Jewish thinker in the twentieth century spoke of "ultimate concern" and the "ground of being"?

Meaning occurs with absolutely obsessive frequency in Heschel's writings, often with such a blatant want of definition and precision that his readers have little choice but to abandon themselves to the flood of raw *sensation* that is Heschel's thought. He was a professor of Jewish mysticism, after all, and, at the risk of offending his ardent admirers, one is sorely tempted to give in to the unschooled impression that *mysticism* refers simply to undisciplined thinking about big metaphysical questions. "For worship is an act of man's relating himself to ultimate meaning," he writes in *God in Search of Man*.[14] "The meaning of history is our profound concern. It is difficult to remain immune to the anxiety of the question, whence we come, where we are, and whither we are going."[15] "It is as an individual that I am moved by an anxiety for the meaning of my existence as a Jew."[16] He writes exultantly of a transcendent meaning that occurs outside the mind in objective things, of a surplus of meaning over being, of "an awareness that something is meant by the universe which surpasses our power of comprehension."[17] But as imprecise and ecstatic as this language is, it bears the clear stamp of Tillich and Tillich's Protestant disciples, all of whom worshiped at the altar of *meaning*. And if Heschel's life and work are a testament to the possibilities of interfaith dialogue, the fact that the language he so easily shared with a Protestant theologian was replete with terms and phrases—*meaning* paramount among them—that never really belonged in *any* conventional theological tradition helped make those possibilities a reality.

"Purpose," "value," "goal," "direction," "explanation," "thing that's missing when we experience existential anxiety," "what symbols point to," "essence," "grand metaphysical essence"—this doesn't even exhaust the list in the Age of Anxiety. *Meaning* can carry one or more of these senses, but whichever of these senses it does carry, even if it's the grand metaphysical essence, the word remains *meaning*, with its suggestion of signification and revelation, not to mention human intention. In an era when popular magazines were sporting images of white middle-class church-goers and the Gallup Organization was reporting record-high levels of "yes" answers to the question "Do you believe in God?," the meaning-obsessed theologians who captured the lion's share of popular attention had long since taken religion in a direction that effectively robbed the question of ... meaning.

And in the next phase, *meaning* will increasingly become a suggestive term, undefined, unspecific, and preponderantly secular, designed to conjure in our minds the idea of something grand, mysterious, and unnamed that, owing to our particular life circumstances, we must strive for.

8

Meaning Goes Clinical, Therapeutic, and Popular

The Emergence of "Existential Psychotherapy"

Paul Tillich and his family arrived in New York in November 1933. A month or so later, at Union Theological Seminary, where he had taken a faculty position, Tillich met a young divinity student by the name of Rollo May. May (1909–1994), after earning his bachelor of divinity at Union and a PhD in clinical psychology at Columbia, would go on to play a leading role in establishing existential psychotherapy as a major force in the United States in the 1950s and 1960s. He became one of Tillich's most devoted American followers and one of his closest friends. His second published book, *The Springs of Creative Living* (1940), was dedicated to Tillich, who would remain a strong intellectual presence in May's work till the end of his life.

Whether or not as a direct result of May's association with Tillich, the book is filled with references to meaning. The very first chapter, in fact, is titled "The Thirst for Meaning." Here the author tells us, "People suffer personality breakdowns because they do not have meaning in their lives."[1] And more grandiosely: "Call it confidence in the universe, trust in God, belief in one's fellow-men, or what not, the essence of religion is the belief that something matters—the *presupposition that life has meaning*."[2] Perhaps there is an echo, however slight, of Tillich in the chapter titled "What Is Healthy Religion?," where May makes these two claims: "Healthy religion is the affirming of God without demanding that God affirm oneself. It is the confidence that life has meaning without the insistence that that meaning be identical with oneself. This is, then, an *objective affirmation* of God." "We have a right only to ask that *there be* salvation and damnation—*that there be ultimate meaning*, in other words—that there be a God who is not ourselves."[3]

Nowhere is the controlling power of Tillich's thought more evident than in a book by May that serves as an emblem of the era in which it came out. It was titled *The Meaning of Anxiety* (1950), and, as the reader quickly finds out, *meaning* in the title refers not only to the meaning (and corresponding concept) of the word *anxiety* but also to *meaning* in the grander senses we're exploring in this book. May had begun his academic journey as a literary scholar, so, after some unremarkable comments about the general state of anxiety in society in this era, he offers an account of the concept in W. H. Auden, Camus (whose works had recently started to be translated into English), and Kafka before moving on to the fields of sociology, philosophy and religion, and, finally, psychology. Meaningfulness and meaninglessness lie at the heart of anxiety. The four characters in Auden's poem, May writes, face the possibility that they will be "drawn into the mechanical routine of meaninglessness" and, "symbolizing all of us, have lost the capacity for faith in, and meaningful communication with, other selves, their fellow human beings."[4] Similarly, the hero of Kafka's *The Castle* "devotes his life to a frantic and desperate endeavor to communicate with the authorities in the castle who control all aspects of the life of the village, and who have the power to tell him his vocation and give some meaning to his life."[5]

The lone two figures covered under philosophy and religion are Paul Tillich and Reinhold Niebuhr. May draws on Tillich's article on existential philosophy in order to establish what will be some of the guiding ideas in *The Meaning of Anxiety*: anxiety is "man's reaction to the threat of *nonbeing*," the threat of non-being lies in "the threat of *meaninglessness* in one's existence," and "the threat of meaninglessness is experienced negatively as a threat to the existence of the self" (though anxiety can be confronted affirmatively as well).[6] He cites Tillich's description of the existential thinkers' project as "the desperate struggle to find a new meaning of life in a reality from which men have been estranged, in a cultural situation in which two great traditions, the Christian and the humanistic, have lost their comprehensive character and their convincing power."[7] Kierkegaard is central here, as he had been for Tillich, because anxiety (like *meaning*) is several things at once. In its more conventional senses, it can be the anxiety occasioned understandably by world circumstances in 1950 ("the uncontrolled atom bomb," for example), the anxiety aroused by a pervasive sense of social insecurity peculiar to this age, or anxiety stemming from other poorly understood social factors and leading to suicide, mental disorders, and divorce, to name just three. But May dwells at great length on Kierkegaard's book on anxiety, and even though the book was available in English at the time only in the translation that rendered the Danish title word (*Angest*) as "dread" rather than "anxiety," May sought and received permission from Walter Lowrie, the translator, to render the word as *anxiety* in the passages that he cites. The issues that matter for May are those that interested Tillich and anyone else connected with existentialism (at least as they understood it): freedom and the will to be oneself, to both of which anxiety serves as an impediment. May does not speak the language of *meaning* in his section on Kierkegaard, but Tillich had already done so for him, in speaking of the "new meaning of life" toward which we strive in an age of anxiety and estrangement.

By the time May wrote his next book, *Man's Search for Himself* (1953), he had adopted a yet more orthodox Tillichian vocabulary. Though he mentions Kierkegaard a number of times in the book, May seems here to be concerned primarily with anxiety as a clinical mental health issue. Once again, we read of "the age of anxiety" and all the factors associated with it that make people anxious. In fact, as May makes clear in his first chapter, the concern in this book is not strictly pathological. "This book will be chiefly concerned with the normal anxiety of the person living in our age of transition," he writes. Not surprisingly, given May's background and outlook, religion comes to play a role. This is where meaning asserts itself most forcefully and where May reflects most noticeably the influence of his German mentor. Where God seemed to be an externally existing being in *The Springs of Creative Living*, here May has adopted the increasingly edgy existential terms of Tillich's conception. In a passage that looks ahead to Thomas J. J. Altizer's "Christian atheism" (1966, also heavily inflected with Tillichian concepts and chock-full of references to meaning), May writes this (in language that almost plagiarizes a passage from Tillich's *Systematic Theology* that I quoted in Chapter 6): "It is as atheistic to affirm the existence of God as to deny it. God is being itself, not *a* being. . . . We define religion as the assumption that life has meaning. . . . Wonder is a function of what one holds to be of ultimate meaning and value in life."[8] What does *meaning* mean in the usage of Rollo May? Of course, nowhere does he define the term, so, as with so many other writers, we're on our own when we try to understand it. "Purpose," "value," and "reason to go on living" appear to be candidates for definitions, when May refers to meaning in life or a life that has meaning. And nowhere in May's work is *meaning* featured as *the* guiding principle or as the basis of a psychotherapeutic method.

That would begin to happen at the end of the 1950s. If you were browsing your local bookstore in 1956, you might have stumbled across a book titled *Meaning: Antidote to Anxiety*, by a certain Henry Clay Lindgren, and you might have thought, "Yes, I suffer grievously from anxiety; perhaps what

I need is some meaning." Or you might have seen the full-page ad for the book in *The New York Times* featuring the screaming, large-type warning "Anxiety can kill you!" Your emotional issues, the ad promised, "can all be helped by simply understanding the *real* meaning of your personal motivations, your fears and inhibitions, your relationships with others."[9] Lindgren, a psychology professor at San Francisco State College (before it received university status, in 1972), began his book, "These are strange, tense days we are living in." He quotes Paul Tillich (who apparently had become a mandatory presence in books about meaning) as saying that anxiety is "the state in which a being is aware of its possible nonbeing."[10] So, what is meaning, and how shall I use it to cure my anxiety? Unhappily, in over two hundred pages, Lindgren has supplied no good answer to this question. He tells us that the dictionary definitions include such terms as *significance, sense, intent, purport,* and *import,* but that he is using *meaning* differently. " 'Meaning' as we are using it here is a *relationship*," he explains. And he gives this definition: "*Meaning is the perceiving of a sense-making relationship.*"[11] Needless to say, this is not very helpful, first because *meaning* starts out *being* the relationship and then becomes the *perceiving* of the relationship (not to mention that we don't know what "sense-making" means) and, second, because Lindgren goes on to use the word in a plethora of other senses that make it all but impossible to learn how in the name of all that's holy (or meaningful) I can count on this thing to cure my anxiety.

The Puzzling Case of Viktor Frankl and His Legacy

But the true revolution in psychotherapy that relied on *meaning* as the key concept, at least in English-speaking lands, followed on the publication of *Man's Search for Meaning* by Viktor Frankl in 1959.

What to say about Frankl (1905–1997) and his book? First, let's say something about Frankl and his history. He was an Austrian Jewish psychiatrist who, despite the Nazi annexation of his homeland (the Anschluss, 1938), was able to work in his profession till an astonishingly late date. He and his family were finally deported in late 1942 to Theresienstadt (in what is today the Czech Republic), originally conceived as a "model ghetto" for high-status Jews. Of course, it was anything but a model ghetto, and conditions there were horrific, but Frankl was lucky enough to be assigned duties that included practicing psychotherapy. He remained in Theresienstadt, where he worked as a physician in the mental hospital, for about two years. He was then transported to Auschwitz and then almost immediately sent to Dachau, where he remained, in two sub-camps, till his liberation in April 1945. Strictly speaking, Frankl was never *in* Auschwitz. He was "in depot" there, which meant that the camp was merely a way station to his next destination. He was never registered as an inmate of the camp, and the total time he spent in depot was two or three days (even though *Man's Search for Meaning* gives the impression—and his readers all appear to believe—that he was imprisoned there for a considerable time).[12] When he was finally liberated at the end of the war, he received the unimaginable news that his wife and his entire family, with the exception of a sister who had managed to emigrate to Australia, had perished in the camps.

Man's Search for Meaning started out in German as *Trotzdem Ja zum Leben sagen: Ein Psychologe erlebt das Konzentrationslager* (Nonetheless saying yes to life: a psychologist experiences the concentration camp). Not surprisingly, it is filled with references to *Sinn* and specifically *der Sinn des Lebens*. The setting is certainly as compelling as it could be, for two closely related reasons. First, as Frankl tells it, finding *Sinn* turns out to be the key to survival—or at least to a chance at survival. Second, the reason it's the key to survival is something that was, even before Frankl's deportation, and remained for the rest of his life, a cornerstone not only of his outlook on life but also of his therapeutic methods.

A perfect illustration of the first point is a story Frankl tells about a moment of general despair in the camp (one of the Dachau sub-camps to which he was moved from Auschwitz). Camp authorities were cracking down on the prisoners for any number of minor offenses and punishing the offenders with death by hanging. A large group, having refused to turn in a fellow inmate who had stolen some potatoes, was enduring a twenty-four-hour fast as punishment. As Frankl tells the story, the block warden (that is, a Jewish prisoner whose job was to enforce camp rules among his fellows) asked him to speak to the prisoners. If we are to believe him, Frankl launched into a short, carefully reasoned disquisition. He spoke not only about seeking *Sinn* but about filling life with it. "And then finally I spoke of the multitude of possibilities of filling life with *Sinn*," he wrote (I'm leaving *Sinn* untranslated). "I explained to my comrades . . . that human life always and under all circumstances has *Sinn* and that this infinite *Sinn* of existence includes within itself also suffering and dying, hardship and death. And I begged these poor devils who were listening to me attentively in the pitch-black barracks [the electrical power had failed], to look at things and our situation straight in the face and nonetheless not to despair but rather, in the awareness that even the hopelessness of our camp could not harm its *Sinn* and its value, to take courage." Their sacrifice, too, had *Sinn*, Frankl explained. When he finished his speech, an electric lamp miraculously lighted up, so Frankl was able to see his fellow prisoners limping toward him, with tears in their eyes, to thank him.[13]

It seems highly unlikely that the incident played out in the precise way that Frankl recounts it in his book, with the almost instantaneous turnabout in the attitude of his listeners in these grimmest of circumstances. Perhaps he allowed himself a measure of narrative liberty in order to enhance the impact of the story on his readers—and who would presume to challenge the truthfulness of a witness to these horrors? But, for purposes of assessing Frankl's thinking and the therapeutic methods he devised, we should examine the claim he's making about *Sinn*, for, to credit the story, this word is the key to the success of Frankl's short speech. What does it mean here, and how does it achieve its power? "Purpose"? "Value" (with which it is explicitly paired at one point)? Perhaps the proper way to approach the word is not to substitute other single words for it (in English, German, or any other language) but instead to offer phrases that appear to match Frankl's message in sentences that include it. That message is "Please don't give up; find something that will serve *you* as a reason to go on living." *Sinn*, with its capacity to suggest "purpose" and "sense" (as in the sense of something that "makes sense"), appears to serve Frankl's intention admirably. What about our *meaning*, as in something signified that gets revealed as the result of an interpretive act? Not so much in this story, I think, which is why the English word could quite possibly be misleading here. But that is the word that the English translator used in the majority of instances in this book. What about the title? The German title makes no reference to *Sinn*, and the original English title, when the translation was first published in 1959, was *From Death-Camp to Existentialism: A Psychiatrist's Path to a New Therapy*. But once Frankl embarked on a long and highly visible career as the author of books written originally in English, the word *meaning* was called in to denote the fundamental concept in the worldview and the therapeutic methods that he so successfully promoted and marketed for the rest of his life. I'll return to those in a moment.

And this brings me to the second point. A few pages before the passage I just quoted, in a section titled "Nach dem Sinn des Lebens fragen" (Asking about the *Sinn* of life—the English translation did not include section titles), we read this (again, I leave *Sinn* untranslated):

In the end, to live means nothing other than to bear responsibility for correctly answering life's questions, for fulfilling the tasks that life imposes on each individual, for fulfilling the requirement of the hour.

This requirement, and with it the *Sinn* of existence, changes from person to person and from moment to moment. The *Sinn* of human life can therefore never be given in a universal way, nor can the question of this *Sinn* be answered in a universal way—life, as it is meant here, is not something vague but rather something entirely concrete for each, and so also are the requirements of life entirely concrete for each of us. This concreteness carries with it the destiny of a person, which for everyone is singular and unique. No person and no destiny may be compared with another; no situation repeats itself.[14]

The entire topic of the *Sinn* of existence or the *Sinn* of human life is thus framed as a question of responsibility (*Verantwortlichkeit*). What Frankl does not state here is that this collection of ideas had their own history in his prewar career. He had already devoted a considerable portion of his career to suicide prevention. In 1937, while working in the female suicide ward of a state hospital, he published an article in the *Zentralblatt für Psychotherapie*, the official journal of the medical institute run by Henri Mathius Göring, cousin of Reich Marshall Hermann Göring. The article was titled "Zur geistigen Problematik der Psychotherapie" (On the spiritual problematics of psychotherapy). Frankl devoted much of the article to establishing a position relative to his celebrated Viennese precursors in psychotherapy, Sigmund Freud and Alfred Adler. For his own reasons, Frankl had viewed the central concept in Freudian psychoanalysis as *adaptation* (that is, of our instincts to the reality principle) and the central idea in Adlerian psychotherapy as *arrangement* (that is, of reality by the individual ego). The breakthrough idea in Frankl's article was his proposal of a third dimension, *responsibility*, encompassing the ideas of *Sollen* (should), obligation, and will.[15]

Frankl had always been firmly opposed to suicide and had never accepted the idea of acceding to an individual's intention to take his or her own life. Approaching life with a sense of responsibility and with a strong will would allow an individual to find the *Sinn* of that life and resist the urge to end it, Frankl thought. The article repeatedly affirmed the connection between the *Sinn* of life and the notion of personal responsibility. Frankl wrote this:

If [the patient] . . . in the course of psychotherapy reveals his struggle for the meaning [*Sinn*] of his existence by raising the question of the meaning [*Sinn*] of life, we must above all make him conscious of the fact that he is ultimately not the one asking the question but rather the one being asked; that it would correspond more to the primeval nature of responsibility in existence if, instead of continually asking about the meaning [*Sinn*] of life, he were to experience himself as the one being asked, as a person to whom life, for its part, constantly poses questions, as a being thrust into the midst of a plethora of tasks. But psychology teaches us that the grabbing of meaning [*Sinn*] belongs to a higher level of development than the giving of meaning [*Sinn*]. So, we psychotherapists must lead the patient toward the capacity to grab meaning [*Sinn*] for his own life, in all its singularity and uniqueness, the capacity to find meaning [*Sinn*] independently.[16]

This is a model that assigns us responsibility, represents us as taking bold action, and identifies *Sinn* as the target of that action. And here is where we run into a thorny issue. Timothy Pytell tells the story of Frankl's activities during the years between the start of the war and his deportation to Theresienstadt. The focus of his work was suicide prevention. It must be understood here that while Frankl had always considered it his moral and professional duty to prevent suicide, his position matched the official policy of the regime once the deportations started. In the years leading up to those mass deportations, the regime was all too happy to learn of Jewish suicides: every such suicide, so the thinking went, would rid the world of one more Jew. But then everything changed, and the regime adopted an official policy of criminalizing and preventing suicide. As Christian Goeschel put it grimly in his book on suicide in Nazi Germany, the police and the Gestapo, once they were committed to a deportation policy whose aim was to take in *all* Jews, saw themselves as being "cheated" by Jewish suicide.[17] Suicide deprived the state of its ability to carry out justice in its own way, for example, in the gas chambers at Auschwitz. Since Frankl appears from early in his career to have regarded suicide as a cowardly act that allowed desperate individuals to avoid responsibility for their destiny, his own practices aligned with the reigning attitude among the authorities and, consequently, among medical professionals in the regime. And so Frankl set out, unhindered, not only to prevent suicide but to revive those who had attempted it. He even managed to publish an article on his methods in a medical journal as amazingly late as 1942, just before he himself was deported.

The notion of responsibility reached a zenith of importance in Frankl's thinking shortly after the war, in a book titled *Der unbewußte Gott*, which was translated into English many years later, with unavoidable ambiguity, as *The Unconscious God* (it means the God of whom we are not conscious, not the God who has fainted and lost consciousness). In the original German, Frankl used a number of related words, all containing *Antwort*, "answer," to convey the idea of responsibility (*Antwortlichkeit*). But he asserts the essential nature of the concept straightaway, in the first chapter, and predictably it has to do with *Sinn* (here I translate from the German). He now refers to his therapeutic methods as "existential analysis."

> If we wanted, in just a few words, to take a look back at the path on which existential analysis arrived at responsibility [*Verantwortlichsein*, literally "being-responsible," as a noun] as the essential feature of human existence, we would have to start from the inversion that we were obliged to carry out in posing the question of the *Sinn* of existence: we endeavored to demonstrate the task-based nature of life but, at the same time, the responsible character [*Antwortcharakter*] of existence: it is not man, we explained, who must pose the question of the *Sinn* of life; rather it is inverted, so that man himself is the one being asked, he himself is the one who has to answer, [and] he himself must answer the questions that his life puts to him.[18]

So, what is Frankl saying here? The logic is rather tangled, but it appears in this book that he has attempted to bring together two lines of thought. The first one, as expressed in this passage, holds that responsibility, the fact of being *answerable* (*antwortlich*) for our actions and of exerting our will in order to bring about actions that are "right," is part of the essence of being human. The second is striking, and it occupies the following two chapters: it holds that the origins of our conscience and therefore of our religiousness lie in our unconscious and are therefore also part of the essence of being human. Responsibility and conscience are both *Urphänomene*, primal phenomena, existing in advance of all experience.

A subsequent enlarged English edition, published long after the original German and including two chapters written in English in, respectively, 1975 and 1985, made the book out to be a kind of sequel to the prison camp memoir. It was titled *Man's Search for Ultimate Meaning*. This was an odd choice of title, because the phrase "ultimate meaning" occurs only once in the portion of the book corresponding to the original German edition—in the rather non-specific sense of what an irreligious person, who stops his search short of the goal, is looking for.[19] What's more, there is no corresponding phrase in the original German. Frankl wrote simply of *Sinnfindung* (*Sinn-finding*), without qualifying *Sinn* in any way at all.[20] The chapter written in 1985 bears the title given to the entire book, "Man's Search for Ultimate Meaning," and it contains numerous instances of "ultimate meaning," which serves here as a kind of substitute expression for "God," very much as this same phrase and the phrase "ultimate concern" functioned for Paul Tillich.

I mentioned that Frankl saw the will as the driving force in a responsible life and that leading a responsible life was inextricably connected with the notion of *meaning* (because it has to do with answering the question of the meaning of life or existence). So, it seems inevitable that Frankl would come up with "the will to meaning"—and he did, first in the English edition of his concentration camp memoir and later in a book with the title *The Will to Meaning*, written in English and published in 1969. But here the concept intersects with Frankl's therapeutic methods, and we should say something about those. He called his style of therapy "logotherapy." It's the therapy referred to in the subtitle of the first edition of *Man's Search for Meaning*. Part Two of that book was titled "Logotherapy in a Nutshell." Logotherapy, Frankl explained there, is "meaning-centered," because by its methods, "the patient is actually confronted with and reoriented toward the meaning of his life."[21] Where does the name *logotherapy* come from? "*Logos*," Frankl explains, "is a Greek word which denotes 'meaning.'" It doesn't, but perhaps that's not important. For him, the word *logotherapy* denotes a style of psychotherapy based on the central concept of *meaning*.[22]

Meaning is central precisely because, like responsibility and conscience, the search for it appears to be an *Urphänomen*. Each of us is driven by a "will to meaning," or as Frankl explains it, his Third Viennese School of Psychotherapy "focuses on the meaning of human existence as well as on man's search for such a meaning. According to logotherapy," he writes, "this striving to find a meaning in one's life is the primary motivational force in man. That is why I speak of a *will to meaning* in contrast to the pleasure principle (or, as we could also term it, the *will to pleasure*) on which Freudian psychoanalysis is centered, as well as in contrast to the *will to power* on which Adlerian psychology, using the term 'striving for superiority,' is focused.'"[23] From this brief account, we would probably conclude that the will to meaning is simply our strong desire to find meaning (however we understand *meaning*).

The Will to Meaning: Foundations and Applications of Logotherapy was based on a lecture series that Frankl gave at Southern Methodist University in 1966. By this time, though logotherapy had not become an international movement (the first institute of logotherapy did not open till 1979), it is safe to say that it was widely known, if only through the popularity of Frankl's earlier books. Here we learn about the three pillars of logotherapy, pillars that continue to the present day to serve as basic principles in the field: (1) freedom of will, (2) the will to meaning, and (3) the meaning of life.[24] Having stated the three pillars, Frankl muddies the waters a bit with this statement about the construction of the word *logotherapy*: "In addition to meaning 'meaning' [it doesn't], 'logos' here means 'spirit' [it never does]—but again without any primarily religious connotation. Here 'logos' means the humanness of the human being—plus the meaning of being human!"[25] I suppose, for purposes of a term that you've invented to denote your field of study and practice, *logos* can mean whatever you say it means. But if we're looking for an understanding of *meaning* here, we're likely to be disappointed. For Frankl, *logos* means "meaning," it means "spirit," and it means "the meaning of being human." So, what does *meaning* mean?

You might expect to find the answer in a section titled "What Is Meant by Meaning?" But there, once again, you'll be disappointed, for, at least to my mind, the section starts out confusing and then descends into complete incoherence. Take, for example, this passage: "This tension [between subject and object] is the same as the tension between the 'I am' and the 'I ought,' between reality and ideal, between being and meaning. And if this tension is to be preserved, meaning has to be prevented from coinciding with being. I should say that it is the meaning of meaning to set the pace of being."[26] A few pages later: "Man is responsible for giving the *right* answer to a question, for finding the *true* meaning of a situation. And meaning is something to be found rather than to be given, discovered rather than invented."[27] And further: "In other words, our contention is that there is a meaning of life—a meaning, that is, for which man has been in search all along—and also that man has the freedom to embark on the fulfillment of this meaning."[28] I can't say for certain that these statements contradict one another, but at the same time, if they don't, I'm quite sure I don't understand them.

What about the will to meaning, which, to judge by the title of the book, ought to be given fairly thorough coverage? Apart from listing "will to meaning" as one of the three pillars of logotherapy, Frankl does not really say what it is or what the function of the will is. Of the three pillars, only the first, "freedom of will," merits an explanatory passage, but that consists in nothing more than the unsensational claim that freedom of will is opposed to determinism. There is no explanation of the role of the will in our quest for meaning, unless we are simply to understand that having a strong desire to find something indicates that we'll need to exert our will in order to do so.

Part Two of *The Will to Meaning* is titled "Applications of Logotherapy," and here we might expect to find out how all these ideas work in actual practice. After all, if the therapy works in practice, who cares whether or not the ideas designed to support it are coherent and consistent? Here Frankl has recourse to a truism that had filled the pages of his own writings as well as the writings of others in the psychotherapeutic world of the Age of Anxiety in the 1950s: that, especially in the United States, the big forces confronting and threatening us every day are conformism (the pressure on members of white middle-class families to be just like all other members of white middle-class families) and totalitarianism (above all, the Soviet Union). These forces create an "existential vacuum," in response to which, of course, we must find meaning. Frankl sets out what purports to be a word-for-word transcript of a conversation he had with a patient suffering from anxiety. In the conversation (which I estimate lasted roughly ten minutes), Frankl patiently and flawlessly explains how to search for meaning, refers to Moses, Jesus, Muhammad (his spelling), Buddha, Sartre, and Camus, and finishes off by quoting Pascal's famous saying about how the heart has its reasons that reason doesn't know. We're to think that the patient's suffering was immediately allayed by this speech.[29]

In the conclusion to the book, Frankl is back to the ideas on religion that he had introduced two decades earlier in *The Unconscious God*, but with a rather confusing turn. For example, having claimed that logotherapy merely "leaves the door to religion open" and lets the patient decide whether or not to pass through that door, he goes on to write, "I would say that the ultimate meaning, or as I prefer to call it, the supra-meaning is no longer a matter of thinking but rather a matter of believing. We do not catch hold of it on intellectual grounds but on existential grounds, out of our whole being, i.e., through faith."[30] And then this, which reads a bit like a salad of ideas drawn from Paul Tillich: "But it is my contention that faith in the ultimate meaning is preceded by trust in an ultimate being, by trust in God . . . The ontological difference between being and things or for that matter the dimensional difference between the ultimate being and human beings, prevents man from really speaking of God. Speaking of God implies making being into a thing."[31] Is this an echo of Tillich's identification of God with "ultimate being" and his contempt for the objectified "theistic God"? At the very end of the book, Frankl claims that he was interviewed for the "Is God Dead?" issue of *Time* (though his name did not end up in the cover article). If we are to credit the story, the "local reporter" who phoned Frankl (John T. Elson, who wrote the article?) apparently just put the question to him, "Is God dead?," and Frankl's answer, for the ages, was allegedly this: "I would say that God is not dead but silent."[32] He ends his book with a passage from Habakkuk about rejoicing in the Lord in the face of great adversity, admonishing us to learn from *The Will to Meaning* the lesson that the Jewish prophet had voiced more than two thousand years earlier.[33]

So, what about Frankl's methods and practice? At one point in *Man's Search for Ultimate Meaning*, the author states not so much that his methods were successful as that empirical evidence presented in scientific publications had irrefutably demonstrated the existence of a "will to meaning."[34] Some of the authorities he cites were indeed practitioners in the field.[35] Nowhere is there anything resembling the irrefutable proof that Frankl refers to. And here, I think, is the core of the problem. As we've seen, Frankl's key terms and phrases, especially those associated with *meaning*, are extraordinarily fluid and changing, as is the word *meaning* (and German *Sinn*) itself. Despite his claim of validation from the scientific work of colleagues in his field, much of his own published work tends to be speculative and (for want of a better word) philosophical, rather than based on the results of carefully designed experimental work of his own. In fairness, it must be said that logotherapy did indeed spawn a large scientific literature based on numerous empirical studies.[36] As best I can tell, in many instances studies use survey questionnaires that aim to establish, first, the degree to which the respondent shows a successful quest for "meaning" or "meaningfulness" and, second, the degree to which a high level of "meaning" or "meaningfulness" correlates with improvements in mental health. Thus, for example, in the case of terminal cancer patients, a study documenting the success of logotherapeutic or other meaning-based techniques will show that patients who found "meaning" also showed a renewed will to go on living, despite the death sentence of their medical condition. More easily measurable than the will to go on living and its association with the notion of *meaning* are the results presented in studies of addiction and dependency, where presumably, having established a level of "meaning in life," with the attendant *imprecision* of this concept, one can also measure *with precision* the level of drug and alcohol usage.

Frankl's logotherapy is not the only form of psychotherapy that centers on *meaning*. Meaning-centered psychotherapy (MCP), developed by Dr. William Breitbart, a psychiatrist at Memorial Sloan Kettering Cancer Center in New York City (as of this writing), while inspired by Frankl's ideas, is designed expressly for terminal cancer patients and aims "to diminish despair, demoralization, hopelessness, and desire for hastened death by sustaining or enhancing a sense of meaning, even in the face of death."[37] Meaning is, of course, the central concept in MCP. It is not defined in the MCP literature any more precisely than it is in the logotherapy literature, and yet Breitbart and his colleagues have documented the success of their methods.

I am not at all competent to judge the validity of those methods or of results in the field of psychotherapy and would not presume to challenge the findings of researchers and practitioners in this field. Interviews with two prominent practitioners, one specifically of logotherapy, the other Breitbart himself, have left me with the somewhat unsettling but encouraging impression that (1) the definition of *meaning*, the core concept in logotherapy and similar therapies, simply does not come up in clinical practice, because (2) both patients and clinicians appear to have an intuitive understanding of what it is they're talking about when they use the word, and (3) the proof is in the documented results.[38] While I would certainly not impute to the mental health professionals who practice meaning-based therapy a deliberate effort to invest the central word of their discipline with ambiguity, it's evident that the fluidity of that word, its ability to signify or suggest a host of meanings and nuances, thus its ability to function productively for many different patients, is no doubt precisely what gives it the power to produce the documented therapeutic results.

The Biochemistry of Finding Meaning

But there actually is a field of science that measures with biochemical precision the impact of meaning on mental states. The field is referred to as "well-being studies," and it has drawn together a number of distinguished researchers. Barbara Fredrickson is Kenan Distinguished Professor of Psychology and Neuroscience and Director of the Positive Emotions and Psychophysiology Laboratory at the University of North Carolina, Chapel Hill. The primary focus of her work for years has been mental states of well-being. A paper published in 2013 draws an explicit connection between meaning and the biochemical basis of a mental state. "A Functional Genomic Perspective on Human Well-being" begins with a distinction that is fundamental to the study of human well-being and that appears throughout the literature in this field: between *hedonia* (not an actual Greek word but derived from the word *hēdonē*, "enjoyment," "pleasure," the basis for the word *hedonism*) and *eudaimonia* (a Greek word signifying a fuller sort of happiness than the raw pleasure of *hēdonē*). Here is how Fredrickson and her co-authors present the distinction at the beginning of the paper: "Philosophers have long distinguished two basic forms of well-being: a 'hedonic' form representing the sum of an individual's positive affective experiences, and a deeper 'eudaimonic' form that results from striving toward *meaning and a noble purpose* beyond simple self-gratification. Both dimensions of well-being are deeply implicated in human biology and evolution, with hedonic well-being hypothesized to motivate basic physiological and psychological adaptations, and eudaimonic well-being hypothesized to motivate more complex social and cultural capacities."[39]

Here (from my non-expert vantage point) is the biochemistry of hedonic vs. eudaimonic states: our sense of well-being is founded, in part, on the expression of genes involved in inflammation and those involved in the opposing process of antibody synthesis, which is to say *in response to* inflammation. CTRA (stress-related conserved transcriptional response to adversity, "transcriptional" because it has to do with transcription, or the copying of segments of DNA onto RNA) is a process that produces an increase in the expression of proinflammatory genes and a decrease in the expression of antibody genes. Thus "upregulation" of CTRA tends to lead toward a less healthy physical state, "downregulation" toward a healthier physical state. Fredrickson and her colleagues found that people in a hedonic state show upregulated expression of CTRA, while those in a eudaimonic state show downregulated expression of CTRA. In other words, the hedonic state is associated with unhealthy stress on the organism of the sort associated with poorly controlled inflammation, while the eudaimonic state is associated with relative physical well-being.

So, *meaning* is integral to a state of eudaimonia. How do we detect its presence? Again, as in logotherapy and MCP, a survey is used, the survey includes the term *meaning*, and the respondents are apparently trusted to know what *meaning* means. In this instance, the survey was a short version of the widely used Flourishing Scale, and curiously enough, *meaning* is here associated with *direction* (as we have seen in the German word *Sinn*). Here is how Fredrickson and co-authors summarized the survey in the "Methods" section of their paper (the words in parentheses have been added by the authors):

> Short Flourishing Scale, e.g., in the past week, how often did you feel . . . happy? (hedonic), satisfied? (hedonic), that your life has a sense of direction or meaning to it? (eudaimonic), that you have experiences that challenge you to grow and become a better person? (eudaimonic), that you had something to contribute to society? (eudaimonic); answered on a six-point frequency metric whereby 0 indicates never, 1 indicates once or twice, 2 indicates approximately once per week, 3 indicates two or three times per week, 4 indicates almost every day, and 5 indicates every day.[40]

Subsequent work by Fredrickson and her colleagues gave a greater role to *purpose*, in fact, to the extent that *meaning* and *purpose* were essentially two different ways of saying the same thing. While the biochemical picture grew somewhat more complicated (as researchers came to recognize that hedonia and eudaimonia, rather than being largely distinct from and opposed to each other, were intertwined), the vocabulary for defining eudaimonia was modified to include not only *purpose* but also *self-transcendence*. In one study, the reason for this was that the survey for capturing mental states of well-being used *purpose in life* as a category and *meaning* in the individual items under that category (such that the respondent who scores high on *purpose in life* "feels there is meaning to present and past life," while the respondent who scores low "lacks a sense of meaning in life"). In addition, here Fredrickson broadened the vocabulary for describing eudaimonic states: such states, she writes, are "self-transcendent experiences of purpose, meaning, contribution, and interconnectedness."[41] But once again, the key words must, at least in part, match those that are used in the surveys in order to demonstrate the presence of one or the other of the two states of well-being. And once again, the whole study appears to stand or fall on our acceptance or rejection of the implicit claim that investigators and subjects hold one and the same understanding of those key words. Or does it? What do *meaning* and *purpose* actually mean in these surveys? *Purpose* probably does not require a definition, yet no survey that I'm aware of ever defines *meaning*. But, whatever *meaning* means, it apparently *functions* in such a way that when a subject responds that he or she *has* what it denotes or suggests—in addition to *purpose*—the researcher may safely infer that that subject is describing a eudaimonic state, not a hedonic state. And if one can demonstrate that such responses correlate positively with suppressed CTRA (that is, *low* inflammation and *high* antibody levels), then one can claim to have identified the biochemical substrate of the impact, on our mental state, of a feeling of meaning and purpose— without having stated what *meaning* is, because it might well be something different from subject to subject and from researcher to researcher.

The Self-Help Movement

If there is a manifestation of our culture that shows the universal acceptance of *meaning*, in the absence of any definition, as an extremely important something to be sought, it is popular psychology and the closely associated self-help movement. It would be impossible to offer a survey of the vast literature on meaning that you would find in the self-help or psychology–personal growth section of a bookstore (or would have found, back when there were still bookstores). I will give two examples that strike me as representative and that also show the pervasive presence of Viktor Frankl in popular consciousness.

Emily Esfahani Smith, a writer and columnist who works on community- and purpose-building projects in the United States, has written *The Power of Meaning: Crafting a Life That Matters* (2017). Smith cast her net wide for the book, speaking to people from a variety of cultures and walks of life in a variety of places in the United States. Her premise is that there is a "meaning crisis" ("The Meaning Crisis" is the title of her first chapter) and that the way to address it is through a quest for a meaningful life. Drawing on a number of cultural, philosophical, and religious traditions, she concludes that meaning is the key to, well, a meaningful life, "a life that matters," and that there are four "pillars of meaning": belonging, purpose, storytelling, and transcendence. And because the pillars appear to be not a set of prescriptive rules that the author herself has devised but rather categories that she has discovered in her travels, geographical, intellectual, and spiritual, they are available to anyone who chooses to explore them. "Both with and without religion," she writes, "individuals can build up each of these pillars in their lives. They are sources of meaning that cut through every aspect of our existence. We can find belonging at work and within our families, or experience transcendence while taking a walk through the park or visiting an art museum. We

can choose a career that helps us serve others, or draft our life story to understand how we got to be the way we are."[42]

To each of the pillars she devotes a chapter. The stories of the author's
travels and research are fascinating. The book is beautifully written and filled
with inspiring stories not only of personal challenges and triumphs but also
of thinkers and investigators who have contributed to our understanding of
meaning. Smith devotes a few pages to Barbara Fredrickson's research and
the first half of her concluding chapter to Breitbart. The final pages of the
book are devoted to Viktor Frankl. The completely favorable account is based
almost entirely on two of Frankl's books and two extremely laudatory books
about him. It is essentially the story that Frankl himself told in *Man's Search
for Meaning*, ending with the assertion that, in the view of Viktor Frankl,
love is where we find the true meaning of life. Smith concludes the book like
this: "That's the power of meaning. It's not some great revelation. It's pausing
to say hi to a newspaper vendor and reaching out to someone at work who
seems down. It's helping people get in better shape and being a good parent or
mentor to a child. It's sitting in awe beneath a starry night sky and going to a
medieval prayer service with friends. It's opening a coffee shop for struggling
veterans. It's listening attentively to a loved one's story. It's taking care of a
plant. These may be humble acts on their own. But taken together, they light
up the world."[43]

Smith includes no explicit definition of *meaning*. The paragraph before
the final one in the book begins, "The act of love begins with the very definition of meaning: it begins by stepping outside of the self to connect with
and contribute to something bigger."[44] But *definition* is used metaphorically in that sentence, to mean "epitome" or "essence." In the book's own
terms, this "stepping outside of the self" is a *means to achieve* meaning, but
it would be inaccurate to say that it *is* meaning. Don't we find meaning *in
the connection*, rather than saying that meaning is the connection itself?
So, I wrote to Smith and asked if she could give me a definition. She did.
"Psychologists and philosophers," she wrote, "define meaning as connecting
and contributing to something beyond yourself (see Nozick, Tolstoy, and
Martin Seligman). According to research psychologists, meaning has three
parts: significance, purpose, and coherence. I like this definition because it
encompasses meaning-as-value (significance/purpose) and meaning-as-
understanding/interpretation (coherence). I argue that the pillars are what
bring us meaning (i.e., significance, purpose, and coherence). They also
enable us to connect with and contribute to something beyond ourselves."

Meaning, as used in Smith's book, is thus polyvalent from the start, as she explicitly acknowledged.

And here is something exceedingly important: meaning-as-value and meaning-as-understanding. Rarely in the vast literature of *meaning* in the senses that I've been looking at in this book is there a reference to anything like this distinction. Meaning-as-value is something we've seen repeatedly, and though it might remain a mystery how *meaning* comes to mean "value," there it is, again and again. But meaning-as-understanding/interpretation does not often get explicitly mentioned, and yet it is a rare instance of the word that stems from its own original meaning. If you seek and find meaning-as-understanding/interpretation, you have applied your interpretive powers to something that is apparently mysterious on first inspection but that yields to your interpretation and leaves you understanding it. What is the meaning of the frog die-off? Let me look into it. Oh, now I understand: turns out it was a fungus. In the world of psychotherapy, if I, a patient, am suffering (for example, I am a terminal cancer patient) or have suffered grievously (say, I suffer from PTSD or have experienced a traumatic loss), doesn't it make sense for me to seek meaning where meaning brings an explanation, understanding, and enlightenment, where the quest for it is literally or figuratively an act of interpretation, and where the "text" that yields up its meaning (in the original sense) to me is the mystery of my suffering?

Smith is right: the distinction does appear in the literature of psychotherapy, particularly psychotherapy devoted to the treatment of grief. A classic study is one published by three psychologists at University of Michigan and Stanford in 1998, titled "Making Sense of Loss and Benefiting from the Experience: Two Construals of Meaning."[45] The authors began from the premise that "finding meaning" is essential for adjusting to a loss, and they use the phrase, as do others in the profession, without defining *meaning*. But they refer to the imprecision of *meaning* (as discussed, they say, by no less a figure than Viktor Frankl) and then present two similar pairs of "construals" of meaning: sense-making vs. benefit-finding and meaning-as-comprehensibility vs. meaning-as-significance (roughly the same as the distinction that Smith cited). The simple idea in the study was to show the extent to which test subjects were able to cope with their loss (1) by "making sense" of it and (2) by finding a benefit in it. Making sense of the death of someone near to you meant coming to an understanding of that loss, such that "finding meaning" in the experience was very much like finding the meaning of a hitherto mysterious natural occurrence, though the meaning may not have been a scientific explanation, such as a ranicidal fungus. For example (my example, not the authors'), if I've experienced a terrible loss, I might think, "I was wondering how God could have allowed such a thing to happen, but now I understand. That's the meaning I found. My loss makes sense now."

This study found its way into the other self-help book I have in mind. David Kessler is a world-famous grief counselor, and the title of his book is *Finding Meaning: The Sixth State of Grief.* A word of explanation about the title: Years ago, Kessler worked with Elisabeth Kübler-Ross, the celebrated psychiatrist who, in her 1969 international bestseller, *On Death and Dying,* changed the way we think about death and grief. Her book presented what came to be the classic list of stages of grief in response either to one's own certain, imminent death (if one is, say, a terminal cancer patient) or to the death of a loved one: denial, anger, bargaining, depression, acceptance. *Meaning* was clearly not an important topic in this book, for there are scarcely any references to it. Shortly before Kübler-Ross herself died, she and Kessler co-authored *On Grief and Grieving: Finding the Meaning of Grief Through the Five Stages of Loss* (2005). Then, twelve years later, Kessler lost an adopted son to a drug overdose and thus, in the cruelest manner, came to live the experience for which he had previously counseled thousands. One consequence of the new, personal experience of grief was Kessler's discovery that there was a sixth stage. No longer was it a question of "finding the meaning of grief"; now, meaning was a sixth stage unto itself.

This is the way Kessler describes the "Making Sense of Loss" study: "A decade after Elisabeth Kübler-Ross's assertion that positives could be found in loss and death, psychologist Christopher Davis and his colleagues wrote an article . . . in which they asserted that having any understanding of meaning was preferable to having none, and that the content of that understanding did not seem to matter. Some people will find meaning in belief in afterlife. Others will find meaning in the memories of their loved ones. Still others will find meaning in simply being able to be present for their loved ones' last hours." But that's not at all what Davis and his colleagues wrote in the article. The point was precisely *not* that "any understanding of meaning was preferable to having none" or that there were unlimited "understandings of meaning"; rather, the investigators were interested in two specific construals of *meaning,* one of which consisted of "understanding," "making sense of," the loss. The study established that while most respondents found some of each construal, those who, later in the process, primarily "made sense" experienced less relief from their suffering than those who, later in the process, primarily found a benefit. (It should be noted that the word *meaning* was not built into the questions designed to elicit from the test subjects the "making sense" vs. "finding a benefit" distinction—it was strictly the investigators' umbrella term for both processes.)

That Kessler should have interpreted the study in the way that he did is understandable, for *meaning* never receives any sort of definition at all in his book. To judge from the huge variety of ways in which it is used, it appears to mean quite a few different things. Some examples: "What does meaning look like? It can take many shapes, such as finding gratitude for the time they had with loved ones, or finding ways to commemorate and honor loved ones, or realizing the brevity and value of life and making that the springboard into some kind of major shift or change."[46] "For all of us, meaning is a reflection of the love we have for those we have lost. Meaning is the sixth stage of grief, the stage where the healing often resides."[47] "Your loss is not a test, a lesson, something to handle, a gift, or a blessing. Loss is simply what happens to you in life. Meaning is what *you* make happen."[48] "When you are drowning in sorrow, meaning becomes a life raft."[49] So, if we were to compile a dictionary entry for the word *meaning* as Kessler uses it, here are a few possible sub-definitions: "benefit" (finding gratitude), "understanding" (realizing the brevity of life), "evidence of our love," "an adjustment in our understanding" (what you make happen).

I repeat, maybe it doesn't matter if a fussy observer can't discern a clear definition of the word *meaning*, or finds many different definitions, or can't quite figure out for many of those definitions why and how the word *meaning*, instead of some other word or collection of words, fits. In fact, maybe a fussy observer *should not be able* to discern a clear definition. Even the Davis study starts out with an acceptance of *meaning* apparently in the broad sense of thing-to-be-found-for-comfort-during-grieving and *then* moves on to introduce a construal that happens to conform partially to the original sense of *meaning*. Since there does not appear to be an extensive literature devoted to how patients and clients understand this word in the world of psychotherapy and grief counseling, let alone a literature devoted to how the reading public understands it in the world of self-help, we seem to have little choice but to look at the results, while hazarding a few guesses about the *range* of meanings of *meaning* and speculating on why *meaning* might properly resonate in these worlds.

My unscientific conjecture is that the Davis study provides an important clue. Given the history that I've covered so far, it's safe to say that by the time such figures as Tillich and, particularly, Frankl have made inroads into the popular consciousness of an English-speaking country such as the United States, the association of *meaning* with value, grand metaphysical truth, supreme being, and, above all, purpose is already pretty solid. But in the world of psychotherapy and counseling, where the fundamental challenge is to relieve suffering—whether from common anxieties that afflict people in comfortable circumstances or from traumatic events on a grand scale—and where an important component of relief is some sort of understanding, *meaning*, with its connotation of explanation, understanding, answer, signified thing, fits the bill.

Then why not just say "explanation"? Because *meaning* carries a bonus: the polyvalence and ambiguity that allow it to point tenuously at a whole collection of sub-senses that it has accumulated over a couple of centuries.

9

Meaning Bridges the Secular and the Sacred

Secularization/Secularity/Secularism

There is a group of words that have haunted the pages of debates and conversations about religion in the United States for decades: *secularization*, *secularity*, and *secularism*. The first is broadly understood as referring to the process by which members of a society lose or abandon conventional religious faith; the second refers to the condition that results from the loss of religious faith; and the third generally refers to a worldview from which religious faith is missing. Loss or absence of religious faith is the common element. Much has been written in recent decades about secularization/secularity/secularism. Not surprisingly, those who comment on what they see as an increasingly secular United States require a new terminology for the type of thinking that characterizes what they regard as a secular worldview. And guess which terms top the list: *meaning* and *purpose*, often as if they were a single word.

Secularization and its consequences are the subject of Charles Taylor's *A Secular Age* (2007), which I briefly mentioned in the Introduction. I don't dare attempt to summarize the contents of this long, often brilliant, but exasperating book. Weighing in at close to nine hundred pages, it is, as UC Berkeley historian Martin Jay accurately put it in a review, "maddeningly prolix, repetitive, and haphazardly organized."[1] But for our purposes, here is what I think Taylor was trying to get at.

As the title suggests, we are living in a secular age. So, to begin with, who are "we"? The opening paragraph, where Taylor answers this question, will give you a good sense of the challenges that readers of this book face:

> What does it mean to say that we live in a secular age? Almost everyone would agree that in some sense we do: I mean the "we" who live in the West, or perhaps Northwest, or otherwise put, the North Atlantic

What Do We Mean When We Talk About Meaning? Steven Cassedy, Oxford University Press. © Oxford University Press 2022. DOI: 10.1093/oso/9780190936907.003.0010

world—although secularity extends also partially, and in different ways, beyond this world. And the judgment of secularity seems hard to resist when
we compare these societies with anything else in human history: that is,
with almost all other contemporary societies (e.g., Islamic countries, India,
Africa), on one hand; and with the rest of human history, Atlantic or otherwise, on the other.[2]

Yes, that's pretty vague, and regrettably it's characteristic of Taylor's writing,
which continually invites you to just kind of catch on to what the author
is trying to say. Taylor writes from his home country, Canada, but we can
safely say that this "we" includes the United States. His explanation of what
he means by *secular* or, rather, *secularity* might also come across as a bit
imprecise, but it's very much what I've been discussing here. Secularity for
Taylor consists not simply in "the falling off of religious belief and practice,
in people turning away from God, and no longer going to Church." That, he
says, is roughly what has happened in much of western Europe. A broader
sense includes the United States, which, as Taylor claims, is "the Western society with the highest statistics for religious belief and practice." "The shift to
secularity," he writes, "consists, among other things, of a move from a society
where belief in God is unchallenged and indeed, unproblematic, to one in
which it is understood to be one option among others, and frequently not the
easiest to embrace." Further, he writes, "the change I want to define and trace
is one which takes us from a society in which it was virtually impossible not
to believe in God, to one in which faith, even for the staunchest believer, is
one human possibility among others."[3]

In order to make his case, Taylor draws a contrast between this current,
secularized world and what came before it. It isn't enough to say something
as glib and pedestrian as "In the old days everyone believed in God, but
now that's changed." Instead, Taylor sets up an opposition between an older
world, of roughly five hundred years ago, which was *enchanted* and the present one, which is *disenchanted*, a pair of opposites whose source is German
sociologist Max Weber (about whom more in a moment). The enchanted
world of the past, Taylor writes, "is the world of spirits, demons, and moral
forces which our ancestors lived in." In that enchanted world, Taylor claims,
the human self was "porous," that is, susceptible to penetration by the spirits,
demons, and moral forces that surrounded it. In the modern, disenchanted
world, the self is "buffered," that is, the self is able to throw up a barrier between the mind and the outside world.

Whatever the merits of this distinction, the discussion soon comes to focus on *meaning*, and this is where things get interesting—and rather confusing. Here's how Taylor starts out explaining what sets the disenchanted apart from the enchanted: the disenchanted world is one in which "the only locus of thoughts, feelings, spiritual élan is what we call minds; the only minds in the cosmos are those of humans . . . and minds are bounded, so that these thoughts, feelings, etc., are situated 'within' them." In characteristic fashion, Taylor realizes he needs to clarify all of this, so, also in characteristic fashion, he offers this new, equally meandering explanation (which includes the passage I quoted in the Introduction):

> What am I gesturing at with the expression "thoughts, etc."? I mean, of course, the perceptions we have, as well as the beliefs or propositions which we hold or entertain about the world and ourselves. But I also mean our responses, the significance, importance, meaning, we find in things. I want to use for these the generic term 'meaning,' even though there is in principle a danger of confusion with linguistic meaning. Here I'm using it in the sense in which we talk about "the meaning of life," or of a relationship as having great "meaning" for us. Now the crucial difference between the mind-centred [that is, disenchanted] view and the enchanted world emerges when we look at meanings in this sense. On the former view meanings are "in the mind," in the sense that things only have the meaning they do in that they awaken a certain response in us, and this has to do with our nature as creatures who are thus capable of such responses, which means creatures with feelings, with desires, aversions, i.e., beings endowed with minds, in the broadest sense.[4]

The initial definition of *meaning* is certainly confusing in its own right, as I mentioned in the Introduction. But what is more confusing is that, having defined it in this way, Taylor appears immediately to use the word in a rather different sense. It's *not* "linguistic meaning," he insists, leading us to think that it has nothing to do with signifying; it's *meaning* (singular), as in "the meaning of life." And he appears to be distinguishing simple perceptions of and beliefs about the world from, perhaps, how we judge those things (significance, importance). But then suddenly there are *meanings* (plural) in the mind and things that have *meanings*. The *meanings* (plural) that "things" have cannot possibly be the same as the *meaning* (singular) that life has. These meanings that things have sound much more like *significations* and *explanations*, especially since we're drawing such a large distinction between how the enchanted mind *understood* things (in the past) and how the disenchanted mind *understands* things (today). What do things mean? How do they make sense? How can I explain them? Is it all about spirits and demons? Yes, if I'm living in the enchanted world. No, if I'm living in the disenchanted world. There, my buffered mind, rather than being invaded by spirits and demons, is able to grasp the explanations of modern science, even though I am not, say, a physicist. As Taylor writes of the disenchanted world, "On the naive level, I have no experience of the molecular constitution of things. But that is no bar to my believing what I am taught in physics class. Only these beliefs have a certain specific locus in my picture of the world; I know that they are available to me only through a complex theoretical activity of search, which has been carried through by others."[5]

The source of the term *disenchantment* is a famous lecture, subsequently published as an essay (1919), by Max Weber (1864–1920), titled "Science as Vocation" ("Wissenschaft als Beruf"). The title is misleading, for the essay, while nominally about the German university system, is really about roughly the same distinction Taylor makes between a much older understanding of the world and the current (for Weber) understanding, based in science. Weber made the ingenious claim that, paradoxically, primitive people "knew" more about their world than we do, that is, in the sense that they had ready explanations (though false and irrational to our modern-day minds) for what they observed around them. By contrast, Weber asks, in the modern world who can explain in detail, without preparation, how a streetcar works? But the difference is that in the modern world, "if one merely *wanted to*, one *could* always come to know it in such a way that in principle there would be no secret, incalculable forces that come into play, that rather in principle one could through *calculation gain mastery over* all things." And here is where he introduces the term that had such an impact on Taylor and others. "But this means: the disenchantment of the world," he wrote.[6] The German word, *Entzauberung*, might more accurately be translated as "demagification" (if such a word existed in English), since it denotes specifically the removal of magic (*Zauber*). Once I gain the confidence that allows me to know that all things will yield to a scientific explanation, even though I myself lack the expertise in many instances to supply such an explanation, then the world is devoid of both magic and the corresponding confidence that allowed those living in a magical world to know that magic is what causes otherwise incomprehensible things to happen.

But, said Weber, our confidence comes at a price. "Does 'progress' as such," he asks, "have a recognizable meaning [*Sinn*] that goes beyond the merely technical, such that thereby service to it becomes a meaningful [*sinnvoll*] calling?"[7] At an even more fundamental level, Weber suggests, is the error that the natural sciences commit in presupposing that "the ultimate laws of cosmic happening are worth [*wert*] knowing" in the first place, either for practical reasons or for their own sake. This presupposition, Weber says, "is itself simply not demonstrable. Even less demonstrable is whether this world that it [science] describes is worthy of existing, whether this world has a 'meaning' [*Sinn*], whether existing in it has any meaning [*Sinn*]."[8] Given the connotations that the German *Sinn* had accrued by the time Weber spoke (and wrote) these words, especially the association with *value* (are the laws *worth* knowing?—*Wert* as a noun means "value"), it is not difficult to grasp what he was asking. Do our lives have something of value now because we fancy that we, as humans, have the capacity to explain all that we see?

Weber has given a concrete example to illustrate what he means by *Sinn* or, to be more precise, *sinnlos* (meaningless): the works of Tolstoy, where we see in stark relief how the cultured life, which is to say the life of the privileged, with their access to education and therefore to the notion of scientific progress, can find no meaning in as profound and ultimate an experience as death. The big question for Tolstoy, Weber thought, was "whether death is a meaningful [*sinnvoll*] phenomenon or not." And Tolstoy's answer, Weber thought, was "for the man of culture, no. And the reason, of course, is that the civilized life, the individual life extended out into 'progress,' into the infinite, by its own immanent meaning [*Sinn*] is supposed to have no end. For there is always another progress [that is, another step forward in the quest for scientific understanding] that lies before the one who is standing there; no one who dies stands at the peak that lies in infinity." Death for Tolstoy is thus a "meaningless occurrence [*eine sinnlose Begebenheit*]."[9] Tolstoy, we saw, generally wondered about the meaning of *life*, especially in the face of death, but Weber is certainly right to implicate culture—with the understanding, of course, that culture includes not only nice clothes, refined manners, and lots of money but also a secular, scientific education—as the force that, according to Tolstoy, is responsible for rendering life and, by extension, death meaningless (or senseless, or valueless). Though Weber does not pursue the point, presumably in Tolstoy the world of magic would be represented by illiterate, earthy, and therefore wise peasants of the sort that enlighten the author's landowning gentlemen heroes on the meaning of life (of course these peasants themselves are not sufficiently advanced to formulate thoughts that include such phrases as "the meaning of life," those thoughts and phrases existing only for the masters).

This is fairly simple. Compare it with the muddle that Taylor has offered, where the disenchanted, buffered self has an array of options that includes not only the scientific worldview that Weber described but also belief in God. And, as for *meaning* or *meanings*, Taylor at first tells us that they reside in the buffered, disenchanted mind but not in the porous, enchanted mind. But then, in a number of places, Taylor returns to a more conventional use of the word *meaning*, one closely aligned with Weber's *Sinn*. He writes, for example, about "the search for meaning," particularly in connection with religion. Toward the end of the book, he introduces a section by writing, "My aim in the last pages has been to raise a number of ways in which our modern culture is restless at the barriers of the human sphere. I have mentioned: the search for meaning, the deepening of our sense of life through our contact with nature and art, death as a denial of the significance of love, but also death as an escape from the confines of life, to the paramount vantage point in which life shows its meaning."[10] At one point, he even asserts (accurately) that "the issue about meaning is a central preoccupation of our age."[11] In a contribution commissioned for an edited, multiauthor collection of essays called *The Joy of Secularism* (2011), Taylor reprinted a long excerpt from *A Secular Age* but added a new concept, that of "reenchantment"—no doubt in keeping with the theme of the volume (that there is joy to be found in secularism). If we wish to find reenchantment, Taylor suggests, we must do so by restoring the *meanings* that used to be there when the world was enchanted. The big question, one that Weber raised but that Taylor had not really raised in his book, was whether disenchantment has "voided the universe of any human meaning." The key to rediscovering enchantment, he maintains, is to rediscover a "sense of awe and wonder." Most important, he thinks, is to avoid "a reductive account of human life" (by which he means a strictly scientific account).[12] These uses appear to be something quite different from what he intended in the passage about the meanings we find in things. I'm at a loss to reconcile Taylor's various uses and senses of *meaning*. Perhaps it's sufficient to say that he has highlighted some of the paradoxes and questions that a secular age presents, while also showing how almost automatically the term *meaning* arises in a discussion of those paradoxes and questions.

Whether or not we agree with what we take to be Taylor's analysis and description of our secular age, we can certainly agree that, even in the United

States, we increasingly live in one. This circumstance has spawned an enormous number of books that offer further commentary on our secular age and, more often than not, advice on how to live in that age. *Humanism*, a concept closely aligned with secularism, shows up frequently as an alternative to conventional religion. A very small sampling: Greg Epstein, humanist chaplain (yes, there is such a thing) at Harvard and MIT, one of whose specialties, as listed on the Harvard chaplain website, is "meaning and purpose beyond religion," wrote *Good Without God: What a Billion Nonreligious People* Do *Believe* (2009), including a chapter on the meaning of life. A. C. Grayling, a professor of philosophy at the New College of the Humanities in London, has written *The God Argument: The Case Against Religion and for Humanism* (2013). Grayling includes a chapter on "the good life," which he defines as "the well-lived, meaningful, fulfilled life." *Meaning* for Grayling is "the set of values and their associated goals that give a life its shape and direction."[13] Journalist Katherine Ozment is the author of *Grace Without God: The Search for Meaning, Purpose, and Belonging in a Secular Age* (2016), which lists "meaning and purpose" as a single item in the index and contains dozens of references to *meaning*, both with and without *purpose*—but with no definition. Elizabeth Drescher, who teaches religious studies at Santa Clara University, has written *Choosing Our Religion: The Spiritual Lives of America's Nones* (2016) ("nones" meaning the religiously unaffiliated, that is, those who would check the box marked "none" in response to the survey question "What is your religious affiliation?"). Drescher has found through extensive interviews with the unaffiliated that many of them are indeed searching for and finding spiritual experiences outside conventional religious belief and practice. She discovered that the group divided themselves into twelve different categories, including "Atheist," "Weak Agnostic," "Strong Agnostic," and, toward the end of the list, "All of the Above," defined as "someone who understands existential meaning-making as moving throughout life through different modes of spiritual, religious, or non-religious self-understanding."[14]

Philip Kitcher, a highly respected philosopher at Columbia University, has offered a remarkably thoughtful and sensitive account of religion, and secular humanism as an alternative to religion, in *Life After Faith: The Case for Secular Humanism* (2014). Like quite a few (but not all) recent proponents of worldviews that can be alternatives to those of conventional religious faith, Kitcher started out religious and lost his faith. For some with a similar story, the early religious life, often characterized as brutally imposed by parents, clergy, or both, produces an almost violent animus toward religion of all sorts. Kitcher is different. In the preface to *Life After Faith*, he tells us that despite having repeatedly, over the years, sought to explain why he no longer finds religious doctrines to be credible, "I resist the now dominant atheist idea that religion is noxious rubbish to be buried as deeply, as thoroughly, and as quickly as possible."[15]

Nonetheless, the aim of Kitcher's book is to present secular humanism as a preferable alternative to religion. I'll skip over the chapters that broadly characterize religious belief and practice and focus on the one in which *meaning* plays the most prominent role. The title is "Mortality and Meaning," and the aim is to show that on matters of life and death, particularly death, secularism has more to offer than religion. Kitcher presents the issue as a choice between the life everlasting that religion promises (or that some religions promise) and the alternative that a secular outlook can present—namely, a successful quest for a meaningful life. The way Kitcher sees it, our fear of death (and, for the religious, the consequent desire to live eternally) stems not so much from a fear of death itself as from a fear of *premature* death. Here is how he puts it: "Deaths count as premature when they prevent lives from attaining meaning: the challenges of mortality and meaning connect. But aren't all deaths premature? Can any finite life be meaningful?"[16]

What is *meaning*, and what is a meaningful life? While Kitcher never defines *meaning*, he does speak of how meaning gets conferred and attained. Like many others who write about meaning and the meaning of life, Kitcher associates meaning with *mattering*. "Human lives," he writes, "sometimes attain meaning through individuals' developing conceptions of who they are and what matters to their existences, through their pursuit of the goals endorsed by those conceptions, and by some degree of success in attaining them."[17] Meaning is not unique to the secular, humanist point of view. Religion has it too—or at least religion as a secularist such as Kitcher sees it. The difference lies in what *confers* it. "Mattering to others is what counts in conferring meaning. . . . For the religious challenger, no set of characteristics of finite lives, or of relations among finite lives, can substitute for the connection to the transcendent that alone confers meaning and value."[18] So, that's the difference: "mattering to others" (secular humanists) vs. "connection to the transcendent" (religious folks). Kitcher reiterates the point after describing how, for secular folks, ordinary lives can attain meaning in small, local ways. But not for the religious: "Religious people might concede that the features I have focused on mark differences among human lives, while denying that they can confer meaning. Detached from any connection to the transcendent, these features, however richly present, are always insufficient. . . . Without filiations to something transcending human life, no amount of the qualities secularists prize could achieve real significance. No link to the transcendent, no meaning."[19] So, meaning appears not to be the exclusive property of the secular; the secular simply have better (more meaningful?) meaning than religious people.

Charles Taylor, a practicing Catholic, has approached our secular age with a sense of regret over something that has allegedly been lost: the enchantment of a bygone era "in which it was virtually impossible not to believe in God." The other writers I have just discussed accept the secular world as a given—at least for those who themselves are secular—and, on the supposition, explicit or implicit, that something is missing, explore options for life in such a world. If *meaning* and *purpose* invariably show up in these discussions as what we need to find if we no longer have, or never had, conventional religious faith, it appears to be because of a widely held assumption that a need to find meaning and purpose is universal: if you're conventionally religious, you find meaning and purpose in the core ideas of your faith, and if you're not, your task is to find them elsewhere.

Meaning Becomes an Outreach Tool Among the Conventionally Religious

Meaning has been pervasive in the works of conventionally religious writers (in addition to Tillich, Niebuhr, and Heschel) since the mid-twentieth century—and often not in any of the specialized theological senses that we find in those writers. Here are some examples.

The Catholic Church Discovers the Power of Meaning

It might come as a surprise to some, for example, that, beginning with Pope Paul VI (pontificate 1963–1978), who assumed his position during the Second Vatican Council (after the sudden death of John XXIII), the official papal decrees of every single pope down to the present (with the exception of John Paul I, whose papacy lasted only thirty-three days, in 1978) have been richly filled with the word *meaning* and the phrase "meaning of life" (or equivalent in other languages). And what is remarkable about the decrees of all the popes, from Paul VI to Francis, is how much the references to meaning appear to mimic the popular usage in psychotherapy and self-help manuals, as if the popes felt the need to reach those Catholics for whom conventional theological terms had become literally, well, meaningless. This is hardly surprising, given that the Council represented, to many, the triumph of ecumenicalism over parochialism and lay inclusiveness over hierarchical authority.[20]

I won't give a lengthy list, but if we take a look at a few examples, we can see the extent to which the meaning of life, of existence, of reality found a comfortable place in official proclamations on the most serious topics confronting the Church. *Gaudiam et spes* (Joy and hope, 1965) is one of the four Apostolic Constitutions of the Second Vatican Council and is devoted to the mission of the Church in the modern world. Owing to the year of its promulgation, it is attributed to Paul VI. I should mention that the extent to which an individual pope is involved in the actual composition of a particular decree varies considerably depending both on the type of decree and on the pope. An Apostolic Constitution is by its very nature a collective enterprise, especially in this case, since the document was designed to reflect the collective wisdom of the bishops who had been brought together for the recently concluded Council (1962–1965). An additional complicating factor, when it comes to language and style, is that while the official version of all decrees is the one published in Latin, decrees, up till John Paul II, were generally composed in Italian (though other languages are possible, given the diversity of nations from which bishops and others are drawn) and then translated into Latin. The official translations that the Vatican issues in other languages have generally been made from that Latin version. In the case of *Gaudiam et spes*, it would be difficult to assign responsibility to particular individuals for particular phrases, and yet it's noteworthy that we find in it the word and phrases that had become so common in English and other European languages in the middle of the twentieth century. The role of the Church in the world, we read, is directly linked to *meaning*: "Since it has been entrusted to the Church to reveal the mystery of God, Who is the ultimate goal of man," the bishops wrote, "she [the Church] opens up to man at the same time the meaning of his own existence, that is, the innermost truth about himself. . . . For man will always yearn to know, at least in an obscure way, what is the meaning of his life, of his activity, of his death."[21]

Six years after *Gaudiam et spes*, Paul VI issued what was probably his most controversial decree, the encyclical *Humanae vitae* (Of human life). Rejecting the recommendation of the Pontifical Commission on Birth Control, which met periodically from 1963 to 1966 and, by an overwhelming majority, endorsed the approval of artificial birth control, Pope Paul reaffirmed traditional Church teaching. The passage containing the very core of the argument against birth control includes an explicit nod to the modern linguistic usage. People must recognize, we read, "that an act of mutual love which impairs the capacity to transmit life which God the Creator, through specific laws, has built into it, frustrates His design which constitutes the norm of marriage, and contradicts the will of the Author of life. Hence to use this divine gift while depriving it, even if only partially, of its meaning and purpose [*significationem et finem*], is equally repugnant to the nature of man and of woman, and is consequently in opposition to the plan of God and His holy will."[22]

John Paul II (1978–2005) presents an exceptional case among the Bishops of Rome. First, he came to the papacy with a rich corpus of philosophical work, written in Polish, from the time of his youth and not always on strictly theological topics. Second, he tended to author his own encyclicals—again, in Polish. Here the process was (1) a Polish original, which was (2) translated into Latin, and from there (3) translated into the other languages in which the Vatican released official papal decrees. So, John Paul's encyclicals can largely be considered his own compositions. In addition, more than his predecessors and more than his immediate successor (Benedict XVI), John Paul appears to have sought a personal and universal tone in his official writings. A papal encyclical opens with a salutation to its addressees—all members of the Church hierarchy down to the clergy. In some instances, before John Paul, this list was followed by the phrase "and to all Men of Good Will," suggesting that the intended readership included laypeople. John Paul's principal encyclicals fall into this category, though by 1978, when he became pope, he saw the need to reword the phrase so as to include women: "to all men and women of good will," intending a readership even beyond the Catholic Church.[23]

John Paul made frequent use of the word *meaning* and the phrase "meaning of life." Writing in a popular and accessible style for an all-inclusive readership in his encyclicals, he generally steered clear of technical and esoteric theological concepts and issues, preferring instead to discuss familiar Christian notions in such a way that they would be easily comprehensible not only to a lay Catholic but also, presumably, to any non-Catholic man or woman "of good will." The pope used his first encyclical, *Redemptor hominis* (Redeemer of man), to introduce himself to the Church and to the world. It is distinguished by its intimately personal style (he tells a bit of his own life story) and by the choice of familiar and basic Christian ideas, which the pontiff explains in this same informal style. At one point, he writes of the "deep amazement at man's worth and dignity," adding that one name for this amazement is *Christianity*. There follows his simple explanation of the central place of redemption and sin in Catholicism: "Unceasingly contemplating the whole of Christ's mystery, the Church knows with all the certainty of faith that the Redemption that took place through the Cross has definitively restored his dignity to man and given back meaning to his life in the world, a meaning that was lost to a considerable extent because of sin."[24] Such language, I'm confident, would have been incomprehensible to a nineteenth-century pope. And, a little farther on: "In Christ and through Christ God has revealed himself fully to mankind and has definitively drawn close to it; at the same time, in Christ and through Christ man has acquired full awareness of his dignity, of the heights to which he is raised, of the surpassing worth of his own humanity, and of the meaning of his existence."[25] As in the world of self-help and psychotherapy, there is no attempt to explain such phrases as "the meaning of his existence"; John Paul appeared to assume that everyone would simply get it.

Among John Paul's most significant decrees, addressing such sensitive issues as sexuality, birth control, abortion, and capital punishment, were the apostolic exhortation (a missive, less formal than an encyclical, to the entire Catholic Church) *Familiaris consortio* (official English title: "On the Role of the Christian Family in the Modern World," 1981) and the encyclical *Evangelium vitae* (The gospel of life, 1995). The former, clearly written at what the pontiff regarded as a moment of decline in morality, includes this pronouncement: "It becomes necessary, therefore, on the part of all, to recover an awareness of the primacy of moral values, which are the values of the human person as such. The great task that has to be faced today for the renewal of society is that of recapturing the ultimate meaning of life [*significatio ultima vitae*] and its fundamental values."[26] And, in the latter decree: "Human life, as a gift of God, is sacred and inviolable. For this reason procured abortion [as distinguished from "indirect" abortion, where a fetus that cannot survive outside the womb is evacuated as the result of an otherwise permissible medical procedure] and euthanasia are absolutely unacceptable. Not only must human life not be taken, but it must be protected with loving concern. The meaning of life is found in giving and receiving love [*significationem suam invenit vita*, literally, "life finds its meaning"], and in this light human sexuality and procreation reach their true and full significance [*veritatem*, "truth"]."[27]

More recently, Pope Francis (2013–), who famously takes a collaborative approach to his official decrees, had this to say about the Incarnation, in the encyclical *Lumen fidei* (The light of faith): "Far from divorcing us from reality, our faith in the Son of God made man in Jesus of Nazareth enables us to grasp reality's deepest meaning [*altissimam eius significationem*, "its highest meaning"] and to see how much God loves this world and is constantly guiding it towards himself."[28] And later, in a passage that, *mutatis mutandis*, sounds a little like Viktor Frankl: "Christians know that suffering cannot be eliminated, yet it can have meaning [*sensum suscipere posse*, "can receive sense/meaning"] and become an act of love and entrustment into the hands of God who does not abandon us; in this way it can serve as a moment of growth in faith and love."[29]

Meaning as a Vehicle for Evangelizing

What about the world of evangelical Christianity? In the Introduction, I mentioned Rick Warren and *The Purpose Driven Life*. Pastor Warren, I said, appears to equate *meaning* with *purpose* and uses the two words together as one phrase a couple of times. *Meaning* is ubiquitous in his book. Even apart from the frequent occurrence of this word, *The Purpose Driven Life* reads very much like a self-help manual, which is essentially what it is. Emily Esfahani Smith urges us to look for meaning in a highly ecumenical list of "pillars." Tony Robbins urges us simply to find it, in *anything*, so that we can acquire wealth "in its deepest sense." Pastor Warren instructs us to find meaning in God alone, and not within ourselves or elsewhere. This advice is fully consistent with the role of an evangelizing leader: the self-help he urges us to accept consists quite naturally in committing ourselves to God. Early in the book, he appears to be mindful of his competition in this publishing genre, mindful, that is, of the possibility that some of his readers might already have been looking for *meaning*, but in the wrong places—in secular places or in various forms of non-Christian metaphysical thought. "Contrary to what many popular books, movies, and seminars tell you," he writes, "you won't discover your life's meaning by looking within yourself. You have probably tried that already. . . . It is only in God that we discover our origin, our identity, our meaning, our purpose, our significance, and our destiny. Every other path leads to a dead end."[30] And a bit later in the book: "Knowing your purpose gives meaning to your life. We were made to have meaning. This is why people try dubious methods, like astrology or psychics, to discover it. When life has meaning, you can bear almost anything; without it, nothing is bearable. . . . Without God, life has no purpose, and without purpose, life has no meaning. Without meaning, life has no significance or hope."[31]

There are dozens and dozens of Christian websites that offer explanations of the meaning of life. A constant theme running through them is the contrast between secular views and the Christian view. Christianity.com, for example, features a page under the title "What Is the True Meaning of Life? Finding Your Purpose in Life from the Creator of Life." "We, humans," the author begins, "are born in this world without knowing exactly who we are (*identity*), where we come from (*origin*), why we are here (*meaning*), what to live for and how we should live (*purpose*), and where we are going (*destiny*)." The very first topic is "Secular and Christian Views on the Meaning of Life." Here the author dismisses popular, secular conceptions of the meaning of life ("Love. Wealth. Happiness. Self-development. Wisdom. Influence. Service") as inadequate and then moves on to a list of biblical passages that purport to show us what the meaning actually is. Once again, nowhere in the Jewish scriptures or the New Testament is there any word that might be translated as *meaning*, but if *meaning* means "purpose" or "goal," then there is no shortage of passages that could be adduced as answers to the modern question "What is the meaning of life?"

Meaning as an Outreach Tool in a Hassidic Sect

Meaning shows up in contemporary Judaism as well—and in a place that few of us would expect. Chabad-Lubavitch is a movement within Hassidic Judaism. To the outside world, it is distinctive for its outreach activities—especially its outreach to less observant fellow Jews, with the aim of attracting them to Orthodox forms of observance. You may have observed young male members of the movement positioned on busy sidewalks in neighborhoods known to have a significant Jewish population, asking passersby, "Excuse me, are you Jewish?"—in the hope of starting a conversation and perhaps inviting them to join a Sabbath dinner at the home of an observant family. Chabad represents a centuries-old rabbinical dynasty, the most renowned recent figure in which was Rabbi (*Rebbe* in Yiddish) Menachem Mendel Schneerson (1902–1994). The Rebbe wrote prolifically, but he taught primarily by means of Sabbath-day *farbrengens* (gatherings) at which he would speak in Yiddish (the lingua franca of Hassidic Judaism) for several hours to his devoted followers. So revered was he that his home synagogue in Crown Heights, Brooklyn, the global headquarters of the Chabad movement, arranged to have a group of "reviewers" attend his *farbrengens* for the purpose of transcribing his discourses. Because Jewish law forbids writing or using recording devices on the Sabbath, the reviewers were required to memorize verbatim the entire contents of the Rebbe's talks, in order to write them down once the Sabbath was over.

One such reviewer was Rabbi Simon Jacobson, who spent years of his life heading up the group responsible for transcribing and publishing Rabbi Schneerson's talks. Today Rabbi Jacobson runs the Meaningful Life Center (MLC), adjacent to the global headquarters building. In 1995, he published *Toward a Meaningful Life*, which he describes in the book's introduction as "a practical distillation of the philosophy of Rabbi Menachem Mendel Schneerson"—which is to say that most of the contents were written by Jacobson, with a few direct quotations from Schneerson (translated from Yiddish).[32] Not surprisingly, given the title, the book is filled with references to *meaning*. One of the passages directly attributed to Schneerson is this: "The rebellion of youth must be directed against the status quo and toward the sublime, toward G-d [Orthodox Jews do not spell out in full the name of the deity], and toward a higher meaning."[33] In the judgment of Jacobson, *meaning* exists at the very core of the great Rebbe's teachings.

A primary concept in those teachings is the distinction and relationship between the body, dominated by the senses, and the soul. The idea is that life, true life, is independent of the senses. "So we are fully alive without our senses," Jacobson writes, channeling the thought of Schneerson. "Without the soul, though, there is no life. Yes, there is the bodily struggle to survive, but life as we understand it is all about the pursuit of meaning, the search for our soul, the quest for G-d."[34] Ideally body and soul exist in harmony: "This harmony between your body and soul carries over to the world at large, helping unite the body and soul, the matter and spirit, of the entire universe. The key to meaning and happiness in your life, then, lies in your own hands: understanding the symmetry and rhythm of your own body and soul."[35] The Rebbe spoke, too, about wanting "a world with meaning and a value system," about young people who are "hungry for meaning," about "finding a deeper meaning in everything you do."[36] It would of course be dishonest and deceptive to remove these remarks completely from their larger context, but what first struck me about them is how little, taken by themselves, they appear to depend on specifically Jewish religious ideas. While Schneerson (again, as presented by Jacobson) mentions God, refers from time to time to passages from the Jewish scriptures, and cites famous rabbis, the conception of the human person he presents, it seemed to me, could easily be derived from any number of religious, non-theistic, or vaguely "spiritual" belief systems.

So, what about Rabbi Jacobson himself? As I examined the MLC's website, I was struck right away by how much of it appeared to bear no connection with what I had always assumed to be Chabad beliefs and practices or, for that matter, with Judaism at all. *Meaning* and *meaningful* are, of course, all over the place. Photographic images on the site show attractive young people bearing no signs of any religious affiliation—and certainly not the garb of Hassidic Jews. From time to time, you encounter a statement that the principles being taught at the MLC are based in Torah, but there is no mention (at least that I could find) of the strict rules that govern Orthodox Jewish life—or, for that matter, of the less stringent rules that govern even non-Orthodox Jewish life. Torah appears to be simply a universally applicable source of wisdom, good advice, and . . . meaning. I was puzzled and intrigued, so I interviewed Rabbi Jacobson (by Zoom).

To begin with, I wondered what Yiddish word Schneerson had used that Jacobson translated into English as *meaning*. After thinking for a moment, he gave me four: *meynung*, corresponding to German *Meinung*, "intention"; *tsil*, corresponding to German *Ziel*, "goal" or "purpose"; *takhles*, a Hebrew word (*takhlit*, as pronounced in modern Hebrew) that could be translated principally as "purpose," but also as "the main point" or "serious business" (in the Jewish scriptures, it signifies "end," "limit," "perfection"); and *kavone*, a Hebrew word (*kavanah*, as pronounced in modern Hebrew) meaning "intention," "devotion," a state of mind reached during prayer. I thought that none of those would readily be translated into English as *meaning*, nor does any Yiddish-English or Hebrew-English dictionary include *meaning* among the English equivalents of these words. So, unless we are understanding *meaning* exclusively in the vaguely understood metaphysical senses that we've been examining, it's not the word that would immediately come to mind when you came across these four words. If Yiddish were to follow German, its closest modern linguistic cousin, the word would be *zinen*, corresponding to German *Sinn* and suggesting the "sense" of a word (thus signification), a "sense" for something, or something that "makes sense." But Rabbi Jacobson never mentioned this word as one that the Rebbe had used.

To say that the Rebbe developed a philosophy of *meaning* and that he spoke of a "meaningful life" is to make the assumption that *meynung, tsil, takhles,* and *kavone* (1) overlap considerably with each other and (2) mean what we English-speakers mean when we use such expressions as "the meaning of life," "searching for meaning," and "toward a meaningful life."

Rabbi Jacobson assured me that the Rebbe spoke English, that he had had plenty of conversations and had written plenty of letters in the language of his adopted homeland (he and his wife succeeded in immigrating to New York from Europe in 1941), and that he had frequently used the English words *meaning* and *purpose*. Still, to the extent that the Rebbe's wisdom was gleaned from his discourses and writings in Yiddish, as the bulk of it was for Jacobson's book, *meaning* clearly had to be the author's own choice. And why not? To him, a native speaker of English, the word covered the same terrain as the two Germanic words and the two weighty Hebrew words that he listed for me. And once he made this choice, *meaning* took on its life in the English-speaking world as the word occupying the center of Rebbe Schneerson's teaching, just as it did for Paul Tillich and Viktor Frankl (with the obvious difference that those two men themselves came to write in English and to accept the English word as the equivalent of German *Sinn*).

So, for purposes of the MLC, I wondered, where English is spoken, where clients might not encounter the name of the great Rebbe, what is Jacobson's own definition of the *English* word? His initial response was not helpful (I do not reproduce our conversation verbatim, though Rabbi Jacobson has vetted and approved the following paraphrases). Let's define it by contrast with its opposite (or negative), he said, that is, with the view that life has no meaning or significance, that everything is meaningless, that there is no purpose to life. Yes, I asked, but how do you define *meaning*? A meaningful life, he answered, is one that has a purpose, a life filled with cosmic and permanent significance. A meaningful life, he continued, is driven by the belief in a designer of life, the belief that each one of us was sent to this world with an indispensable mission. Just as an engineer builds an instrument and an artist paints a portrait, the divine architect built this world and every aspect of it with purpose and design. It therefore follows that a truly happy and fulfilling life is possible only when one actualizes and realizes his or her purpose. It is a life driven by direction and goals toward a specific objective and destination.

Once again, I thought, much of this, expressed in this way, is entirely unspecific to Judaism and must place the MLC's mission outside the boundaries of what is taught and practiced in a Chabad synagogue such as the one right next door. Is the MLC ecumenical? I asked. Do you accept clients regardless of faith or lack thereof? Yes, absolutely, he replied. Chabad has two elements to it: (1) its religious infrastructure, a shul (synagogue) and a school, which cater to Jews of all backgrounds, and (2) its universal philosophy, which addresses all people, including non-Jews, people of different faiths or no faith. The MLC focuses primarily on the second element, he said. Our goal is to present these teachings as a universal blueprint for life, leading our clients and all those interested toward a discovery of their own spiritual self. My jaw dropped. Really? I asked. Let me get this straight, then: if a lapsed Catholic comes to you and the quest for a spiritual center that she undertakes at the MLC results in her return to devout Catholicism, that, to you, is an acceptable outcome? Yes, he answered without a moment's hesitation. After all, he remarked, ours is not a proselytizing religion, so we wouldn't be asking non-Jews to convert to Judaism in any case. Our objective, he continued, is to help people of all backgrounds to find and cultivate their spiritual mission. He added jokingly that he's been accused in his community of being "the atheist rabbi." But it was important to understand that the element of universality came from Schneerson himself. As Jacobson put it in the introduction to his book, "While utterly faithful to Jewish tradition and law, the Rebbe presented the Torah's universal truths in an accessible and relevant manner, providing instruction to people of all races and all beliefs. The Rebbe put special emphasis on the obligation to adhere to the Seven Noahide Laws [those given to Adam and Noah before the revelation to Moses on Mount Sinai] and the universal code of morality and ethics that was given *to all humankind* at Sinai [the Ten Commandments]."[37]

Perhaps. But as I listened to Jacobson, I almost had the impression that the core of what's taught in the MLC, absent the explicit references to Torah, could have been conceived just as well by a "spiritual but not religious" thinker as by this Chabad rabbi. For those clients outside Judaism, it seemed to me, the references to Torah serve largely as confirmation and enhancement, not as foundation. And so here, I thought, was a consummate example of the power of *meaning* in the modern world. Its frequent refusal to attach itself uniquely to any particular body of beliefs allowed an adherent of one very distinctive body of beliefs to construct a methodology and a set of principles for his organization that feature a fully ecumenical reach.

This Highly Charged Bridge Word

I won't pretend to know exactly what motivated individual popes (and their collaborators), evangelical pastors, and a Hassidic rabbi to choose the word *meaning* and such phrases as "the meaning of life." But it strikes me that the function of the word and phrases is not difficult to detect. If the intended readership of the papal decrees includes ordinary Catholics and if, as evidenced by the very fact of the Second Vatican Council, the Church was struggling both to hold on to its faithful and to attract back into the fold those who had strayed, then it made sense to resort to this ambiguous word. For *meaning* had clearly come to straddle the divide between secularism and conventional religious belief—but to do so *because of* secularism. For those errant and doubting souls who have slipped into the realm of secular uncertainty and the secular smorgasbord of choices, *meaning* is the generic term capable of suggesting something of great value that lies outside the arid realm of empirical facts and scientific inquiry. The papal decree invites such souls to complete their search for *meaning* by returning to the Church. "You're looking for what you call meaning?" it appears to say. "Come back. You doubt, or you don't understand, the notions of redemption, of the Incarnation, of the sanctity of all human life? Let me explain it to you in terms that will make sense even to a secular mind such as yours."

The aim of the evangelical pastor, given the nature of evangelizing, is different. To be sure, the intended audience includes doubting souls who have wandered or lost their faith, but it is made up also of those who have not yet found that or perhaps any faith. How to explain to them what they will find if they join our numbers? Simply to use the conventional religious and theological terms is to reinforce the off-putting and foreign nature of those terms. But if we can promise something that is phrased in language they can understand, then perhaps we stand a chance of attracting them. "You're looking for what you call meaning?" the evangelical pastor appears to say. "We have what you're looking for, but it isn't something secular, nor is it the salad of unruly ideas you find in the metaphysics section of your bookstore."

As for Rabbi Jacobson, the devoted reviewer of Rabbi Schneerson, the emphasis on outreach led, with an apparently inexorable logic, to a self-help movement similar to the ones we've already looked at. The result? Just look at the mission statement: "The Meaningful Life Center (MLC) is a spiritual health center that empowers you to find meaning in everything you do, and discover your personal mission in life. Through a wide variety of live and

published programming, videos, webcasts, podcasts, articles and personally customized counseling and materials, the MLC offers you empowering
and potent life skills that improve every aspect of your life. From love and
relationships to work and finance, from fear and anxiety to joy and celebra-
tion, from birth to death [and] all life cycles in between, you can look forward to an exhilarating journey, which will both stimulate and provoke you
to actualize your enormous potential and reach unprecedented heights."[38] Is
there any mention of dietary laws or of Sabbath observance? No. Who would
ever guess that these words were penned by any religiously affiliated person,
let alone by a Chabad rabbi—something you learn only when you turn to a
separate page about Rabbi Simon Jacobson? And of course, as is universally
true in the self-help movement, *meaning* is never defined. On its face, this
looks like a *secular* philosophy.

Meaning, this gloriously ambiguous and polyvalent word, has now come
to serve as a kind of bridge. Religious writers appear to be saying, "If you're
looking for it under that name, you've probably approached it from the secular side—otherwise, why would you be using the word *meaning*? But over
here, on the side of religious faith, you can find what you've been looking
for—call it *meaning* if you like; it's just that it resides not in you, not in the
outside world, not in the world of astrology or psychics, but in the teachings
of our faith." Rabbi Jacobson takes an opposite tack: "It *does* reside in you,
whatever your faith and even if you have none." Small wonder that it's often
not defined at all or defined with such imprecision when it *is* defined. It
functions naturally—and better—when it's not.

Conclusion

The Marvel of *Meaning*

And so we return to where we began. I started this book with two central observations about the word *meaning* that struck me—and still do—as odd. First, almost no one ever pauses to define it. Second, when someone does pause to define it, the attempt almost always fails—that is, the proffered definition cannot simply be substituted for the word in any given sentence.

And yet, of all words, this one appears not only to function but to *flourish* in the absence of a conventional definition. Even providing several definitions can misleadingly suggest that in some instances the word means precisely one thing while in others it means some slightly different thing. No, even when *meaning* is held to carry several definitions and appears, in the work of a single person, to function differently in slightly different settings, those definitions bleed into each other in such a way that it's always a matter of differing emphases rather than distinct definitions.

Providing a definition freezes the word, actually prevents it from carrying out its mission. At least that's one, conventional way of looking at it. Another would be to say that it is precisely the slipperiness of the word that allows it to function the way it does. Its success is, in fact, the result of our inability to define it.

The ambiguity, polyvalence, and fluidity of this word mean that those who use it can't assume that their readers will understand it as carrying a certain precise set of nuances and sub-senses in one passage and another precise set in another passage. For one thing, it's far from evident that those who use this word have a clear notion of what they themselves intend to convey with it in a particular setting; for another, there are many forums in which they actually *rely* on individuals who hear or read this word to form understandings that are unique to *them*. We saw this in the case of psychotherapy, where we have no idea how each patient or subject understands survey questions that include the word *meaning* but where the therapist or researcher can point to the (presumably) measurable results—for confirmation not of the word's meaning but of its successful functioning. Does it really matter what terminal cancer patients think the word *meaning* means on questionnaires or in therapy sessions, if the use of the word in a therapeutic setting somehow leads to a hopeful attitude that provides them with a measure of comfort and even optimism?

Think of where this quintessentially modern word came from and the sub-senses it has accrued: "signification," "sense," "direction," "purpose," "value," "goal," "explanation," "thing that's missing when we experience existential anxiety," "what symbols point to," "grand metaphysical essence," and many more. Think of *how* it accrued all these senses. Its German precursor traveled through hazy forms of Romantic idealism, where the emphasis was on the mystery behind the veil separating two worlds, the alleged power of poets to penetrate the veil, and the consistent failure of the same poets to do so. If *Sinn* suggested signification and interpretation (and it didn't always or only do so), and if interpretation suggested the actual recovery of something concrete (as in Daniel: "God has numbered your kingdom and brought it to an end"), then actual interpretation never really took place, for the meaning had always "gone missing." It had to: how could a Romantic poet state that the "meaning/*Sinn* of the world is . . ." and finish the sentence?

But of course neither English *meaning* nor any of its precursors and rough equivalents in other languages consistently had to do exclusively with signifying and interpreting. *Meaning* became almost limitlessly suggestive. It became interchangeable with *purpose*, which is understandable, given the easy slippage from *meaning* (intending) something, to conceiving a purpose, to simply calling that purpose *meaning*. The word's various nuances and sub-senses, while often hazy and indeterminate, were, from the beginning, grand in scope. "Looking for meaning" almost never means looking for something small, and when, as in Emily Esfahani Smith's book, we discover meaning in small happenings, it's the happenings that are small, not the meaning. Meaning is big.

And so, it effortlessly became equivalent to various notions of the ultimate or absolute—God, for instance, or qualities that God possesses. The beautiful thing about the word in this role is that when you use it, you're specifically *not* naming the ultimate. Much as I've criticized the lack of precision in Charles Taylor's writing, I admire his phrase "gesturing at" ("What am I gesturing at with the expression 'thoughts, etc.'?").[1] It's what *meaning* does, thanks to its intrinsic fluidity, ambiguity, and polyvalence. And it's what makes it the quintessential modern word. When Rabbi Jacobson uses it, he's surely gesturing in part at G-d, but he's also gesturing at a whole array of notions, more and less concrete and limpid, that might dwell in the minds of the non-Jewish and, especially, the altogether non-religious—notions of which he himself may not be aware. How can he possibly guess the meaning whose discovery or rediscovery brings a particular lapsed Catholic back to Catholicism? When Rick Warren uses it, he's gesturing at some quality that both the religious and the non-religious seek, a quality that (in his view) exists in a superior form when you find it in God but that (he must assume) is nonetheless comprehensible to those who have not yet found their way to God. He surely can't know what conceptions of meaning the individual non-believers he targets might be entertaining as they consider whether to join his movement. When Philip Kitcher uses it, he's gesturing at an array of notions that include those of the conventionally religious (as he conceives them)—or that at least in some way capture elements common to the religious and the secular (again, as he conceives them).

And yet . . . I've repeatedly spoken of how *meaning* has strayed from its "primitive" meaning, which has to do with *signifying*. When it is closely paired with *purpose*, for example, as it so often is, it suggests a goal, the object of a quest of some sort. When God is renamed "ultimate meaning," the word suggests something infinitely grand. The question was "Why, then, use the word *meaning* if what you really mean is 'purpose,' or 'God'?" And the answer was that *meaning* carries around other associations that are perhaps missing in the words *purpose* and *God*—some intrinsic to it and others that it has accrued as part of the process that I've described in this book. But perhaps here is the place, at the end of the book, to say that we should not forget the primitive meaning of *meaning*, that is, "meaning" itself, the "thing signified" and the closely associated idea of interpreting. Nor should we forget the peculiar status of our English word as a verbal form: something or someone *means*, with everything that this suggests. The mere hint, when we speak of *meaning* in any of the grand senses that we've examined here, that there is something initially hidden being pointed to, that there is an answer or explanation waiting to be uncovered, that there is something *doing* the meaning or signifying, implying that we can exercise our interpretive faculties in at least an effort (even though the effort will almost certainly fail) to uncover that something, is, to a considerable extent, what gives this word the power, the promise, and the mystique that it holds.

Notes

Introduction

1. Tony Robbins, *Money, Master the Game: 7 Simple Steps to Financial Freedom* (New York: Simon & Schuster, 2014), 582.
2. Rick Warren, *The Purpose Driven Life: What on Earth Am I Here For?* (Grand Rapids, MI: Zondervan, 2002), 19.
3. Roy F. Baumeister et al., "Some Key Differences Between a Happy Life and a Meaningful Life," *Journal of Positive Psychology* 8, no. 6 (November 2013): 506 (preview).
4. Charles Taylor, *A Secular Age* (Cambridge, MA: Harvard University Press, 2007), 31. I have discussed the same passages from Taylor's *A Secular Age* and made similar remarks in "Where's the Joy in Secularism?," *The European Legacy* 18, no. 3 (2013): 245–257.
5. John Cottingham, *On the Meaning of Life* (London: Routledge, 2003), 1–15.
6. Terry Eagleton, *The Meaning of Life* (Oxford: Oxford University Press, 2007), 64, Eagleton's emphasis.
7. Dennis Ford, *The Search for Meaning: A Short History* (Berkeley: University of California Press, 2007), iv.
8. Thaddeus Metz, *Meaning in Life: An Analytic Study* (Oxford: Oxford University Press, 2013), 3–4.
9. The most substantial etymology I am aware of is the one in the *Oxford English Dictionary*, which gives the impression that the original, primitive sense of the Germanic forebears of English *to mean* has to do with human agency, as in Middle Dutch: "*mēnen* to intend, signify, think, hold a good opinion of, love." But the earliest examples listed under Branch I, "to intend," appear to be no older than those listed under Branch II, "to signify; to convey or carry a meaning, significance, consequence, etc."
10. Abraham Joshua Heschel, *Man Is Not Alone: A Philosophy of Religion* (1951; rpt., New York: Harper Torchbooks, 1966), 89.
11. Warren, *The Purpose Driven Life*, 228.
12. Robbins, *Money, Master the Game*, 582.
13. Heschel, *Man Is Not Alone*, 109.
14. Albert Camus, *Le Mythe de Sisyphe: Essai sur l'absurde* (Paris: Gallimard, 1942), 16.

Chapter 1

1. Thanks to my colleague and Hebrew Bible scholar William Propp for this information about the dating of Ecclesiastes.

2. Heartfelt thanks to the late, kindly, gentle, prodigiously learned David Goodblatt, *olev ha-sholem*, who over the years generously helped his much less learned colleague with matters scriptural in Judaism. Any errors in this chapter are, of course, my own.

3. *Cratylus*, 393a.

4. *De interpretatione*, 16a.

5. *Rhetorica*, 1404a.

6. Ibid., 1404b.

7. Ibid., 1405b.

8. *Iliad*, 1:62–64.

9. Ibid., 1:69–72.

10. Ibid., 1:85.

11. Joseph Fontenrose, *The Delphic Oracle: Its Responses and Operations, with a Catalogue of Responses* (Berkeley: University of California Press, 1978), 196–232.

12. *Fragmenta*, 93, 1.

13. *Agamemnon*, 1080–1113.

14. Ibid., 1241.

15. Ibid., 1113.

16. Ibid., 1095, 1213.

17. Ibid., 1255.

18. *Timaeus*, 72a6–72c1.

Chapter 2

1. Hans Blumenberg, *Die Lesbarkeit der Welt* (Frankfurt am Main: Suhrkamp, 1981), 50–51. My translation.

2. *Sancti Avrelii Avgvstini Enarrationes in Psalmos*, in *Corpus christianorum, series latina* (Turnhout: Typographi Brepols, 1956), 38:521–522. Part of this quoted in Blumenberg, *Die Lesbarkeit der Welt*, 49. My translation from the Latin.

3. See F. F. Bruce, *The Canon of Scripture* (Downers Grove, IL: InterVarsity Press, 1988), 197–207; Lee Martin McDonald, *The Biblical Canon: Its Origin, Transmission, and Authority*, 3rd ed. (Peabody, MA: Hendrickson, 2007), 308–310.

4. In Johannes Kirchhofer, *Quellensammlung zur Geschichte des Neutestamentlichen Kanons bis auf Hieronymus* (Zürich: Meyer and Zeller, 1844), 7–9.

5. Augustine, *De doctrina christiana*, II.8.13. My translation from the Latin.

6. On Augustine and the biblical canon, see Anne-Marie La Bonnardière, "Le canon des divines Écritures," in *Saint Augustin et la Bible*, edited by Anne-Marie la Bonnardière, 287–301 (Paris: Éditions Beauchesne, 1986). In English translation: "The Canon of Sacred Scripture," in *Augustine and the Bible*, edited and translated by Pamela Bright (Notre Dame, IN: University of Notre Dame Press, 1986), 26–41.

7. Harry Y. Gamble, *Books and Readers in the Early Church: A History of Early Christian Texts* (New Haven: Yale University Press, 1995), 54–59.

8. Ibid., 93.

9. Ibid., 141.
10. *De doctrina christiana*, II.1.1.
11. Ibid., II.1.2.
12. Ibid., II.2.3.
13. Ibid.
14. Ibid., II.3.4.
15. Ibid., II.13.19.
16. Ibid., II.31.49–II.32.50.
17. *Enarrationes in Psalmos*, 8:7–8.
18. Hugh of St. Victor, *Eruditio didascalica*, VII, 4. Quoted in Blumenberg, *Die Lesbarkeit der Welt*, 53. My translation from the Latin.
19. St. Bonaventura, *Collationes in hexaëmeron sive illuminationes ecclesiae*, in *Opera omnia* (Quaracchi: Ad Claras Aquas, 1891), 5:389–390. My translation from the Latin.
20. Peter Harrison, *The Bible, Protestantism, and the Rise of Natural Science* (Cambridge: Cambridge University Press, 1998), 120.
21. Ibid., 263–264.
22. Ibid., 266.
23. *An Essay Towards a New Theory of Vision*, sect. 147.
24. Ibid., sect. 159.
25. Kenneth P. Winkler, "Berkeley and the Doctrine of Signs," in *The Cambridge Companion to Berkeley*, edited by Kenneth P. Winkler (Cambridge: Cambridge University Press, 2005), 125–165.
26. *A Treatise Concerning the Principles of Human Knowledge*, sect. 107.
27. Ibid., sect. 109.
28. See, for example, T. E. Jessop, "Berkeley's Philosophy of Science," *Hermathena* 97 (July 1963): 23–35; John W. Davis, "Berkeley, Newton, and Space," in *The Methodological Heritage of Newton*, edited by Robert E. Butts and John W. Davis (Toronto: University of Toronto Press, 1970), 57–73; James Lawler, "From Berkeley to Hume: The Radicalization of Empiricism," in *Matter and Spirit: The Battle of Metaphysics in Modern Western Philosophy Before Kant* (Rochester, NY: University of Rochester Press, 2006), 204–232.
29. For this view, see Péter Losonczi, "Berkeley's Wonderful Divine Language: Apology and Biblical Realism," in *Philosophy Begins in Wonder*, edited by Michael Fund Deckard and Péter Losonczi (Cambridge: James Clarke, 2011), 190–210.

Chapter 3

1. A number of commentators have written about the kenotic element in Hamann's theology. See, for example, Katie Terezakis, *The Immanent Word: The Turn to Language in German Philosophy, 1759–1801* (New York: Routledge, 2007) and Kenneth Haynes, in Johann Georg Hamann, *Writings on Philosophy and Language*, edited by Kenneth Haynes (Cambridge: Cambridge University Press, 2007), xiii.

2. Johann Georg Hamann, *Sämtliche Werke* (Vienna: Verlag Herder, 1949–1957), 2:204.

3. Ibid., 1:302.

4. Ibid., 1:298.

5. Ibid., 1:308.

6. Thanks to Christian Danz, at the Institut für Systematische Theologie und Religionswissenschaft der Evangelisch-Theologischen Fakultät, of the University of Vienna, for his assistance with this section.

7. German philosopher and logician Gottlob Frege devoted an article to the distinction between *Sinn* and *Bedeutung*, asserting that *Bedeutung* is used to suggest that the word or sentence in question carries a truth value and points to a referent, while *Sinn* refers to the thought that is expressed and grasped. See Gottlob Frege, "Über Sinn und Bedeutung," *Zeitschrift für Philosophie und philosophische Kritik*, NF 100 (1892): S. 25–50.

8. For example, entry for *Sinn*, in Friedrich Kluge, *Etymologisches Wörterbuch der deutschen Sprache*, edited by Elmar Seebold (Berlin: Walter de Gruyter, 1995), 764; entry for *Sinn*, *Digitales Wörterbuch der Deutschen Sprache*, edited by Berlin-Brandenburgische Akademie der Wissenschaften, https://www.dwds.de/wb/Sinn.

9. Entry for *Sinn*, *Deutsches Wörterbuch von Jacob Grimm und Wilhelm Grimm*, http://dwb.uni-trier.de/de/.

10. Genesis 40:5: "Und es träumte ihnen beiden, dem Schenken und dem Bäcker des Königs von Ägypten, in einer Nacht einem jeglichen ein eigener Traum; und eines jeglichen Traum hatte seine *Bedeutung*." (New Revised Standard Version: "One night they both dreamed—the cupbearer and the baker of the king of Egypt, who were confined in the prison—each his own dream, and each dream with its own *meaning*.") Genesis 41:32: "Daß aber dem Pharao zum andernmal geträumt hat, *bedeutet*, daß solches Gott gewiß und eilend tun wird." (NRVS: "And the doubling of Pharaoh's dream *means* that the thing is fixed by God, and God will shortly bring it about.") Daniel 5:17: "Da fing Daniel an und redete vor dem König: Behalte deine Gaben selbst und gib dein Geschenk einem andern; ich will dennoch die Schrift dem König lesen und anzeigen, was sie *bedeutet*." (New International Version: "Then Daniel answered the king, 'You may keep your gifts for yourself and give your rewards to someone else. Nevertheless, I will read the writing for the king and tell him what it *means*.'")

11. Hamann, *Sämtliche Werke*, 1:305. I've corrected Hamann's Greek by adding aspiration and accent marks (which, for some reason, he always left out). I've used the older English spelling *Cabbala* since it's the spelling that Hamann uses.

12. Immanuel Kant, *Theorie-Werkausgabe Immanuel Kant, Werke in 12 Bänden* (Frankfurt: Suhrkamp, 1968), 2:926. My translation.

13. Ibid., 2:978–979.

14. On Kant's "precritical project" and the role that Swedenborg's work played in its collapse, see Martin Schönfeld, *The Philosophy of the Young Kant: The Precritical Project* (New York: Oxford University Press, 2000), chapter 10, "The Reductio and Collapse of the Precritical Project," 229–244. See also Ernst Cassirer, *Kant's Life and Thought*, trans. James Haden (New Haven: Yale University Press, 1981), 77–91; and Henry

E. Allison, *Kant's Conception of Freedom: A Developmental and Critical Analysis* (Cambridge: Cambridge University Press, 2020), 162–175.

15. Kant, *Theorie-Werkausgabe*, 2:983.

16. Ibid., 3:30–32/Bxxiv–xxviii.

17. Ibid., 3:28/Bxxii.

18. Ibid., 3:33/Bxxix; 3:338/B395.

19. Ibid., 2:614.On this early writing, see Henry E. Allison, *Kant's Transcendental Deduction: An Analytical-Historical Commentary* (Oxford: Oxford University Press, 2015), 13.

20. Kant, *Theorie-Werkausgabe*, 3:199/A155/B194.

21. Ibid., 3:147/B149.

22. Ibid., 4:375/A369.

23. Novalis, *Schriften*, edited by Paul Kluckhohn and Richard Samuel (Stuttgart: Kohlhammer, 1977–), 2:562.

24. Will Dudley writes of the early German Romantics, among them Novalis, "Poetic and experimental language—including the use of metaphors, fragments, aphorisms and irony—confront the reader with the task of active and ongoing interpretation, and so embody the view that the truth always lies beyond what can be explicitly or literally said." See *Understanding German Idealism* (Stocksfield: Acumen, 2007), 188.

25. Novalis, *Schriften*, 3:250.

26. At issue was the notion that the seat of the soul is the brain. In the footnote, Kant writes of the stimulation (*Reizung*) of nerves and of the "stimulable parts" (*der reizbaren Teile*) of the brain. Kant, *Theorie-Werkausgabe* 2:932–933n.

27. In the early pages of the work, Kant writes of the "subjective" senses, smell and taste, and of the action of a stimulus (*Reiz*) on them. Kant, *Theorie-Werkausgabe*, 12:455. I have written about the history of the term *stimulus* in (and have here borrowed phrases from) "A History of the Concept of the Stimulus and the Role It Played in the Neurosciences," *Journal of the History of the Neurosciences* 17, no. 4 (2008): 405–432.

28. Novalis, *Schriften*, 2:546.

29. Ibid., 2:550.

30. *Novalis: Philosophical Writings*, edited and translated by Margaret Mahony Stoljar (Albany: State University of New York Press, 1997), 61–63. Stoljar's translation roughly matches the one I made, with the word *meaning* instead of *sense*.

31. Novalis, *Schriften*, 1:89–90.

32. Novalis, *The Disciples at Saïs and Other Fragments by Novalis*, translated by Una Birch (London: Methuen, 1903), 110.

33. Novalis, *The Novices of Sais*, translated by Ralph Manheim (New York: Curt Valentin, 1949), 47.

34. Novalis, *Schriften*, 1:90.

35. Novalis, *Disciples* (trans. Birch), 111–112; Novalis, *Novices* (trans. Manheim), 49.

36. Novalis, *Schriften*, 1:85.

37. It's worth pointing out that Johann Gottlieb Fichte, who was in a sense a mentor to the members of this generation of German romantics, used *Bedeutung* in connection with life. His popular account of his own (otherwise difficult) philosophy, *Die Bestimmung*

des Menschen (usually translated "The vocation of man"), contains a couple of prominent examples. Here is one, in the chapter titled *Glaube* (faith): "To listen to this [the voice of my conscience], to hearken to it sincerely and impartially, without fear and mental trickery, this is my own vocation [*Bestimmung*], the entire goal of my existence. My life ceases to be empty play without truth and meaning [*Bedeutung*]." Fichte, *Die Bestimmung des Menschen*, ed (Berlin: Berliner Ausgabe, 2014), 65.

38. Johann Wolfgang von Goethe, *Gesamtausgabe der Werke und Schriften in zweiundzwanzig Bänden* (Stuttgart: J. G. Cotta, 1961–), 7:139.

39. Ibid., 16:234.

40. Novalis, *Schriften*, 2:577.

41. Ibid., 2:594.

42. Ibid., 2:545. *Geistererscheinung* here is a play on words: normally it means a ghostly apparition, but this is a Kantian context where *Geisterseher*, "spirit-seer," refers to someone with direct access to a non-empirical world of spirits that appear (*erscheinen*) without mediation.

43. Ibid., 2:545.

44. Ibid., 1:79.

45. Wm. Arctander O'Brien, *Novalis: Signs of Revolution* (Durham, NC: Duke University Press, 1995), 199.

46. For the role of Sanskrit and "the Orient" in Novalis's work, see Debra N. Prager, *Orienting the Self: The German Literary Encounter with the Eastern Other* (Rochester, NY: Camden House, 2014), 119–188.

47. O'Brien, *Novalis*, 111.

48. *Kritische Friedrich-Schlegel-Ausgabe*, edited by Ernst Behler (Munich: Ferdinand Schöningh Verlag, 1962), 2:182.

49. Ibid., 5/1:82.

50. Friedrich Daniel Ernst Schleiermacher, *Kritische Gesamtausgabe* (Berlin: Walter de Gruyter, 1980–), I/2:212.

51. Ibid., I/2:260–261.

52. Ibid., I/12:346–347.

53. The work in question was Johann Salomo Semler's *Vorbereitung zur theologischen Hermeneutik* (Preparation for theological hermeneutics, 1760–1769). See editor's introduction to *Kritische Gesamtausgabe*, II/4:xviii.

54. In his translation of Herder's essay, Michael N. Forster translates *Besinnung* as "taking-awareness" and *Besonnenheit* as "awareness." See *Herder: Philosophical Writings*, edited and translated by Michael N. Forster (Cambridge: Cambridge University Press, 2004), 82n33.

55. Johann Gottfried Herder, *Frühe Schriften, 1764–1772*, edited by Ulrich Gaier (Cambridge: Chadwyck-Healey, 2001), 717.

56. Ibid., 719.

57. Ibid., 711. See Forster's Introduction to *Herder: Philosophical Writings* for an excellent summary of Herder's theory of interpretation.

58. Schleiermacher, *Kritische Gesamtausgabe*, II/4:132.

59. Ibid., II/4:140.

Chapter 4

1. Volker Gerhardt, "Sinn des Lebens," in *Historisches Wörterbuch der Philosophie* (Basel: Schwabe, 1971–2007), 9:817; and Christoph Fehige, Georg Meggle, Ulla Wessels, eds., *Der Sinn des Lebens* (Munich: Deutscher Taschenbuch Verlag, 2000), 21.

2. Søren Kierkegaard, *Either/Or: A Fragment of Life*, abridged and translated by Alastair Hannay (London: Penguin, 1992), 48–49.

3. Ibid., 49.

4. Søren Kierkegaard, *The Concept of Anxiety: A Simple Psychologically Oriented Deliberation in View of the Dogmatic Problem of Hereditary Sin*, translated by Alastair Hannay (New York: Norton, 2014), 131.

5. Søren Kierkegaard, *Fear and Trembling/Repetition*, edited and translated by Howard V. Hong and Edna H. Hong (Princeton: Princeton University Press, 1983), 175.

6. Thanks to my former student Anders Engberg-Pedersen, University of Southern Denmark, for his help with Kierkegaard's Danish.

7. Charles Frederick Harrold, "The Nature of Carlyle's Calvinism," *Studies in Philology* 33, no. 3 (July 1936): 476.

8. Charles Frederick Harrold, *Carlyle and German Thought: 1819–1834* (New Haven: Yale University Press, 1934), 27.

9. Harrold, "The Nature of Carlyle's Calvinism," 478.

10. Thomas Carlyle, "Novalis" (1829), in *Critical and Miscellaneous Essays* (Boston: Phillips, Samson, 1858), 176.

11. Ibid., 177.

12. Ibid., 176.

13. Ibid., 174.

14. Ibid., 176.

15. Novalis, *Schriften*, edited by Ludwig Tieck and Friedrich von Schlegel, 5th ed. (Berlin: Reimer, 1837), 1:89–90.

16. Carlyle, "Novalis," 179.

17. Novalis, *Schriften*, xxxi–xxxii.

18. Carlyle, "Novalis," 186.

19. Thomas Carlyle, *Sartor Resartus* (1833–1834), edited by Kerry McSweeney and Peter Sabor (Oxford: OUP, 1987), 56.

20. Ibid., 75.

21. Ibid., 166–167.

22. Ibid., 169.

23. Ibid., 195.

24. Ibid., 140.

25. Ibid., 127.

26. Thomas Carlyle, *Of Heroes, Hero Worship, and the Heroic in History*, edited by David R. Sorensen and Brent E. Kinser (New Haven: Yale University Press, 2013), 170.

27. Ibid., 181.

28. Ibid., 182–183.

29. For Emerson's acquaintance with *Wilhelm Meister*, see Frank T. Thompson, "Emerson and Carlyle," in *Studies in Philology* 24, no. 3 (July 1927): 440. For his acquaintance with the Novalis essay, see René Wellek, "Emerson and German Philosophy," in *Confrontations* (Princeton: Princeton University Press, 1965), 188n5.

30. Fred Kaplan, *Thomas Carlyle: A Biography* (Ithaca, NY: Cornell University Press, 1983), 232.

31. Leon Jackson, "The Social Construction of Thomas Carlyle's New England Reputation, 1834–36," *Proceedings of the American Antiquarian Society* 106 (April 1996): 167–191; and "The Reader Retailored: Thomas Carlyle, His American Audiences, and the Politics of Evidence," *Book History* 2 (1999): 146–172. The letter from Francis is quoted on p. 146 of the latter article. Jackson gives this citation for the letter: Convers Francis to Ralph Waldo Emerson, October 14, 1835, Ralph Waldo Emerson Memorial Association, Houghton Library, Harvard University.

   Thanks to my nephew Tim Cassedy, Department of English, Southern Methodist University, for bringing the Jackson articles to my attention.

32. Jackson, "Social Construction," 180.

33. Carlyle, *Critical and Miscellaneous Essays*, 26–30.

34. Samantha C. Harvey, "Reading the 'Book of Nature': Emerson, the Hunterian Museum, and Transatlantic Science," in *The Edinburgh Companion to Atlantic Literary Studies*, edited by Leslie Elizabeth Eckel and Clare Frances Elliott (Edinburgh: Edinburgh University Press, 2016), 325–339.

35. *Ralph Waldo Emerson: The Major Prose*, edited by Ronald A. Bosco and Joel Myerson (Cambridge, MA: Harvard University Press, 2015), 30.

36. Ibid., 31. Emphasis added.

37. Ibid., 43–44.

38. Ibid., 47–48.

39. Robert D. Richardson Jr., *Emerson: The Mind on Fire: A Biography* (Berkeley: University of California Press, 1995), 198.

40. *Emerson: The Major Prose*, 54–55.

41. Ibid., 49.

42. Ibid., 54.

43. Ibid., 165–166.

44. Ralph Waldo Emerson, *Letters and Social Aims* (Boston: James R. Osgood, 1876), 13–14.

45. Ibid., 14.

46. Ibid., 15.

47. Ibid., 18.

Chapter 5

1. Alexandra Popoff, having gained first-time access to extensive archival materials, recently exposed the full extent of Chertkov's manipulative, unscrupulous, and

downright treacherous relationship with an astonishingly docile Tolstoy, in *Tolstoy's False Disciple: The Untold Story of Leo Tolstoy and Vladimir Chertkov* (New York: Pegasus Books, 2014).

2. Vladimir Chertkov, ed., *O smysle zhizni: Mysli L. N. Tolstogo* (Christchurch, Hants, England: Izdanie "Svobodnago Slova," 1901), 10. My translation.

3. Ibid., 26.

4. Vladimir Dal', *Tolkovyi slovar' zhivogo velikorusskogo iazyka* (Moscow: Gosudarstvennoe Izdatel'stvo inostrannykh i natsional'nykh slovarei, 1956), entry for *smysl*.

5. Chertkov, *O smysle zhizni*, 5–6.

6. Tolstoy, *Polnoe sobranie sochinenii*, ed. Vladimir Chertkov (Moscow: Gosudarstvennoe Izdatel'svto "Khudozhestvennaia Literatura," 1929–1958), 46:30–31. Abbreviated *PSS* hereafter.

7. *PSS*, 10:77–78.

8. *PSS*, 10:295–296.

9. *PSS*, 12:50–51. I have quoted and discussed the same passage, in similar language, in "Dostoevsky and the Meaning of 'the Meaning of Life,'" in *Dostoevsky Beyond Dostoevsky: Science, Religion, Philosophy*, edited by Svetlana Evdokimova and Vladimir Golstein, 111–128 (Brighton, MA: Academic Studies Press, 2016). The relevant part appears on pp. 118–119.

10. *PSS*, 12:229–230.

11. *PSS*, 19:376.

12. *PSS*, 19:378.

13. *PSS*, 19:380.

14. *PSS*, 19:399.

15. *PSS*, 23:16–17.

16. *PSS*, 23:21–22.

17. *PSS*, 23:47.

18. *PSS*, 23:48.

19. *PSS*, 23:52.

20. *PSS*, 23:56–57.

21. *PSS*, 23:57.

22. Irina Paperno makes this point in an excellent discussion of the confession genre and Tolstoy's *Confession* in *Who, What Am I? Tolstoy Struggles to Narrate the Self* (Ithaca, NY: Cornell University Press, 2014), 60–80.

23. *PSS*, 26:317.

24. *PSS*, 26:322.

25. *PSS*, 26:328.

26. *PSS*, 26:365–366.

27. Count Leo Tolstoi, *The Kingdom of God Is Within You: Christianity Not as a Mystic Religion but as a New Theory of Life*, trans. Constance Garnett (New York: Cassell, 1894), 368.

28. Rosamund Bartlett makes the claim about the number of people reading Tolstoy in translation in "Tolstoy Translated," *Financial Times*, August 8, 2014.

29. *The New York Times*, March 7, 1909, SM1.

30. *The New York Times*, March 21, 1909, SM4.

31. William James, *The Varieties of Religious Experience* (New York: Barnes & Noble Classics, 2004), 138–139.

32. Léon Tolstoi, *Ma confession*, trans. Zoria (Paris: Albert Savine, 1887), *passim*.

33. James, *Varieties of Religious Experience*, 17.

34. Ibid., 44.

35. Many of the ideas and much of the language in this section appeared in Cassedy, "Dostoevsky and the Meaning of 'the Meaning of Life,'" 121–128. They appear here with permission of the publisher and editors of the volume in which it appears.

36. Dostoevsky, *Polnoe sobranie sochinenii v tridtsati tomakh* (Leningrad: Nauka, 1972–1990), 30/1:63. Abbreviated hereafter as PSS.

37. *PSS*, 14:210.

38. *PSS*, 14:214.

39. *PSS*, 24:472.

40. Partly quoted in *PSS*, 24:472; quoted at greater length, in the original Russian, in Irina Paperno, *Suicide as Cultural Institution in Dostoevsky's Russia* (Ithaca, NY: Cornell University Press, 1997), 294–295. Paperno tells the story of this episode in Dostoevsky's career on pp. 162–184.

41. *PSS*, 24:49.

42. *PSS*, 24:50.

43. *PSS*, 24:54.

44. *PSS*, 29/2:280.

45. *PSS*, 29/2:280–281, ellipsis in the original.

46. Paperno, *Suicide as Cultural Institution*, 202.

47. Albert Camus, *Le Mythe de Sisyphe* (Paris: Gallimard, 1942), 15–16.

48. Ibid., 142–143.

49. In *Dostoevsky's Religion* (Stanford, CA: Stanford University Press, 2005), I claimed that Dostoevsky showed a peculiar capacity for adopting—*sincerely*—opposing points of view and systems of belief. See chapter Four, "Belief Is Expressed in Antinomies," 87–113.

Chapter 6

1. One example each from Sartre and Camus: In *Being and Nothingness*, in the context of "my death," Sartre wrote this: "As such, [death] influences the entire life against the current; life limits itself with life, becoming like the world of Einstein, 'finite but unlimited': death becomes the meaning [*le sens*] of life as the resolving chord is the meaning [*le sens*] of the melody." It's worth mentioning, however, that, in this context, *le sens* carries, as it often does in French, the idea of direction. Jean-Paul Sartre, *L'être et le néant; essai d'ontologie phénoménologique* (Paris: Gallimard, 1943), 700. In *The Myth of Sisyphus*, Camus wrote this (the passage I referred to in the Introduction): "On

the other hand, I see that many people die because they consider life to be not worth living. I see others who paradoxically have themselves killed for the very ideas or illusions that give them a reason to live (what we call a reason to live is at the same time a reason to die). I judge therefore that the meaning of life is the most pressing of questions." Albert Camus, *Le mythe de Sisyphe: essai sur l'absurde* (Paris: Gallimard, 1942), 16.

2. Martin Heidegger, *Sein und Zeit*, 19th ed. (Tübingen: Max Niemeyer, 2006), 2–4.
3. Paul Tillich, "Existential Philosophy," *Journal of the History of Ideas* 5, no. 1 (January 1944): 44–70.
4. The notion of a book under this title, authored or compiled by Nietzsche himself, has long been discredited.
5. Tillich cites Nietzsche, *Werke. Taschenausgabe* (Leipzig: Naumann, 1906), 10:114. The passage may be found in *Nietzsche Werke: Kritische Gesamtausgabe*, edited by Giorgio Colli and Mazzino Montinari (Berlin: Walter de Gruyter, 1970), sect. 8, vol. 2, 128.
6. Tillich, "Existential Philosophy," 57.
7. Ulrich Barth, *Religion in der Moderne* (Tübingen: J. C. B. Mohr, 2003), 89–123. The quoted passage appears on p. 121.
8. Paul Tillich, *Gesammelte Werke* (Stuttgart: Evangelisches Verlagswerk, 1959), 1:318. Abbreviated hereafter *GW*. An English translation of this work appears in Paul Tillich, *What Is Religion?*, trans. James Luther Adams, Konrad Raiser, and Charles W. Fox (New York: Harper & Row, 1969), 27–101. Adams's translation of this passage appears on p. 57.
9. Tillich, *What Is Religion?*, 19.
10. *GW*, 1:318.
11. Paul Tillich, *Systematic Theology* (Chicago: University of Chicago Press, 1951–1963), 1:11–14.
12. Ibid., 1:14.
13. Ibid., 1:204–205.
14. Paul Tillich, *The Courage to Be* (New Haven: Yale University Press, 1952), 182.
15. Ibid., 186.
16. Ibid., 46–50.
17. Paul Tillich, *Dynamics of Faith* (New York: Harper & Row, 1957), 41–43.
18. Ibid., 45.

Chapter 7

1. Alfred Kazin, "A Devout Russian Iconoclast," *New York Times*, January 6, 1946, BR1. Thanks to the sleuthing skills of Edward Mendelson, who reported in a personal email to me that he found the review of *For the Time Being* in *Time*, September 11, 1944. The passage announcing *The Age of Anxiety*, he reported, was also quoted on the dust jacket of Auden's *Collected Poetry* in 1945.
2. Alan W. Watts, *The Wisdom of Insecurity* (New York: Pantheon, 1951), 14–16.

3. Andrew Finstuen has written about this in *Original Sin and Everyday Protestants: The Theology of Reinhold Niebuhr, Billy Graham, and Paul Tillich in an Age of Anxiety* (Chapel Hill: University of North Carolina Press, 2009), 36–37.

4. This, incidentally, may be an allusion to the original German edition of the book by Viktor Frankl that would soon be published, in English translation, as *Man's Search for Meaning* (see Chapter 8). The German title was *Trotzdem Ja zum Leben sagen: Ein Psychologe erlebt das Konzentrationslager* (Nonetheless saying yes to life: a psychologist experiences the concentration camp).

5. Cleanth Brooks, *Poetry in the Age of Anxiety* (Charlottesville: University of Virginia Library, 1947), 1.

6. For a brief history of English translations of Kierkegaard, see Roger Poole, "The Unknown Kierkegaard: Twentieth-Century Receptions," in *The Cambridge Companion to Kierkegaard*, edited by Alastair Hannay and Gordon D. Marino (Cambridge: Cambridge University Press, 1998), 56–58.

7. Reinhold Niebuhr, *The Nature and Destiny of Man* (New York: Charles Scribner's Sons, 1941), 1:164.

8. Ibid., 1:164.

9. Reinhold Niebuhr, *Discerning the Signs of the Times: Sermons for Today and Tomorrow* (New York: Charles Scribner's Sons, 1946), 152–153.

10. Ibid., 154.

11. Ibid., 247–248.

12. Thomas J. J. Altizer, *The Gospel of Christian Atheism* (Philadelphia: Westminster Press, 1966), 22.

13. Ibid., 81.

14. Abraham Joshua Heschel, *God in Search of Man* (New York: Farrar, Straus and Cudahy, 1955), 119.

15. Ibid., 204.

16. Ibid., 420.

17. Abraham Joshua Heschel, *Man Is Not Alone: A Philosophy of Religion* (1951; rpt., New York: Harper Torchbooks, 1966), 62.

Chapter 8

1. Rollo May, *The Springs of Creative Living* (New York: Abingdon-Cokesbury Press, 1940), 13.

2. Ibid., 19–20.

3. Ibid., 151, 159. Emphasis in the original.

4. Rollo May, *The Meaning of Anxiety* (New York: Ronald Press Company, 1950), 6.

5. Ibid., 7.

6. Ibid., 14.

7. Ibid., 32. The quoted passage is from Paul Tillich, "Existential Philosophy," *Journal of the History of Ideas* 5, no. 1 (January 1944): 67.

8. Rollo May, *Man's Search for Himself* (New York: Norton, 1953), 210–212.

9. *New York Times*, December 14, 1956, BR 19.

10. Henry Clay Lindgren, *Meaning: Antidote to Anxiety* (New York: Thomas Nelson & Sons, 1956), 16. The quote is from *The Courage to Be*, 34.

11. Lindgren, *Meaning*, 34.

12. Timothy Pytell has written about Frankl's "mendaciousness" concerning his experiences in the camps, though Pytell claims (unconvincingly, to my mind) that it was not intentional (perhaps, then, "mendaciousness" is not the right word) but rather "a product of longstanding intellectual interests, and the desire to heal himself and others." See Timothy Pytell, *Viktor Frankl's Search for Meaning: An Emblematic 20th-Century Life* (New York: Berghahn, 2015), 125. Pytell was far less forgiving—and, in my opinion, far more honest and accurate—in an article he wrote a number of years before his book: "The Missing Pieces of the Puzzle: A Reflection on the Odd Career of Viktor Frankl," *Journal of Contemporary History* 35, no. 2 (2000): 281–306.

13. Viktor E. Frankl, *Trotzdem Ja zum Leben sagen: Ein Psychologe erlebt das Konzentrationslager* (Munich: Kösel, 2018), 181–184.

14. Ibid., 170–171.

15. See Pytell, *Viktor Frankl's Search for Meaning*, 67–68.

16. Viktor E. Frankl, "Zur geistigen Problematik der Psychotherapie," *Zentralblatt für Psychotherapie* 10 (1937): 33–45. The quoted passage appears on p. 38. My translation. Quoted in part in Pytell, *Viktor Frankl's Search for Meaning*, 71.

17. Christian Goeschel, *Suicide in Nazi Germany* (Oxford: Oxford University Press, 2015), 107.

18. Viktor Frankl, *Der unbewußte Gott*, 2nd ed. (Vienna: Amandus-Verlag, 1949), 14–15.

19. Viktor Frankl, *Man's Search for Ultimate Meaning* (Boston: Perseus Books, 2000), 67.

20. Frankl, *Der unbewußte Gott*, 79.

21. Viktor Frankl, *Man's Search for Meaning* (Boston, MA: Beacon Press, 2006), 98.

22. According to Timothy Pytell, Frankl may well have derived the term *logotherapy* from the work of pioneering speech therapist Emil Fröschels, who coined the word *logopedics* to name his scientific field. But in Fröschels's coinage, the component *logo-* derives from an understanding of *logos* as "word," which is indeed one of the Greek word's meanings. Fröschels never claimed that *logo-* meant "meaning." See *Viktor Frankl's Search for Meaning*, 51.

23. Frankl, *Man's Search for Meaning*, 98–99.

24. Viktor Frankl, *The Will to Meaning: Foundations and Applications of Logotherapy* (1969; rpt., New York: Plume, 1970), 21.

25. Ibid., 22–23.

26. Ibid., 45.

27. Ibid., 53.

28. Ibid., 58.

29. Ibid., 73–74.

30. Ibid., 109.

31. Ibid., 110.

32. Ibid., 115.

33. Ibid., 117.
34. Frankl, *Man's Search for Ultimate Meaning*, 91.
35. Three of the sources Frankl cites are studies based on surveys conducted by scientists in the field. He cites the Purpose-in-Life Test, designed by James C. Crumbaugh and Leonard T. Maholick, and a Logo-Test devised by Elisabeth S. Lukas. Crumbaugh was known at the time primarily for his work on parapsychology and his lack of success in proving the existence of the effects he was investigating. Maholick was a psychiatrist who had studied with Jung and Frankl before establishing a career in the United States. The Purpose-in-Life Test was a twenty-question test designed to determine whether the respondent was experiencing an "existential void." The relevant item for Frankl, I assume, is one that asks you to finish the statement "My personal existence is . . ." by marking from 1 to 5, 1 being "utterly meaningless, without purpose," and 5 being "purposeful and meaningful." The only other item that might qualify asks you to finish the sentence "As I view the world in relation to my life, the world . . ." where 5 represents "fits meaningfully with my life." It's not clear to me how the results of this survey prove the existence of a "will to meaning." For the study based on the Purpose-in-Life Test, see James C. Crumbaugh and Leonard T. Maholick, "An Experimental Study in Existentialism: The Psychometric Approach to Frankl's Concept of *Noogenic Neurosis*," *Journal of Clinical Psychology* 20 (April 1964): 200–207. Elisabeth S. Lukas's Logo-Test was designed to represent an improvement over the Crumbaugh/Maholick test by replacing questions that explicitly asked about meaningfulness with questions designed to elicit evidence of feelings in the respondent that contribute to a sense of meaningfulness. See Barma Konkolÿ Thege et al., "Development and Psychometric Evaluation of a Revised Measure of Meaning in Life: The Logo-Test-R," *Studia Psychologica* 52 (2010): 133–145. The third source is an unpublished paper by two Czech researchers.
36. See, for example, Alexander Batthyány and David Guttmann, *Empirical Research in Logotherapy and Meaning-Oriented Psychotherapy: An Annotated Bibliography* (Phoenix, AZ: Zeig, Tucker & Theisen, 2006).
37. William S. Breitbart, "Meaning-Centered Psychotherapy (MCP) for Advanced Cancer Patients," in *Logotherapy and Existential Analysis: Proceedings of the Viktor Frankl Institute Vienna*, edited by A. Batthyány, 1:151–163 (Cham: Springer, 2016). The quoted passage appears on p. 151.
38. Alexander Batthyány is the Viktor Frankl Chair for Philosophy and Psychology at the International Academy of Philosophy, University in the Principality of Liechtenstein, and a practitioner in the field of logotherapy. In an email to me, he wrote this, in response to my question about the meaning of the word *Sinn* in German and the word *meaning* in English: "At least in German, and from what I see on the American or English field—patients and clients bring up the question of meaning/*Sinn* on their own. It is not that we have to make them aware of it, or explain the term. There appears to be an intuitive, or pre-reflexive understanding of the term, and we work from there. If you ask about meaning in or of life, people appear to know immediately what is meant—but again, it might be that I have this impression precisely because people who come to us are those who share the same or a sufficiently similar understanding

of the term 'meaning.' In German, however, it is a very prevalent term, precisely with our understanding of it." Dr. Breitbart, in a phone conversation, in response to my question about the meaning of *meaning*, did not offer a simple definition but instead spoke about the feeling (the experience) and the belief (the cognition) that one's life is meaningful and about the experiential sources of meaning: love, a feeling of connection, and an awareness of something greater than oneself. He spoke, too, of the creative sources of meaning, including the idea of creating one's own life, a sense of "who you are," which, he explained, is "an amalgam of your values, attitudes, intentions, motivations, being authentic, becoming who you intend to become." Breitbart emphasized that while MCP utilizes Frankl's basic concept of meaning, its methods are tailored specifically to cancer patients and it differs from logotherapy in that the course of treatment in MCP is brief and tightly structured. The efficacy of MCP, he said, has been demonstrated in a series of four randomized trials.

39. Barbara Fredrickson et al., "A Functional Genomic Perspective on Human Well-being," *PNAS* 110 (33): 13684–13689. The quoted passage appears on p. 13684. Emphasis added.
40. Ibid., 13688.
41. B. L. Fredrickson, "The Eudaimonics of Positive Emotions," in *The Handbook of Eudaimonic Wellbeing*, edited by J. Vitterso, 183–190 (New York: Springer, 2016).
42. Emily Esfahani Smith, *The Power of Meaning: Crafting a Life That Matters* (New York: Crown, 2017), 42.
43. Ibid., 229–230.
44. Ibid., 229.
45. Christopher G. Davis et al., "Making Sense of Loss and Benefiting from the Experience: Two Construals of Meaning," *Journal of Personality and Social Psychology* 75, no. 2 (1998): 561–574.
46. David Kessler, *Finding Meaning: The Sixth State of Grief* (New York: Scribner, 2019), 7.
47. Ibid., 9.
48. Ibid., 8.
49. Ibid., 107.

Chapter 9

1. Martin Jay, "Faith-Based History," *History and Theory* 48 (February 2009): 76–84. The quoted words appear on p. 77.
2. Charles Taylor, *A Secular Age* (Cambridge, MA: Belknap Press of Harvard University Press, 2007), 1.
3. Ibid., 2–3.
4. Ibid., 31–32.
5. Ibid., 31.
6. Max Weber, "Wissenschaft als Beruf," in Max Weber, *Schriften, 1894–1922*, edited by Dirk Kaesler (Stuttgart: Alfred Kröner Verlag, 2002), 488. My translation.

7. Ibid., 489.

8. Ibid., 494–495.

9. Ibid., 488–489.

10. Taylor, *A Secular Age*, 719–720.

11. Ibid., 711.

12. "Disenchantment—Reenchantment," in *The Joy of Secularism: 11 Essays for How We Live Now*, edited by George Levine (Princeton, NJ: Princeton University Press, 2011), 57–73. The quoted passage appears on p. 73.

13. A. C. Grayling, *The God Argument: The Case Against Religion and for Humanism* (New York: Bloomsbury, 2013), 162.

14. Elizabeth Drescher, *Choosing Our Religion: The Spiritual Lives of America's Nones* (New York: Oxford University Press, 2016), 29.

15. Philip Kitcher, *Life After Faith: The Case for Secular Humanism* (New Haven: Yale University Press, 2014), xii.

16. Ibid., 100.

17. Ibid.

18. Ibid., 101.

19. Ibid., 109.

20. See Melissa J. Wilde, *Vatican II: A Sociological Analysis of Religious Change* (Princeton: Princeton University Press, 2007), for an account of the changes brought about by the Second Vatican Council.

21. Section 41. All papal decrees can be accessed, in Latin and in their official translations in a host of European languages, on the Vatican website, w2.vatican.va. I will give section numbers for quoted passages.

22. Section 13.

23. For an excellent account of John Paul II's encyclicals, see Richard A. Spinello, *The Encyclicals of John Paul I: An Introduction and Commentary* (New York: Rowman & Littlefield, 2012). My thanks to Professor Spinello for his help with this section.

24. Section 11.

25. Section 11.

26. Section 8.

27. Section 81.

28. Section 18.

29. Section 56.

30. Rick Warren, *The Purpose Driven Life: What on Earth Am I Here for?* (Grand Rapids, MI: Zondervan, 2002), 21–22.

31. Ibid., 34.

32. Simon Jacobson, *Toward a Meaningful Life: The Wisdom of the Rebbe Menachem Mendel Schneerson* (1995; 2nd ed., New York: HarperCollins, 2004), 5.

33. Ibid., 51.

34. Ibid., 20.

35. Ibid., 26.

36. Ibid., 54, 56, 119.

37. Ibid., 10. Emphasis added.

38. https://www.meaningfullife.com/about/.

Conclusion

1. Charles Taylor, *A Secular Age* (Cambridge, MA: Belknap Press of Harvard University Press, 2007), 31.

Index

For the benefit of digital users, indexed terms that span two pages (e.g., 52–53) may, on occasion, appear on only one of those pages.